THE BIBLE AND LEADERSHIP VALUES

A Book By Book Analysis

by Dr. J. Robert Clinton

Professor of Leadership
School of World Mission
Fuller Theological Seminary

THE BIBLE AND LEADERSHIP SERIES:

Leadership Perspectives for Bible Study
The Bible and Leadership Values—A Book By Book Analysis
Biblical Leaders—Their Strengths and Weaknesses

©   1993 Dr. J. Robert Clinton

ACKNOWLEDGMENTS

I am indebted to several who stimulated me to study the Bible for leadership insights. James M. (Buck) Hatch, helped give me my hermeneutical framework of which the overall perspective laws are the focus of this study. He also gave me the framework for viewing the redemptive story in his Progress of Redemption course years ago in Bible college. The concept of a leadership time-line across the Bible was rooted in that course.

Frank Sells modeled the importance of knowing each book of the Bible and particularly the idea of knowing the unique contribution of each book.

G. Coleman Luck's little book, **The Bible Book By Book** was a tool I used early on in my first several years of personal Bible study, and from time to time in recent years. His idea of display categories for each book in the Bible stimulated me to come up with my own. His important word lists for each book in the Bible was very helpful to me. I have, of course, adapted his and added new words of my own that I have seen.

G. Campbell Morgan's, **Living Messages of the Books of the Bible** (now just recently republished under the title of **Handbook for Bible Teachers and Preachers**) has been a useful tool over the years and more so in the present as the focus of my study has shifted from mastering book content to searching for overall lasting impacts of Bible books. His thoughts are always stimulating. I have used his ideas quite a bit. While I have not quoted him, I do reference his book several times for in-depth follow-up for the interested reader.

Finally, W. Graham Scroggie's book, **The Unfolding Drama of Redemption--The Bible as a Whole,** has been a useful tool over the years. He has been particularly helpful in studying the Kings and Chronicles and the Exilic and Return Periods.

My leadership thinking has been most stimulated by my recent doctoral research done under the able guidance of Paul Hiebert, Sam Wilson, and Sherwood Lingenfelter. All of these and probably many others whom I can't remember have helped shape my thinking and contributed to this Handbook.

Table of Contents

Preface

Three things happened to me in the first six years after my Lordship committal that have forever affected my ministry. And I want to pass them on.

One, my discipler mentor, Harold Dollar, told me, "Bobby, if you don't have a desire to study the Word, then ask God to give you that desire." I saw all those around me, the small group of aspiring Navigators, deeply committed to studying and using the Bible in their lives. So I did! I asked God to give me a desire to study His Word. And He did! I did studies with two mentor coaches, Harold Dollar and Gene Solberg, and then I did studies on my own, self-initiated. And ever since I have been grateful for that little piece of advice.

This advice proved very helpful when I was challenged in my local church situation to really study the Bible. My goal was to accept my pastor's challenge to master the Bible over my lifetime--overwhelming at the time he gave it. A Christian leader has as a major resource the Word and must learn from it all of life. A motivating desire to be in the Word and have the Word in the leader is fundamentally necessary.

Two, I was in a Bible centered ministry which included home Bible studies, tapes with Bible teaching available to any who wanted to borrow them, teaching from the pulpit and at least two Bible Conferences per year. The Bible conferences brought in speakers from all over. I stand amazed when I think of the names that came to that little country-like church on the outskirts of Columbus, Ohio. There was Marmion Lowe from Practical Bible Training School, one of the oldest Bible institutes in the United States, Joe Temple, the noted Bible teacher from Abilene, Texas, Herman Hoyt, then the President of Grace Theological Seminary, Norman Geisler, then at Detroit Bible College and later to move to Dallas Theological Seminary and many other outstanding teachers from the General Association of Regular Baptists. Norm Geisler taught a week long series on *Christ in All the Scriptures*. Scriptures like Matthew 5:17,18 (Christ being the fulfillment of the law), Luke 24:27, 44,45 (Christ seen in every part of the Old Testament), John 5:39,40 (the Old Testament Scriptures testify of Christ), and Hebrews 10:7 (in the volume of the book it is written of Christ) came alive as Geisler presented Christ in so many ways in all the Bible. I was motivated to study the whole Bible. Seeing someone model a Bible centered ministry, partaking of the excitement and the fruit of it, and being challenged to be an active part in that kind of ministry lays the foundation for one's own Bible centered ministry. A Christian leader must have a Bible centered ministry.

Three, I was given hermeneutical tools showing me the importance of synthesis as well as analysis. I began reading Milton Terry on hermeneutics (the guidelines for interpreting Scripture). Then I studied with Mr. Hatch, at Columbia Bible College, who organized hermeneutics into a system of guidelines which I have used ever since. The hermeneutical system included spiritual laws and language laws which fit the notion that the Bible is the Word of God in the words of men. The three spiritual laws had to do with the interpreter who comes to Scripture. 1. TO UNDERSTAND GOD'S REVEALED TRUTH ONE MUST BE A CHILD OF GOD AND THUS POSSESS THE HOLY SPIRIT WHO IS THE REVEALER OF TRUTH. 2. TO UNDERSTAND GOD'S REVEALED TRUTH ONE MUST BE DEPENDENT UPON THE HOLY SPIRIT TO TEACH HIM/HER. 3. TO UNDERSTAND GOD'S REVEALED TRUTH ONE MUST BE YIELDED TO DO THE WILL OF GOD. These set the tone for the general language laws which followed. Each of the general language laws begins with the phrase, *In The Spirit*, which reminds of the priority of these Spiritual Laws. The language laws were broken into 7 general language laws which deal with the general nature of written communication and 7 types of special language laws which dealt with unusual language types seen in the Bible. The following diagram shows this organizational scheme.

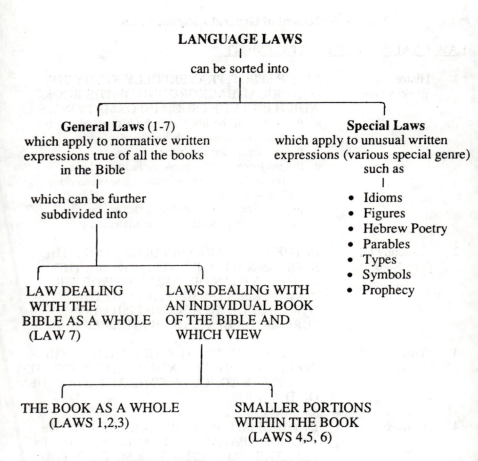

LANGUAGE LAWS
|
can be sorted into

General Laws (1-7)
which apply to normative written
expressions true of all the books
in the Bible
|
which can be further
subdivided into

LAW DEALING
WITH THE
BIBLE AS A WHOLE
(LAW 7)

LAWS DEALING WITH
AN INDIVIDUAL BOOK
OF THE BIBLE AND
WHICH VIEW

THE BOOK AS A WHOLE
(LAWS 1,2,3)

SMALLER PORTIONS
WITHIN THE BOOK
(LAWS 4,5, 6)

Special Laws
which apply to unusual written
expressions (various special genre)
such as

- Idioms
- Figures
- Hebrew Poetry
- Parables
- Types
- Symbols
- Prophecy

Diagram 1. Overall Scheme of Hermeneutical System

Each of these general language laws are stated in Table 1 which follows. Note especially laws 1, 2, 3, and 7.

Table 1. Statement of General Language Laws

LAW	DEALING WITH	STATEMENT
1	Historical Background	IN THE SPIRIT, PRAYERFULLY STUDY THE HISTORICAL BACKGROUND OF THE BOOK WHICH INCLUDES SUCH INFORMATION AS: a. the author of the book and the *historical perspective* from which he/she wrote. b. the *occasion* for the book c. the *purpose* for the book including where pertinent the people for whom it was intended and their situation. d. any geographical or cultural factors bearing on the communication of the material.
2	Structure Of The Book	IN THE SPIRIT, PRAYERFULLY STUDY THE BOOK AS A WHOLE UNTIL YOU SEE THE AUTHOR'S PLAN OR STRUCTURE OR THE WAY HE RELATES HIS PARTS TO THE WHOLE BOOK TO ACCOMPLISH HIS PURPOSE OR DEVELOP HIS THEME.
3	Theme Of The Book	IN THE SPIRIT, PRAYERFULLY STUDY THE BOOK AS A WHOLE UNTIL YOU CAN IDENTIFY AND STATE CONCISELY THE AUTHOR'S THEME OF THE BOOK.
4	Context	IN THE SPIRIT, PRAYERFULLY STUDY THE AUTHOR'S PARAGRAPHS AND SECTIONS IN RELATION TO EACH OTHER SO THAT YOU CAN CONCISELY STATE THE CENTRAL IDEA OF EACH.
5	Grammar/ Syntax	IN THE SPIRIT, PRAYERFULLY STUDY THE AUTHOR'S GRAMMAR (i.e. the way he/she relates words, phrases, and sentences to develop paragraphs and larger sections) IN ORDER THAT YOU CAN STATE NOT ONLY THE CONTEXT OF A PARAGRAPH BUT THE FLOW OF THOUGHT IN DEVELOPING THE CONTEXT IN THE PARAGRAPH OR LARGER SECTION.

Table 1. Statement of General Language Laws continued

<u>LAW</u> <u>DEALING WITH</u>   <u>STATEMENT</u>

| 6 | Words | IN THE SPIRIT, PRAYERFULLY STUDY THE AUTHOR'S WORDS TO DETERMINE THE SENSE IN WHICH HE/SHE USES THEM IN DEVELOPING A GIVEN CONTEXT. |
| 7 | Book And Books | IN THE SPIRIT, PRAYERFULLY STUDY THE BOOK AS A WHOLE IN TERMS OF ITS RELATIONSHIP TO OTHER BOOKS IN THE BIBLE (i.e. the Bible as a whole) TO INCLUDE: a. its place in the progress of revelation, b. its overall contribution to the whole of Bible literature, and c. its abiding contribution to present time. |

It is these synthesis laws, 1,2,3 and 7, which form the basis for macro studies of the Bible for leadership information--the focus of this Handbook. Christian leaders need not only desire to learn the Word and to have a Bible centered ministry but must have tools and perspective that will aid them in their actual accomplishment of these worthy goals.

There is a need today for quality leadership. The Bible gives the basic issues on which Christian leadership is founded. Two verses in that most important leadership book, 2 Timothy, add to that advice.

Make every effort to present yourself to God as one approved, a workman who does not need to be ashamed and who correctly handles the word of truth. 2 Timothy 2:15

All Scripture is God inspired and is useful for teaching, rebuking, correcting and training in righteousness, so that the leader of God may be thoroughly equipped for every good work. 2 Timothy 3:16, 17.

Other Scriptures motivate us to study the whole Bible and elaborate on how it equips us.

For everything that was written in the past was written to
instruct us, so that through patient endurance and the
encouragement of the Scriptures we might have hope. Romans
15:4

Now these things happened as examples to keep us from
pursuing evil desires as they did.... These things happened to
them as examples and were written down to warn us, at this
crucial moment in history. 1 Corinthians 10:6,9

Remember your former leaders, who spoke God's Word to you.
Remember how they lived and how they finished. Imitate those
qualities of faith which made them what they were. Hebrews
13:7,8

Christian leaders need to know their Bibles and to center their lives and
ministry around its teaching. But few know the Bible well. Still fewer have
studied the Bible seriously with a view to learning what it can teach about
leadership.

My own studies of the Bible concerning leadership have led me to
identify the following approaches or kinds of Bible literature (genre) which
prove useful for leadership information. Recognizing the different sources
of leadership information is a first step. Getting tools to study each type is a
second. The Handbook series of which this Handbook is one, gives these
tools and some findings from each of these kinds of Bible genre.

1. Biographical: Joseph, Moses, Joshua, Caleb, Jephthah, etc.
2. Historical Leadership Acts: Samuel's final leadership act 1Samuel 12.
3. Actual leadership contexts: e.g. 1 Peter 5:1-5
4. Parabolic leadership literature: e.g. Stewardship parables
5. Indirect--passages dealing with Christian character or behavior
    which also apply to Christian leadership as well.
6. Study of Bible books as a whole: placing them in their context--
    hermeneutically and in terms of leadership development.
7. The Study across Books for common themes and lessons on
    leadership.

It is these last two approaches which are the thrust of this Handbook. They
require the use of language laws 1,2,3 and 7. Other Handbooks deal with the
other approaches or types.

Many Christian leaders can do something with language laws 4, 5, and 6. But they leave their hearers with details that have no overall meaning, no integrated coherence. Few can synthesize from the parts to the whole. And fewer still have done so in terms of what the Bible says about leadership. We must learn to handle correctly the Word of God, from cover to cover. We need to be equipped by it. And we desperately need the perspectives on leadership that the Bible has to offer us.

This handbook seeks to give two basic overall frameworks that help synthesize the Bible as a whole.

The *Redemptive Story time-line* helps us understand each book in the Bible in terms of what it is doing in terms of the redemptive story--that is, its major reason for being in the Bible. The *Structure, Theme, Purposes* and *Why Important* categories given for each Bible book seek to get at this perspective.

The *Bible leadership time-line* seeks to give an overall framework for viewing leadership development historically. Our Bible studies of leadership must be done in terms of the state of development of leadership at the time it occurred in the Scriptures. And then we seek to identify leadership lessons from these specific studies which may have broader usefulness. The *Where It Fits, Leadership Lessons*, and *Further Leadership Study* categories given for each Bible book seek to unravel insights in terms of the Bible leadership time-line.

Part I of the Handbook gives the frameworks through which I have worked to synthesize my studies of Part II of the Handbook. Part II then gives each book of the Bible and applies the language laws 1,2,3 and 7 to get leadership findings in their proper historical context.

(This page is deliberately left blank)

PART I. FOUNDATIONS

<u>Summary Preview</u>

Part I gives two major analytical frameworks which provide overall perspective for studying macro issues of leadership.

The first analytical framework is the **Time-Line of the Redemptive Story**. This time-line contains six sections,

> Introduction,
> Chapter 1. The Making of A Nation,
> Chapter 2. The Destruction of A Nation,
> Chapter 3. Messiah,
> Chapter 4. The Church, and
> Chapter 5. The Kingdom.

This story is briefly explained in a Running Capsule of the Redemptive Story. The story traces **what God does** and **what He says** throughout the Bible. And it shows that there is a progressive revelation of God throughout the whole drama. The Bible is unified around this salvation history. Once this is recognized then the notion of intentional selection becomes important. Each book in the Bible is there for a purpose and contributes something to this salvation story.

This overall time-line is then broken down into four time-lines which give more details about the books and when they occur. The four time-lines, given without comment, provide the framework for studying each book of the Bible. These four include,

> Time-Line 1. Bible Books and Introduction, Chapter 1
> Time-Line 2. Bible Books and Chapter 2
> Time-Line 3. Bible Books and the Return From Exile
> Time-Line 4. Bible Books and Chapters 3, 4, 5

It is this framework which provides the macro context for studying each book of the Bible. Where is the book in the progress of redemption time-line? What does it contribute to it? Why is it there? What would we miss if it were left out? Understanding each book in terms of its own purpose is a preliminary first step that must be done before we can interpret it for leadership findings.

The second analytical framework includes the **Time-Line of Historical Leadership Development.** Throughout the redemptive drama there are different needs for leadership. And there are different responsibilities. God raises up different kinds of leaders to meet the situations that arise. The various books in the Bible will present different kinds of leaders with no comments as to definition, purposes, or functions they accomplish. These must be interpreted. An understanding of this broad framework is helpful when each book is surveyed for leadership lessons. Other handbooks in the series deal with specific details of this time-line. Here it is assumed as an overall framework when seeking to see the fit of each book in terms of leadership findings.

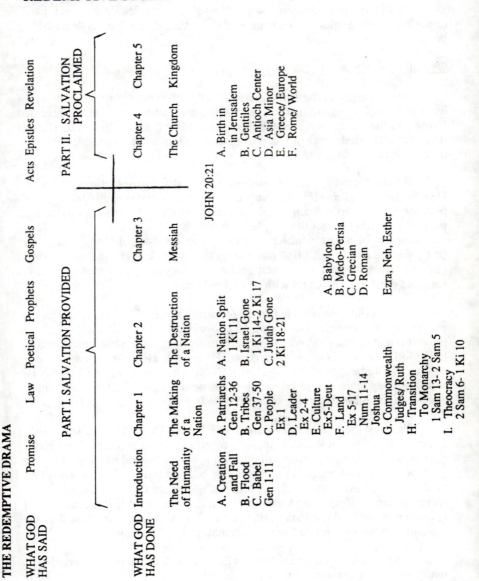

ANALYTICAL FRAMEWORK 1. TIME-LINE OF THE REDEMPTIVE STORY.

THE REDEMPTIVE DRAMA

WHAT GOD HAS SAID	Promise	Law	Poetical	Prophets	Gospels	Acts Epistles Revelation
	PART I. SALVATION PROVIDED					PART II. SALVATION PROCLAIMED
	Chapter 1	Chapter 2		Chapter 3		Chapter 4 Chapter 5

WHAT GOD HAS DONE	Introduction	Chapter 1	Chapter 2	Chapter 3	Chapter 4 Chapter 5
	The Need of Humanity	The Making of a Nation	The Destruction of a Nation	Messiah	The Church Kingdom

JOHN 20:21

The Need of Humanity

A. Creation and Fall
B. Flood
C. Babel
Gen 1-11

The Making of a Nation

A. Patriarchs Gen 12-36
B. Tribes Gen 37-50
C. People Ex 1
D. Leader Ex 2-4
E. Culture Ex5-Deut
F. Land Ex 5-17 Num 11-14 Joshua
G. Commonwealth Judges/ Ruth
H. Transition To Monarchy 1 Sam 13- 2 Sam 5
I. Theocracy 2 Sam 6- 1 Ki 10

The Destruction of a Nation

A. Nation Split 1 Ki 11
B. Israel Gone 1 Ki 14-2 Ki 17
C. Judah Gone 2 Ki 18-21

A. Babylon
B. Medo-Persia
C. Grecian
D. Roman

Ezra, Neh, Esther

The Church   Kingdom

A. Birth in in Jerusalem
B. Gentiles
C. Antioch Center
D. Asia Minor
E. Greece/ Europe
F. Rome/ World

The Running Capsule for the Redemptive Story

I will first give an overview and then give more detail from each part of the redemptive drama. See page 17 for the time-line which is described below.

<u>Overall</u>

At the center of the Biblical revelation is the concept of a God who has intervened in human history. He created the human race. He has revealed himself to that race. That race rebelled against His desires. In its fallen state it continually rebels against His wishes and desires and for the potential that it could accomplish.

So He started again and selected specifically a people through whom He could reveal Himself to the world. God moves unswervingly toward His purpose which is to redeem people and relate to them. He moves toward His purposes whether or not the people He has chosen follow them or not. They can willingly be a part in which they enjoy the blessings of God or they can be by-passed and He will find other ways to accomplish His purposes. He patiently works with them to include them in His purposes. But when all is said and done He moves on with or without them.

All the time He is increasingly revealing more of Himself and His purposes to His people. They come to know Him as a mighty God, all powerful and controlling, yet allowing human beings their choices. He is a holy God, that is, a being of perfection. He reveals His purposes as that of having a Holy people following Him. People who are becoming Holy as He is holy. They learn that to fall short of His demands or standards is to sin against Him and is deserving of retribution if justice is to be satisfied.

Part I of the redemption drama, **SALVATION PROVIDED**, is His selection of a people, which will prove foundational to accomplishing His purposes. Out of that people will come one who is central in the decrees of God. Not an afterthought but mysteriously beyond our thinking, known to God. Look at Revelation 13:8, the Lamb slain before the foundation of the world. In terms of what we know of God today, we see this Part I as revealing to us, God the Father, that is, the God who is source of all that we are and to whom we relate, infinite, eternal, powerful, a spirit.

God protects that line through which He will come over a period of many years and in times of failure on their part to know Him and obey Him as they should.

His incarnation into the world begins Part II of the Redemptive Drama, **SALVATION PROCLAIMED**. Galatians 4:4, in God's time. That incarnate God, manifest in the flesh, to communicate directly with the human race, to be a part of it, to share in its joys and sorrows, finally pays the supreme price of rejection, by a world who wanted to call its own shots, the death of the Cross, perfection paying the perfect price to satisfy God's Holy just demands. The great dilemma was solved, how God could be absolutely just and yet lovingly receive to Himself, those for whom justice demanded the harsh penalty of death. That time in which Jesus lived and walked and taught and did so many things to reveal God to us is the time, as we now know it of God the Son, God revealed to a human race as one of that race. Having accomplished the first portion of His work, the Cross, He ascended to heaven and will yet come again. Having ascended, He sent the Holy Spirit into the world, the intimation of what is to come, the Spirit who indwells those people He has chosen.

In the meantime while we wait we are involved in Part II **Salvation Proclaimed**, which shows that this message was more than just for the Jews but for a whole world. And that is what we are about today, the proclamation of that reconciling message, that God has provided a way in which sinful human beings can be rightly related to Him and progress to live a satisfying and fruitful life, in harmony with His purposes. And as they live this purposeful life, demonstrating the power and presence of God in their time on earth, they know that God is going to make all things right someday--there is a justice coming; the Lord Jesus, now a risen Savior, a life-giving Spirit will return to claim His own. There will be a time of His reigning on earth and then there will be eternity. And we who have been called out, as a people to His name, will reign with Him for all eternity. In terms of what we know today, this is the Age of God, the Spirit.

TIME-LINE FOR BIBLE BOOKS, INTRODUCTION AND CHAPTER 1

TIME-LINE OF BIBLE BOOKS--CHAPTER 1 OF THE REDEMPTIVE DRAMA

PART I. SALVATION PROVIDED...

	Introduction--The Need of Humanity	Chapter 1. The Making of A Nation			
WHAT GOD HAS DONE					
EVENTS		A. Patriarchs	B. Tribes C. People	D. Leader E. Culture	F. Land H. Kingdom G. Pre- Kingdom
WHAT GOD HAS SAID	A. Creation B. Fall C. Flood D. Babel	Gen 12-36 Job	Gen 37-50 Ex 1	Ex 2,3,4 Ex 5-Deut	Gen 15 1 Sam 13- Num 11-14 1 Ki 11 Joshua
	Gen 1,2 Gen 3 Gen 6-9 Gen 11				

<-------Psalms------->

<-----Proverbs------->

Ecclesiastes

Song of Songs

<u>Introduction</u> (See page 20 for the Time-Line which includes Genesis)

Genesis tells us of many beginnings. It tells of the beginning of the creation, the human race, of sin in the world, of the spread of the race, of judgment on the race and a new beginning for the race. It does not satisfy all our questions. We would ask more and want more. But it does give us the backdrop for the salvation story. Humanity is in need. It can not get along with itself. It has alienated itself from God. Left to itself it will be destructive at best. There is a need. And the salvation story which begins in Genesis chapter 12 will give God's response to meet that need.

<u>Chapter 1. The Making of a Nation</u> (See page 20 for Time-Line)

God's basic plan is to choose a people and to reveal Himself and His plans for reconciling the world to Himself through that nation. Chapter 1 tells of the story of God's building of the nation.

If I were to pick out the most important events in the making of a nation, Chapter 1 of the redemptive drama I would say the following would certainly be a part of it.

1. The call of Abraham--the Abrahamic Promise
2. The renewal of the covenant with Isaac
3. The renewal of the covenant with Jacob
4. The deliverance of Jacob and sons through Joseph
5. The call of Moses
6. The power encounters in Egypt and the Exodus
7. The Red Sea deliverance
8. The Spies in the Land/corporate failure of a faith check
9. The Giving of the 10 Commandments/covenant
10. Moses' failure--striking the rock
11. Moses' outstanding leadership in the desert years with a rebellious followership and his transition of Joshua into leadership
12. Crossing of Jordan
13. Circumcision at Gilgal
14. Joshua meets the Captain of the Hosts
15. Capture of Jericho
16. Failure at Ai
17. Success at Ai
18. Gibeonite deception
19. Capture of Land (lack of total obedience)

20. Repetitive Failure--moving from dependence to independence.
    The Cycle of the Judges (need for centralized influence)
21. Samuel's unifying influence
22. Saul's anointing and failure
23. David's anointing and success
24. David's failure and discipline
25. David's preparation for building the temple

Lets examine some of the Bible books which present these events.

From Genesis

From the introduction we know that humanity is not in good shape and is in need of intervention by God. And God has a plan thought out in eternity past.

God chooses one man, Abraham, and promises (THE FIRST GREAT REVELATION--THE PROMISE) to make of him a great nation and to give them land and to bless the world through his offspring. (Gen 12:1-3, 7; 15:4,18, et al) Now God plans to use the nation He will bring forth to be a channel of redemption and revelation of Himself. So He begins to build a nation. For a nation you need people (including numbers) a coherent culture, a land, and a leader.

God begins to work on these things--the people first (the land has people on it who will be judged eventually when they are too evil to be redeemed). From this one man, who exemplifies faith in God's promise, comes a son, Isaac. Isaac has two sons, one of whom, Jacob, becomes the successor of the family line through which God will work--the 12 heads of the tribes: Reuben, Simeon, Levi, Judah, Zebulun, Issachar, Dan, Gad, Asher, Naphtali, Joseph, Benjamin.

Joseph, a son of Jacob's old age and his favorite, is sold into slavery by his jealous brothers (Acts 7:9 Because the patriarchs were jealous of Joseph they sold him as a slave into Egypt. But God was with him and rescued him from all his troubles. He gave Joseph wisdom and enabled him to gain the goodwill of Pharaoh king of Egypt; so he made him ruler over Egypt and all his palace.) Joseph, a person of proven integrity, rises to power through a series of providential appointments in which he shows wisdom from God upon several occasions. God gives some dreams to Pharaoh, the ruler of Egypt, which predict some good years followed by famine years. Joseph gives a wise plan to Pharaoh on how to prepare for it. He is put in charge and is right on target to protect his own family when the famine hits.

The family comes to Egypt and rides through the famine years. It stays and expands in the land. Joseph , never losing sight of God's promise, exacts a promise from his brothers and fellow Israelites that they will take him back into the land when God takes them back. That is how Genesis ends.

From Exodus

Exodus opens many years later. There are many Israelite descendants, so many in fact, that the Egyptian King is fearful of them so he subjugates them. They are slaves and being ill-treated. Persecution takes the form of enforced labor and attempts to cut down the population (executing the boy babies).

God, having fulfilled the first part of his plan, getting a people, now works on the second part--getting a leader. Moses, an Israelite baby is preserved providentially and taken into the palace and educated as an Egyptian royal class person. As he reaches adulthood he recognizes that his people by blood relationship are in great bondage. So he wants to free them. His first attempt to help them is a disaster. He kills an Egyptian and has to flee Egypt. He goes to Midian, settles down, marries a Midianite woman, and has a family. After forty years, God selects him via a miraculous revelation, to go back to Egypt to lead God's people out of Egypt and into the promised land. Moses goes back and after 10 major confrontations with the Egyptian ruler (in which God-given power is seen--Moses certainly has spiritual authority) the people are freed to leave. But on the way the Egyptian ruler has second thoughts and pursues with his military. The military should overtake the Israelites who will be trapped by the Red Sea. God miraculously intervenes and they escape across the Red Sea on dry ground. The sea moves back as the military forces start to cross and they are wiped out. This is the heart of *the Exodus*.

From Exodus and Leviticus

God next begins to build the people culturally into what He will need. He gives them the LAW, the second great revelation and reveals more of Himself, His standards, and His purposes. The tabernacle which He gives the plans for reveals more of who God is in terms of access and revelation. The rest of EXODUS is given to that, revealing who God is as is the whole of LEVITICUS. It is especially in Leviticus that the holiness of God is developed--an understanding of sin and its implications; what atonement is (that is, being made right with God by making up for wrong against Him).

From Numbers

After disobedience and a lack of faith prevent the people from going in to the land (see NUMBERS) they wander for 40 years in the Sinai desert until the older rebellious people die off. During the desert years they learn to trust in God's provision. God reveals Himself primarily through his leader Moses. Near the end of the 40 years they are again ready to go into the land. God has a people, a culture, a leader, Moses, and a leader to take his place, Joshua. Moses prepares them for that push into the land by giving them a series of addresses (DEUTERONOMY--second law). These messages, his final words to them, reflect warnings drawn from their desert experience, remind them of standards of obedience which reflects what they have learned of God, and gives encouragement in the form of expectations as they enter the land. He closes his final words to them with songs of warning and blessing that portend the future. And thus we are ready for the third part of God's plan to build Himself a people--getting them into the land.

From Joshua

Joshua transitions into leadership with some sterling miraculous interventions by God which give him the spiritual authority he will need to follow Moses (a hard act to follow) as leader. Joshua seizes Jericho, after following a supernaturally revealed plan for its capture. He proceeds after an unexpected failure, which teaches an important corporate lesson on obedience, to the people, to split the land in two militarily and then begins to mop up in the north and south. The land is allotted. Each tribe has a portion, just as Moses had planned. They decentralize and begin to settle into their spots--with much trouble. After having been so long in a centralized authoritarian mode, they enjoy being decentralized and having autonomy. But this decentralization eventually leads to spiritual deterioration. This brings us up into the times of the judges.

From Judges

For a long period of time, longer than we in the United States have been a nation, the twelve tribes live scattered. There is frequent civil war in specific locales and much fighting with various surrounding nations and peoples who were not totally destroyed when the land was taken.

In short there is an oft repeated cycle: the people deteriorate spiritually getting far from God, God brings judgment upon them, they finally recognize that their problem is relationship with God--they repent and cry out for God's help. He sends along leaders, very charismatic who usually lead a volunteer army to defeat their enemies. There are at least 13 of these including: Othniel, Ehud, Shamgar, Deborah (Barak), Gideon, Abimelech, Tola, Jair, Jephthah, Ibzan, Elon, Abdon, and Samson. Some of these are more well known than others. Gideon and Samson for example. These are evil times and few there are who follow God.

In a section of the Judges (Judges 2:7) the writer sums it up well, "After Joshua had dismissed the Israelites, they went to take possession of the land, each to his own inheritance. The people served the Lord through out the lifetime of Joshua and of the elders who outlived him and who had seen all the great things the Lord had done for Israel." And then again in the closing portion a repeated phrase haunts us--Judges 21:25, "In those days Israel had no king; everyone did as he saw fit." These are the pre-kingdom years. Corporately the people are negatively prepared for the kingdom which will come.

From Ruth

There is a spark of life during those dreadful times. Ruth introduces us to that life by showing that there were some people of integrity who honored the Lord. This little romantic book shows how God provides and also allows us to see how the line through which the redeemer will later arise progresses.

The Judges and Ruth are pre-kingdom times. They prepared the Israelites to want a centralized structure after so much independence and autonomy. The Israelites were dependent upon voluntary armies raised up in times of crisis. Many times, other of the tribes than the one threatened, were not interested in their local squabbles and would not fight for them. Thus the entire commonwealth of tribes comes to the place where it needs, wants, and will accept a kingdom. Again God steps in and provides a transition leader-- Samuel.

From 1 Samuel

The first thirteen chapters show how Samuel was providentially raised up as a leader. His ministry as judge was not just a momentary deliverance but a continual one. He visited the different tribes and judged them--that is, established law and justice for them. Samuel paves the way for a centralized kingdom. Crises around the people spur the need; Samuel's own sons are not able to replace him. The people demand a king--showing their need for one but also showing that they basically did not trust the unseen King. God gives them one king, Saul, who outwardly is what they would expect. But he fails repeatedly to follow God. His kingdom is spiritually bankrupt. God replaces him with David, whom God describes as *a man after my own heart*. The last part of 1 Samuel describes Saul's fall and David's early pre-kingdom years, in which David is gaining military expertise as a guerrilla warfare leader with a para-military band.

From 2 Samuel and 1 Chronicles and the Psalms

2 Samuel and 1 Chronicles give David's story--one written earlier to it and one written later. David is a long time in getting the kingdom as Saul's descendants try to hold on to the kingdom. After seven years of civil war, David is ruling a smaller part of Israel, the kingdom is united. God gives a covenant to David concerning his descendants. The poetical literature, particularly the Psalms, emerge more solidly from this era. David is an artistic person who spends time alone with God in worship. Many of the Psalms come out of those times alone with God, many spurred on by crises in David's kingdom. The kingdom is established under David and expands. In mid-life David has a major sin which tarnishes his lifetime. He has one of his military leaders killed in order that he might take his wife for himself. It and failure to manage his family well lead to a rebellion by one of his sons Absalom. David is deposed briefly but comes back winning a strategic battle. He is reinstated. Most of the rest of his kingdom is downhill. David's son, Solomon, after some manipulation and political intrigue succeeds David.

A number of the Psalms are ascribed to David. They reveal something of the personal touch--what that great leader was feeling during some of the more important times of his kingdom. They particularly show his need for God and why God calls him a "man after my own heart."

From Proverbs and Ecclesiastes

Solomon has the best start of any king in all the history of Israel. There is peace in the land. The borders have expanded almost to the full extent of God's promise. There is money and resources in the kingdom as well as a good military. Times are stable. Solomon builds the temple for God--a symbol of the centralized importance of religious worship in the capital. Solomon's early years are characterized by splendor. Most likely during the early and middle part of his reign many of the Proverbs were collected. These sayings embody truth that has been learned over the years (times of the Judges, times of the kingdom) about how to live harmoniously with others. Toward the end of his reign, he slips and falls away from following God. In this latter part of his reign, he writes Ecclesiastes which sums up much that he has learned over his lifetime. Its cynical tone shows need for an intimate relationship with God that is missing.

The nation is there. There are people. They know of God and his desires for them. There is a land. But they continually fail to live up to what God wants. During the reigns of David and Solomon the kingdom reaches its zenith. And thus ends Chapter 1, the making of a nation. In it all, God is seen to weave His purpose all around a people who frequently rebel against Him. They freely choose to live as they do, whether following after God or not. But even so He manages to move unswervingly forward to His purposes.

TIME-LINE: BIBLE BOOKS IN CHAPTER 2, DESTRUCTION OF A NATION

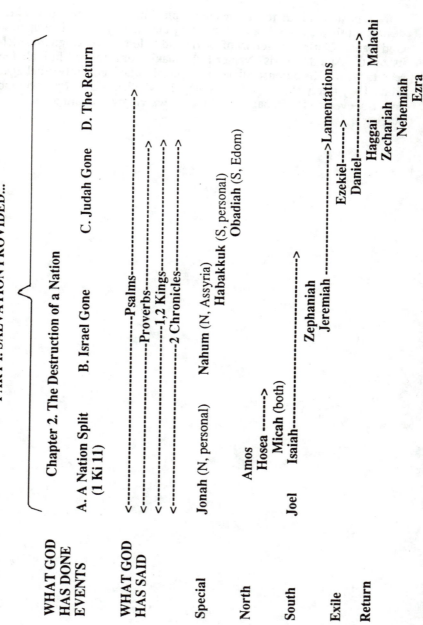

TIME-LINE OF BIBLE BOOKS--CHAPTER 2 OF THE REDEMPTIVE DRAMA

PART I. SALVATION PROVIDED...

Chapter 2. The Destruction of a Nation

WHAT GOD HAS DONE EVENTS	A. A Nation Split (1 Ki 11)	B. Israel Gone	C. Judah Gone	D. The Return

WHAT GOD HAS SAID

```
<----------------Psalms--------------------------->
<---------------Proverbs--------------------------->
<---------------1,2 Kings-------------------------->
<--------------2 Chronicles------------------------>
```

Special   Jonah (N, personal)   Nahum (N, Assyria)
Habakkuk (S, personal)
Obadiah (S, Edom)

North   Amos
Hosea ------>
Micah (both)

South   Joel   Isaiah-------------------------->
Zephaniah
Jeremiah --------------------->Lamentations

Exile   Ezekiel------->
Daniel-------->

Return   Haggai   Malachi
Zechariah
Nehemiah
Ezra

Chapter 2. The Destruction of a Nation (See page 28 for Time-Line)

The story-line of chapter 2 hinges around the following major events:

1. Solomon goes away from the Lord, great warning--had the best start of any king yet did not finish well.
2. Rehoboam (1 Kings 12) makes unwise decision to increase taxes and demands on people--kingdom splits as prophecy said. 10 tribes go with the northern kingdom, Judah with the southern.
3. The northern kingdom under Jereboam quickly departs from God. Jereboam is used as the model of an evil king to whom all evil kings are likened; He had a good start also--God would have blessed him.
4. The southern kingdom generally is bad with an occasional good Kings and partially good kings: Asa, Jehoshaphat, Joash, Amaziah, Uzziah, Jotham, Hezekiah, Josiah. But the trend was always downward. The extended length of life of the southern kingdom more than the northern kingdom is directly attributed to the spiritual life of the better kings. Spiritual leadership does make a difference.
5. During both the northern and southern kingdoms God sent prophets to try and correct them--first the oral prophets (many--but the two most noted were Elijah and Elisha) and then the prophets who wrote.

Now in order to understand this long period of history you should know several things:

1. The History books that give background information about the times.
2. The Bible Time-Line, need to know when the books were written.
3. Need to know the writing prophets: northern or southern kingdom, which crisis, direct or special.

The History Books

The history books covering the time of the destruction of a nation include 1, 2 Samuel, 1,2 Kings, and 1,2 Chronicles. The following chart helps identify the focus of each of these books as to major content.

Chart 1. The History Books--Major Content

1 Samuel	2 Samuel 1 Chronicles	1,2 Kings 2 Chronicles
Samuel Saul David	David	All Kings: Solomon-- Zedekiah

The time-line for the books of the Bible for Chapter 2, see page 28) reveals four categories of prophetical books. Prophetical books deal with three major crises: the Assyrian crisis which wiped out the northern kingdom; the Bablonian crisis which wiped out the southern kingdom; the return to the land after being exiled. There are also prophetical books not specifically dealing with these crises but associated with the time of them. The prophetical books dealing with these issues are:

A. Northern--Assyrian Crisis

Jonah, Amos, Hosea, Nahum, Micah

B. Southern--Babylonian Crisis

Joel, Isaiah, Micah, Zephaniah, Jeremiah, Lamentations, Habakkuk, Obadiah

C. In Exile

Ezekiel, Daniel, Esther

D. Return From Exile

Nehemiah, Ezra, Haggai, Zechariah, Malachi

In addition, to knowing the crises you must know that prophets wrote:

A. Direct to the Issue of the Crisis either Assyrian, Babylonian, or Return To The Land

Amos, Hosea, Joel, Micah, Isaiah, Jeremiah, Ezekiel, Haggai , Zechariah, Malachi

B. Special

Jonah, Nahum, Habakkuk, Obadiah, Zephaniah, Daniel.

The special prophets, though usually associated with one of the crisis times, wrote to deal with unique issues not necessarily related directly to the crisis. The following list gives the special prophets and their main thrust.

1. Jonah--a paradigm shift, pointing out God's desire for the nation to be missionary minded and reach out to surrounding nations.
2. Nahum--vindicate God, judgment on Assyria.
3. Habakkuk--faith crisis for Habakkuk, vindicate God, judgment on Babylon.
4. Obadiah--vindicate God, judgment on Edom for treatment of Judah.
5. Zephaniah--show about judgment, the Day of the Lord.
6. Daniel--give hope, show that God is indeed ruling even in the times of the exile and beyond, gives God's plan for the ages.

TIME-LINE: BIBLE BOOKS DESCRIBING THE RETURN TO THE LAND

TIME-LINE OF BIBLE BOOKS--CHAPTER 2 OF THE REDEMPTIVE DRAMA

PART I. SALVATION PROVIDED...

Chapter 2. The Destruction of a Nation--the Return

	520-518 B.C.	483-474 B.C.	Darius' Letter 456 B.C.	Artaxerxes Decree 442-432 B.C.	445-397 B.C.
WHAT GOD HAS DONE					
Left Hand of God	Cyrus' Decree		Darius' Letter 456 B.C.	Artaxerxes Decree 442-432 B.C.	
Events	Temple built / Temple begun	Esther as Queen Providential Deliverance		Wall Built	
Characters	Zerrubabel leads Remnant back; Zerrubabel (political leader) Joshua (priest) Ezra (priest)? Haggai (prophet) Zechariah (prophet)	Esther Mordecai Haman	Ezra (priest/teacher)	Nehemiah (lay person)	Malachi (prophet)
WHAT GOD HAS SAID	Zechariah Haggai	Esther	Ezra	Nehemiah	Malachi

The Destruction of A Nation--The Return From Exile (see page 32)

Several Bible books are associated with the return to the land from the exile. After a period of about 70 years (during which time Daniel ministered) Cyrus made a decree which allowed some Jews (those that wanted to) to return to the land. Some went back under Zerrubabel, a political ruler like a governor. A priest, Joshua, also provided religious leadership to the first group that went back. This group of people started to rebuild the temple but became discouraged due to opposition and lack of resources. They stopped building the temple. Two prophets, after several years, 10-15, addressed the situation. These two, Haggai and Zechariah, were able to encourage the leadership and the people to finish the temple.

Another thirty or forty years goes by and then we have the events of the book of Esther, back in the land. Her book describes the attempt to eradicate the Jewish exiles--a plot which failed due to God's sovereign intervention via Esther, the queen of the land and a Jewish descendant going incognito, and her relative Mordecai.

Still another period of time passes, 20 or so years and a priest, Ezra, directs another group to return to the land. The spiritual situation has deteriorated. He brings renewal.

Another kind of leader arrives on the scene some 10-15 years later. Nehemiah, a lay leader, and one adept at organizing and moving to accomplish a task, rebuilds the wall around Jerusalem. He too has to instigate renewal.

Finally, after another period of 30 or so years we have the book of Malachi which again speaks to renewal of the people. The Old Testament closes with this final book.

A recurring emphasis occurs during the period of the return. People are motivated to accomplish a task for God. They start out, become discouraged, and stop. They must be renewed. God raises up leadership to bring renewal.

Preparation for the Coming of Messiah--The Inter-Testamental Period

Some 400+ years elapse between the close of the Old Testament and the Beginning of the New Testament. There are significant differences in the Promised Land. The following chart highlights these differences.

Chart. Differences in Palestine--Close of O.T., Beginning of N.T.

The End of the Old Testament Testament	The Beginning of the New
1. Palestine was part of a Persian satrapy, since Persian, an eastern nation was the greatest governmental power in the world at the time.	1. Palestine was a Roman province, since the entire world had come under the sway of the western Nation of Rome.
2. The population was sparse.	2. One of the most dense parts of the Roman empire.
3. The cities of Palestine as a whole were were heaps of rubbish.	3. There was general prosperity throughout Palestine.
4. The temple of Zerubbabel was a significant structure.	4. The temple of Herod the Great was a magnificent building.
5. There were no Pharisees or Sadducees, although the tendencies from which they developed were present.	5. The Pharisees and Sadducees were much in evidence and strong in power.
6. There were no synagogues in Palestine.	6. Synagogues were located everywhere in the Holy Land. There was no hamlet or village so small or destitute as to lack a synagogue.
7. There was little extra-biblical tradition among the Jews.	7. There was a great mass of tradition, among both the Jews of Palestine and those of the dispersion.
8. The Jews were guilty of much intermarriage with the surrounding nations.	8. There was almost no intermarriage between Jews and non-Jews.
9. Palestine was under the rule of a Hebrew.	9. Palestine was under the rule of an Edomite vice-king, Herod the Great.
10. The Hebrew governor was regarded by the Jews as their spiritual leader.	10. The scribes and priest were regarded by the Jews as their spiritual leaders.

Note. This list came from my Old Testament studies with Frank Sells.

In addition to differences, there were some similarities between end of O.T. times and beginning of N.T. times.

1. **Freedom from idolatry.** God had used the Babylonian Captivity to free His people from their oft-repeated tendency to idolatry.

2. **Israel in two great divisions**, the Jews of the Homeland (Isolation) and the Jews of the Dispersion (who were scattered throughout the world). In the time of Malachi a relatively small proportion of God's chosen people was located in Palestine, while by far the larger part was still in exile. Although Palestine was much more thickly populated in the time of Christ than in the time of Malachi, the same general situation prevailed as to the two-fold division of Israel into Palestinian Jews and Jews of the Diaspora (Dispersion), with a far greater number in exile than in the land of Canaan.

3. **Externalism and dead orthodoxy.** A comparison of Malachi (the last prophetical book of the Old Testament) and Nehemiah (the last historical book of the Old Testament) with the Gospels indicates that the outward conformity of the Pharisees to the law which they inwardly revolted from, was but an advanced step of the hypocritical conformity which had marked many Israelites at the end of Old Testament days.

It was during the inter-testamental period that these changes occurred. Daniel had foretold of the various empires that would emerge after Babylon: the Medo-Persian, the Grecian, and the Roman. Each of these were used by God to prepare the way for the coming of Messiah, the next chapter in the redemptive drama.

The Importance of the Inter-testamental Period

During the so called 400 silent years (there is no written revelation) God was active. These years were the climax of several thousand years of Old Testament preparation for the coming of Christ. One major thing this period did was to authenticate fulfillment of Messianic prophecy. The interval between Malachi and Matthew was designed by God to separate the fulfillment from the giving of many Messianic prophecies so as to render impossible any collusion or trickery. These times give the historical background so that we can understand many things in the time of Christ. For example, the fierce patriotism of many Israelites at the time of Christ can only be understood in light of the prolonged warfare during this period. This period of time also helps us understand many prophecies of the book of Daniel.

There were 6 distinct periods during the Inter-testamental era. Each accomplished something that paved the way for Messiah.

1. The Persian Period 538 B.C. to 332 B.C.

Chief Thing: The chief thing which God accomplished during the Persian Period was the re-establishment of the Jews in Palestine.

2. The Macedonian Period--332 B.C. to 323 B.C.

Chief Thing: The chief thing God did during this period was to provide a worldwide cultural vehicle whereby the Gospel could be extended later.

3. The Egyptian Period 320 B.C. to 204 B.C.

Chief Thing: The chief thing which God accomplished during the Egyptian Period was the spread of missionary activity . God used an unsaved man (Ptolemy Philadelphus) to give the Old Testament (Septuagint) to the whole world in the cultural language that allowed it to be read (Greek). Alexandria was developed as a world center of learning. Two of its five zones were Jewish. A wonderful missionary opportunity. People from all over the world were coming to Alexandria and being exposed to God's working through the Jews and the Septuagint.

4. The Syrian Period 204 B.C. to 167 B.C.

Chief Thing: The chief thing which God accomplished during the Syrian period was the humiliation of His people in order that they might be purified and separated from Hellenizing influences.

5. The Maccabean Period 167-163 B.C.

Chief Thing: The chief thing which God accomplished during the Maccabean period was the rededication of the temple and the rededication of God's people to His redemptive purposes. Mattathias Hasmoneus and his five sons (Judas, Eleazar, John, Jonathan and Simon) were called Maccabees from the word "makkab (hammer)' since they were considered to be "the hammer of God" against the Syrians.

6. The Roman Period 63 B.C. to 70 A.D.

Chief Thing: The chief thing which God accomplished during the Roman period was the unification of the world and of the Jews. Since God had already used Nebuchadnezzar, Cyrus, and Alexander the Great as forward steps in the unification of the world, He used the Romans as the climax of this unification in preparation for the coming of His Son. Not only did God use the Roman emperors to unite the world and thus facilitate the spread of the Gospel. He also used Herod the Great to unite the Jews by building he beautiful temple which almost rivaled Solomon's temple for magnificence.

Galatians 4:4 states that Messiah came at the "fullness of time." That is, the time was ready. Some have suggested a fivefold preparation for Christ's Coming.

1. Religious Preparation--both negative and positive
2. Political Preparation--world at peace
3. Cultural Preparation--lack of meaning; cultural vehicle through which to spread the Gospel
4. The Social Preparation--great needs; life under bondage
5. The Moral Preparation

Note. This section on the inter-testamental period was condensed and adapted from Frank Sells' notes on the New Testament.

TIME-LINE: BIBLE BOOKS , CHAPTERS 3, 4, 5 OF REDEMPTIVE DRAMA

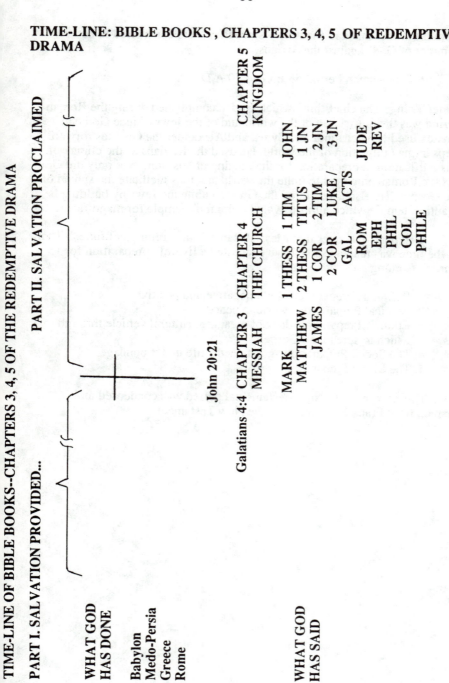

TIME-LINE OF BIBLE BOOKS--CHAPTERS 3, 4, 5 OF THE REDEMPTIVE DRAMA

PART I. SALVATION PROVIDED...

PART II. SALVATION PROCLAIMED

CHAPTER 5
KINGDOM

JOHN
1 JN
2 JN
3 JN

JUDE
REV

CHAPTER 4
THE CHURCH

1 THESS   1 TIM
2 THESS   TITUS
1 COR   2 TIM
2 COR   LUKE/
GAL   ACTS
ROM
EPH
PHIL
COL
PHILE

John 20:21

Galatians 4:4   CHAPTER 3
MESSIAH

MARK
MATTHEW
JAMES

**WHAT GOD
HAS DONE**

Babylon
Medo-Persia
Greece
Rome

**WHAT GOD
HAS SAID**

Chapter 3. Messiah

At the right moment in time--Jesus was born. His miraculous birth attested to his uniqueness.

He was the fulfillment of the Old Testament as to many of its prophecies, types, symbols. He was the seed of the woman who dealt a fatal blow to the seed of the serpent (Genesis 3:15); he was the tabernacle who lived among us (Exodus 25-40); he was the arch type of the brazen serpent, lifted up that people might look, see and be healed (Numbers 21); he was the arch types of the Levitical offerings , the perfect sacrifice (Leviticus 1-5); he was that prophet like unto Moses (Deuteronomy 18); he was the ultimate fulfillment of the Davidic covenant (2 Samuel 7); he was the Messianic Sufferer (Psalm 22); he was the one who was anointed to preach good news to the poor, to proclaim freedom for the captives, and release from darkness those who are prisoners, to proclaim the year of the Lord's favor (Isaiah 61:1ff) and the Suffering Servant (Isaiah 53); he was the righteous branch from David's line (Jeremiah 23); he was the one shepherd, the servant David, the prince of Ezekiel (Ezekiel 37); he was the one greater than Jonah, the sign after three days he arose (Jonah 21); he was the proper leader coming out of obscure Bethlehem (Micah 5:2); and we could go on.

Matthew showed he was the Messiah King, rejected. Mark showed him to be vested with divine power, a person of action and authority. Luke showed him to be the perfect representative of the human race: one of courage, ability, social interests, sympathy, broad acceptance. And John showed him to be Immanuel, God with us, revealing God to us and acting to demonstrate grace and truth, the heartbeat of the divine ministry philosophy.

The bottom line of the story line is given in a quote taken from John, "He was in the world, and though the world was made through him, the world did not recognize him. He came unto his own, but his own did not receive him. Yet to all who received him, to those who believed in his name, he gave the right to become children of God, children born not of natural descent, nor of human source but born of God. The Word became flesh and made his dwelling among us. We have seen his glory, the glory of the One and Only, who came from the Father, full of grace and truth." (John 1:10-14).

The story of this chapter of the redemptive drama ends abruptly. But there is a postscript. Each of the Gospel stories and the Acts tell us of Jesus Christ's resurrection. After His death He arose and was seen for a period of about 40 days upon various occasions. During those days He gave the marching orders for the movement He had begun. The great commissions repeated five times, Matthew 28:19,20, Luke 24:46,47, Mark 16:15, John 20:21, and Acts 1:8. Each of these carry the main thrust which is to go into the world and tell the Good News of salvation, that people can be reconciled to God. Each also carries some special connotation. It is these marching orders which set the stage for Chapter 4, The Church, in the redemptive story.

Chapter 4. The Church

The essence of the story line of chapter 4, is contained in the book of Acts. Its central thematic message is the essence of the story line.

Theme: **THE GROWTH OF THE CHURCH**
- which spreads from Jerusalem to Judea to Samaria and the uttermost parts of the earth,
- is seen to be of God,
- takes place as Spirit directed people present a salvation centered in Jesus Christ, and
- occurs among all peoples, Jews and Gentiles.

This basic phenomenon reoccurs as the Gospel spreads across cultural barriers throughout the world. Though the message of the book of Acts covers only up through the first two thirds of the first century its basic essence reoccurs throughout the church age until the present time in which we live.

About half of the book of Acts tells of the formation of the church in Jerusalem and its early expansion to Jews, Samaritans, and finally to Gentiles. The latter half of the book traces the breakout of the Gospel to Gentiles in Asia and Europe. The structure of the book highlighted by the linguistic discourse markers (the Word of the Lord grew) carries the notion of a God-given church expanding.

Structure: There are seven divisions in Acts each concluding with a summary verse. The summary verses: 2:47b, 6:7, 9:31, 12:24, 16:5, 19:20, 28:30,31

I.	(ch 1-2:47)	The Birth of the Church in Jerusalem
II.	(ch 3-6:7)	The Infancy of the Church in Jerusalem
III.	(ch 6:8-9:31)	The Spread of the Church into Judea, Galilee, Samaria
IV.	(ch 9:32-12:24)	The Church Doors Open to the Gentiles
V.	(ch 13-16:5)	The Church Spreads to Asia Minor
VI.	(ch 16:6-19:20)	The Church Gains a Foothold in Europe
VII.	(ch 19:21-28)	The Travels of the Church's First Missionary To Rome (The Church on Trial in its Representative Paul)

As to details there are many important pivotal events in the Acts, many of which have similarly reoccurred in the expansion of the Gospel around the world and throughout church history. Acts begins with Jesus' post resurrection ministry to the disciples and his Ascension to heaven. Then the disciples are gathered at Jerusalem praying when the Pentecost event, the giving of the Holy Spirit to the church, as promised in Luke's version of the Great Commission, happens and Peter gives a great public sermon which launches the church.

Early church life is described. Peter and John imbued with power heal a lame man at the temple gate and are put in prison. They are threatened and released. An incident with Ananias and Sapphira shows the power and presence of the Holy Spirit.

Stephen an early church servant has a strong witness and is martyred for it. General persecution on the church breaks out. The believers are scattered and preach the gospel where ever they go. Phillip, another early church servant leads an Ethiopian palace administrator to Christ and has ministry in Samaria.

Saul, the persecutor of Christians, is saved on the road to Damascus. Peter demonstrates Godly power in several miraculous events. Peter is divinely chosen to preach the Gospel to a Gentile, Cornelius. Herod kills James and imprisons Peter. Peter is miraculously delivered.

The story line now switches to follow the missionary efforts of Barnabas and Paul (formerly Saul) to Cyprus and Asian minor. It then goes on to follow Paul's efforts which go further into Asia minor and Greece. Paul makes a return visit to Jerusalem where he is accused by the Jewish opposition in Jerusalem. Eventually after several delays and hearings he is ordered to Rome. The book ends with the exciting journey to Rome, including a shipwreck.

The time-line on page 38 shows approximately when the books of the New Testament were written. Many were written by Paul. These generally were letters to the various churches which had resulted from his missionary efforts. Each was contextually specific--written at a certain time, written at a certain stage of Paul's own development as a leader, and dealing with a specific situation--either an individual in a church or to a corporate group, some church at a location or in a general region.

Other New Testament books not written by Paul are also shown on the time-line. The book of Hebrews, author uncertain, John's three letters, Jude's one letter and Peter's two letters all are of a general nature. With the exception of possibly 2nd and 3rd John, these letters were written to believer's in general in scattered regions--probably Asia minor.

All of these, Paul's letters, and the general books, deal with the church. They give us insights into church problems, church situations at that time, and the essence of what the church is and how Christians ought to live. These New Testament books are filled with leadership information. Each of them represents a major leadership act of a leader seeking to influence followers of Christ. Many of them have actual details that reflect leadership values, leadership problem solving, and leadership issues. All of them have important modeling data.

We would have an unfinished story if we were left only with *just these* New Testament books. We would have a task. And men and women would be out and about the world attempting to fulfill that task. But where is it leading. What about those Old Testament prophecies yet to be fulfilled about *that day*. Our story is incomplete. We need to know how this redemptive drama is going to end. And so the Revelation.

Chapter 5. The Kingdom

The final book of the Bible is aptly named. The Revelation (unveiling, revealing, making clear) of Jesus Christ (the unveiling of Jesus Christ) brings closure to the redemptive drama. This final book in the Bible has among others these purposes:

1. to reveal future purposes of Jesus Christ and graphically show the power He will unleash in accomplishing His purposes, which include bringing about justice and bringing in His reign,
2. to show those purposes and power to be in harmony with His divine attributes, and
3. to bring a fitting climax to the redemptive story developed throughout Scripture.

The theme statement of the book of Revelation highlights the fitting climax of the redemptive drama.

Theme: **GOD'S ULTIMATE PURPOSES FOR HIS REDEMPTIVE PROGRAM**
- center in the Person of His Son,
- involve His churches,
- will take place in a context of persecution and struggle--as described cryptically by many visions,
- will focus on the triumph of Jesus and his judgment of all things in harmony with his divine attributes, and
- will be realized in final victory for His people and ultimate justice accomplished in the world.

God's intent from the first of Genesis on has been to bless His people with His eternal presence. Ezekiel closes his book with that thought in mind. Numerous of the prophets point to a future day in which things would be made right and God would dwell with His people. The plan has had many twists and turns but through it all God has sovereignly moved on to His purpose.

Some have followed hard after God and were included in His purposes. Others refused to follow God. They were cast aside. God moved on.

In the New Testament God prepares a way where He can reveal Himself in justice and love and reconcile all people unto Himself. The Cross climaxes all of God's preparation to bless the world. The message of the Cross is seen to be for all. The church goes out into all the world. It has its problems. But always it seeks to be part of God's future purposes looking forward to Christ's return. Were there no Revelation, the Redemptive Story would be incomplete. The Revelation brings to a fitting climax all of God's working to bless the world. There is seen to be an ultimate purpose in history. Justice is meted out. And there is the final blessing--the eternal presence of God with His people.

TIME-LINE OF HISTORICAL LEADERSHIP DEVELOPMENT

TIME-LINE OF BIBLICAL LEADERSHIP

	I. LEADERSHIP ROOTS	II. PRE-KINGDOM LEADERSHIP	III. KINGDOM LEADERSHIP	IV. POST-KINGDOM LEADERSHIP	V. N.T. PRE-CHURCH LEADERSHIP	VI. N.T. CHURCH LEADERSHIP
	A. Abraham B. Isaac C. Jacob D. Joseph E. Job	A. Desert B. Conquering The Land C. Conquered By the Land	A. United B. Divided C. Single Kingdom	A. Exile B. Post Exilic C. Interim	A. Pre-Messianic B. Messianic	A. Jewish B. Gentile
Book	Gen, Job	Ex, Lev, Num, Deut Josh Judges	I,II Sam, I Chron Isa, Hos I, II Ki II Chron, Jer	Eze, Dan, Est Ezra, Neh, Hag Zech, Mal	extra biblical Matt Matt, Mk, Lk, Jn	Acts, 1,2 Peter Jas, Jn, 1,2,3 Jn Acts, Pauline
Cycle	decentralized	centralized centralized decentralized	centralized	decentralized	Quasi-centralized Centralized	centralized decentralized
Dominant Trait	heritage	spiritual authority military charismatic/military	political pol/proph pol/proph	modeling renewal	religious spiritual movement	spiritual institutional
Nature	family	revelatory task crisis	unifying degenerate/corrective	inspirational task	cultic movement Jewish Church	worldwide church
Kinds of Leaders	patriarchical tribal local priests local kings local military	spir/pol/mil clans judges prophets military	political formal relig informal relig prophets military various court	models prophets (priests) administrators military	Scribes, Lawyers Various Roman Rabbis, Priests Political Elders	Apostles Evangelists Prophets, Pastors Missionaries Elders, Overseers Deacons
examples	Abraham Judah Melchezedak Kedorlaomer	Moses, Miriam Joshua, Caleb Othniel Deborah	Saul, David Jereboam Hezekiah	Daniel Ezekiel Ezra Zerubbabel	Theudas Gamaliel Jesus	Peter, Paul, Barnabas Phillip Philemon Luke, Timothy

BRIEF EXPLANATION OF THE LEADERSHIP DEVELOPMENT TIME-LINE

The basic elements common to all leadership are three: leaders, followers, and situations. Characteristics and kinds of all three of these can vary over time. There are perhaps 30 to 40 different kinds of specific leadership types mentioned in Scripture. Some kinds include: patriarchal, tribal, local priests, local kings, local military, clans, judges, mediums, priests, military (various levels), political, prophets, teachers, rabbis, apostles, prophets, evangelists, pastors, elders, deacons. There are several thousand leaders actually mentioned by name in the Bible. There is enough information on about one hundred of these so that profitable biographical studies can be done. Another handbook makes this the thrust of its findings.

In studying a given book of the Bible for leadership findings it is helpful to place it in its leadership context. The leadership time-line identifies six different eras of leadership. We are presently in the sixth era which makes it an important one for us. However, there are important leadership findings that occur all along the various eras which have application today. Leadership, followership, and situational dynamics are generally alike during an era and quite different from another era. Succeeding eras usually introduce new types of leaders to meet the new situational dynamics arising.

Two major factors affect differing leadership types and functions. One factor recognizes the relationships between the basic leadership elements. Because followership dynamics and situational dynamics change over time, so too will leadership types and functions. For example followership in the Leadership Roots era (Patriarchal) has dominantly to do with families and flows along familial authority lines. A leader's sphere of influence is small but pervasive. But followership in the United kingdom era is quite different. David's sphere of influence is much broader than family. It includes several million Israelites united loosely into a kingdom. His sphere of influence though broad is not so pervasive. What a king does, though having some common things with a Patriarch, is generally very different. A second factor has to do with God's progressive revelation of Himself and His purposes to His people. Further generations have more light. This brings higher responsibility for leaders.

So then, when a given book is studied for leadership insights one must remember when it occurred, what kind of leaders were necessary for the era, what their prime functions were, and how much they knew of God's purposes and plans. They must be judged in terms of their own leadership era and not succeeding eras.

20 IMPORTANT BIBLE BOOKS GIVING LEADERSHIP FINDINGS

The following are some important books that are a source of leadership findings. I have listed them in the order that they are important to me. I would not quibble if someone else ordered them differently or even took some off this list and added others. But at least these ought to be studied seriously with a leadership focus.

Book	Focus of Leadership Findings
1. 1 Timothy	Mentoring, local church leadership lessons, consulting ministry, developmental focus
2. 2 Timothy	Mentoring, finishing well, developmental focus
3. Titus	Apostolic ministry, local church leadership, use of spiritual authority
4. Deuteronomy	leadership values, leadership transition, biographical, processing, motivational techniques, finishing well
5. 2 Corinthians	leadership values, processing, spiritual authority
6. Daniel	perspective, leadership lessons, biographical, processing
7. Ezekiel	leadership lessons, processing
8. Joshua	leadership transition, leadership lessons, spiritual authority, biographical, processing
9. Habakkuk	processing, perspective
10. Jonah	processing
11. Haggai	leadership lessons, task oriented leadership, motivational techniques
12. Luke	mentoring, leadership training, processing

Book	Focus of Leadership Findings
13. Nehemiah	leadership lessons, task oriented leadership, motivational techniques
14. Malachi	leadership lessons, renewal issues
15. 1 Corinthians	leadership lessons, problem solving, spiritual gifts
16. Isaiah	perspective, processing, leadership lessons
17. 1, 2 Samuel	biographical, processing, leadership lessons
18. 1,2 Kings	biographical, processing, leadership lessons
19. Hebrews	renewal issues, inspirational leadership
20. Micah	leadership lessons, urban influence

PART II.
BIBLE BOOKS AND THEIR CONTRIBUTION TO LEADERSHIP

Introduction

Each of the books of the Bible has been studied using the analytical frameworks described in Part I of this Handbook. The Bible books are listed as they fall along the time-line (one exception--John is included with the synoptic Gospels since it deals with Messiah).

For each book, the outline categories include those described below in Chart 2.

Chart 2. Outline Categories for Each Book--Thrust of Each

Category	Intent of Category
BOOK	English name for the book.
Author	Gives the name of the author who traditionally is held to have written the book or overseen its organization or contributed the majority of information to it. This category has as its intent use of language law 1 on historical background.
Characters	Lists important persons either acting in the events of the book or those mentioned in the book and important to know in order to understand parts of the book.
Who To/for	Attempts to list who the writing was intended for.
Literature Type	Lists the various types of material that the interpreter must work with such as historical narrative, Hebrew Poetry, visions, prophecies, letters, exhortative passages, didactic (teaching), etc. This is important not only for exegesis (methods of analyzing) but also for asserting validity of lessons found.
Story Line	This gives information which either traces the flow of events through the book or sets the contextual stage around the book and its writing so that the book can be read with the background in mind.

Chart 2. Outline Categories for Each Book--Thrust of Each continued

Category   Intent of Category

Structure   This attempts to determine the author's plan for presenting information, or relating his parts in order to accomplish the purpose or develop the theme.

Theme   The author's theme is made up of a major subject, the most important thing the whole book is about, which synthesizes the overall thrust of the parts and usually a major idea about the subject which comes
from each structural part. The theme statement can be read as one continuous statement or it can be read in terms of subject and each major idea. It is this theme to which all parts, sections, and paragraphs relate. Each should develop something about the theme.

Key Words   This gives important repeated words or phrases. Such repeated items usually help identify the thematic subject of the book, or major ideas.

Key Events   This identifies the major events in the book itself or to which the book alludes. Understanding of these items is usually crucial to getting the flow of ideas in the book or to identifying the development of some subject.

Purposes   There are two kinds of purposes statements included in this category. One type of purpose has to do with identified purposes of the author of the book. Sometimes these are stated. Sometimes they are deduced from the inclusion or exclusion of subject matter or the thrust of the exhortation sections. A second type of purpose has to do with assumptions concerning the contribution of the book to the Bible as a whole. The original author may not have had that purpose in mind. But a study of what the book does in light of other books reveals it. Almost none of these purposes are absolute in nature. They are simply best analytical attempts. They are open to rejection, modification, and additions.

Chart 2. Outline Categories for Each Book--Thrust of Each continued

Category	Intent of Category
Why Important	This category seeks to point out something of the unique contribution of the book. To emphasize why it is in the Bible and important to the redemptive story. This category seeks to apply language law 7, seeing the book in terms of the Bible as a whole.
Where It Fits	This category identifies where on the leadership time-line the book fits in order to help assess the kind of leadership information it may contain.
Leadership Lessons	This category attempts to identify suggestions, guidelines or absolutes which reflect leadership ideas that might be helpful to leaders today. These ideas will range in terms of how certain they are and how applicable to today's situations depending on a number of factors. Where these statements are seen to occur in many different books of the Bible the more they are likely to be toward absolutes. This category applies the two macro analytical approaches, the book as a whole, and the book in comparison with other Bible books. Frequently these are just tentative observations that are suggested by leadership concepts that I have studied both in my research (both secular and Christian). Handbook I will contain detailed explanation of some of these concepts. Sometimes I will give added explanation in footnotes. The leadership models and frameworks that I have identified in my research over the past 12 years often serve as heuristic (discovery) models--that is, they stimulate me to see things in the Bible that I would not have previously seen without these models.
For Further Leadership Study	This category identifies topics, types of material, and other such information worthy of further analysis. This Handbook does expose detailed study on these topics though that may have been done to arrive at the lessons given in the above category.
Special Comments	This is a catch-all. I put what ever I want to here.

BOOK Genesis   **Author:** uncertain, Moses some

Characters	Adam, Eve, Cain, Abel, Enoch, Noah, Abraham, Isaac, Jacob, Joseph
Who To/for	For Israelites
Literature Type	Selected Narrative/ vignettes

Story Line

       Time-Line: Genesis traces redemptive history from the origin of the human race until the death of Joseph.

       Content-Line: It gives the beginnings of the human race, the beginning of sin (and thus separation from God), the beginning of the redemptive story of the people of God--particularly the patriarchal leadership of Abraham, Isaac, Jacob, and Joseph.

       Uniqueness: There is a high degree of intentional selectivity both since so many years are covered and since there is a narrowing of focus to Abraham's line (later called Israel) through which redemption will come.

Structure

I. Gen 1-11, Critical Events of Early Human History
II. Gen 12-50, Early Selection of God's People--
                       Patriarchal History

Theme

GOD'S INTERVENTION IN HUMAN HISTORY INVOLVES
- His creation of the human race and His plans for it,
- His judgment of that race,
- His promise to bless it, and
- His selection of a people for His purposes.

Key Words   generations

Key Events   Creation, Fall of Human Kind, Flood--Judgment, Babel--Judgment, Selection of Abraham and the Promise, Renewal of Covenant with Isaac, Jacob; preservation of Israel via Joseph.

Purposes
- to furnish an account of the beginning of things, (human race, sabbath, marriage, sin, sacrifice, nations, governments)

Genesis continued

- to especially point out the origin of God's peculiar people, known as Israel, from whom a redeemer would come.

Why Important   It explains why things are the way they are. This sets the stage for our understanding of what God is doing. **Most importantly, it gives the promise around which redemptive history focuses.**

Where It Fits   Genesis 1-11 introduces the need of humanity and sets the stage for the whole redemptive drama. Genesis 12-50 is the first part of Chapter 1, The Making of a Nation. It tells about the patriarchs and the initiation of the twelve tribes. In terms of the leadership time-line it occurs in Phase I, Leadership Roots which describes patriarchal leadership.

Leadership Lessons

1. **ESSENTIAL INGREDIENT OF LEADERSHIP.** The presence of God is the essential ingredient of patriarchal leadership. Among other things (guidance, intervention to save, etc.) the blessing and protection of God reveals this presence.
2. **BLESSING FUNCTION.** Patriarchs are to be channels of God's blessing especially to their families but also beyond.
3. **CONTAGIOUS BLESSING.** Contagious blessing describes the situation where those associated with patriarchal leadership are blessed in their affairs because of that association and recognize that it is the Patriarch's God who is responsible (see Abraham/Abimelech: Gen 20:17, 21:22; Isaac/Abimelech 26:28; Jacob/Laban Gen 30:27; Joseph/Potiphar, Jailer, Pharaoh, 39:2-6, 20-33, 47:13ff).
4. **REALITY DEMONSTRATED.** Patriarchs are to demonstrate the reality of the living God.
5. **LOYALTY TO GOD.** Patriarchs are to have supreme loyalty to the living God.
6. **INSPIRATIONAL FUNCTION.** Patriarchal leadership dominantly deals with the inspirational function of leadership.
7. **HERITAGE IMPLICATIONS.** One inspirational function has to do with passing on a heritage with God to the generation to come.
   a. Part of the heritage passed on is that of loyalty to God. God must be supreme.
   b. They are to pass on a heritage of obeying God,

Genesis continued

     c. They are to especially pass on their deep experiences with God and His promises made to them.

     d. Part of the heritage passed on is that of destiny with God. The notion of a chosen people for a special purpose.

8. **POWER BASE--FULL RANGE.** Family leadership allows for the full range of power components (Wrong's continuum) force, coercive, inducive, positional, competent, personal). The natural tendency is from left to right as the followers (descendants) mature.

For Further Leadership Study

1. The first leadership mandate is given in Genesis 1:26-28. Let us make mankind in our image, in our likeness, and let **them rule** over the fish of the sea and the birds of the air, over the livestock, over all the earth, and over all the creatures that move along the round. What are the implications of this joint mandate given before the fall?
2. See Genesis 3:16, he will rule over you . What are the implications of this in terms of leadership?
3. The Characters Abraham, Isaac, Jacob, Joseph should be studied as biographical sources.
4. The wives: Sarah, Rebekah, Leah, Rachel should be studied. In a male dominated study notice that the power form of manipulation is used frequently by the wives. These women exerted influence.
5. Notice the cultural forms of leaders: city princes, leaders of bands, a priest (Melchezedak), military leaders.
6. Social structure should be carefully studied in order to see the different kinds of leadership roles and influence. The concept of steward is given during the leadership roots era. How the wives and concubines related and its impact on their children is important.

Special Comments:

Key verses: Gen 12:1-3; one of my favorite chapters Genesis 15; one of my favorite characters--Joseph. Moses probably wrote at least some of this book.

BOOK	**Job** **Author:** uncertain, maybe Job
Characters	Satan, Job, Eliphaz, Bildad, Zophar, Elihu
Who To/for	Israelites
Literature Type	Poetry, A series of dialogues in poetical format between Job and his friends: Eliphaz, Bildad, Zophar. Finally, Elihu speaks. Then God concludes. Much figurative language.
Story Line	Job, a righteous patriarch in early times, worships the living God and obeys the revelation he has about that God. He is tested to see if he will serve God no matter what. The tests are instigated by Satan--a powerful evil being under the final control of God. Job goes through the loss of family, friends, wealth, and finally health. As he suffers he is trying to understand why. His friends Eliphaz, Bildad, and Zophar come to help him think it through. Each gives his opinion two or three times and Job rejects their views each time. Finally, a younger friend Elihu summarizes. God then speaks. Job sees God in the situation and repents. God blesses Job.

Structure

I. (ch 1,2)   Behind The Scenes--Unraveling the Mystery of Suffering
II. (ch 3-37)   The Pain and Confusion of Suffering
III. (ch 38-42)   God Through the Suffering

Theme

THE MYSTERY OF A RIGHTEOUS PERSON'S SUFFERINGS
- is confusing to sufferer and friends,
- challenges current explanatory views, and
- becomes clearer when it is seen that God allows it and uses it to bring unreserved consecration to the sufferer.

Key Words   affliction--11; righteous--21, arrows of the almighty

Key Events   Job's loss of material possessions, family, and health

Job continued

Purposes
- to teach us unconditional responsiveness to God
- to teach us how paradigm shifts occur
- to teach us about patriarchal leadership--major traits: loyalty to God, faithful to revelation, pass on to heirs Godly heritage,
- to teach us about isolation
- to give insights into spiritual warfare
- to stress God's overall providential control

Why Important   Suffering is a fact of life throughout the world. We need answers. We only get a partial answer in Job. The New Testament elaborates. But the answer we get is important. We must respond to God in the midst of the suffering. He has his purposes which may not always be clear to us. And most importantly we would not know about **Satanic influence in the physical world nor know of God's purposes in it.**

Where It Fits   Job like Genesis occurs during either the introduction or chapter 1 of the redemptive drama. We are not told. It does not directly deal with the on-going redemptive drama but instead deals with suffering a subject fitting anywhere along the redemptive drama. It occurs in the time of patriarchal leadership and gives great lessons on how God shapes the character of a leader. It is the classic treatment in the Old Testament of isolation processing.

Leadership Lessons

1. **ISOLATION PROCESSING.** Isolation processing is always meant to take us deeper with God. This book deals with causes and responses in isolation processing. For details on isolation processing see the position paper on *Isolation Processing* [1] which treats this subject comparatively across several Bible characters. See also the biographical treatment of Job in Handbook II.

---

[1] This Isolation paper is available through Barnabas Publishers, 2175 North Holliston Avenue, Altadena, CA 91001.

Job continued

2. **PARADIGM SHIFT**. An experiential paradigm shift is often needed before we can see the cognitive essence behind it. Job also shows the importance of a processing that leads to a paradigm shift[2]. See especially the biographical treatment of Job.
3. **CHARACTER TESTING**. Character testing is one of God's ways of developing a leader.
4. **CONTAGIOUS BLESSING**. God frequently blesses others because of their association to a leader He is using. The concept of contagious blessing is seen with Job.
5. **EXCLUSIVE LOYALTY**. The patriarchal leadership trait of exclusive loyalty to God is illustrated in Job.
6. **BLESSING FUNCTION**. Job also illustrates the blessing aspect of patriarchal leadership both in regards to his children but also to his friends for whom he prayed in God's blessings.
7. **CONTINUANCE OF HERITAGE**. Job enforces the patriarchal leadership duty of passing on a Godly heritage to children.

For Further Leadership Study

1. Study Job for its indications of how God gives revelatory information.
2. Study Job for the progress of knowledge about the world known during the patriarchal age.
3. Study Job for findings on paradigm shifts (why they are opposed, how God breaks through) and for isolation processing (the various stages one goes through in deep processing).
4. Study Job in order to understand the Wider Hope[3] view of salvation.

Special Comments

   The 929 chapters of the Old Testament contain 2274 questions. Of individual books Job stands first with 329 questions (Jeremiah next with 195). That is the nature of suffering, isolation, and crises--we question things--want to know why. Need to understand Hebrew poetry to get into Job: same, opposite, progressive. Some favorite verses: 13:15; 19:25,26; 38:2; 42:2. Job speaks much more than anyone--one thing we must do is learn to listen well to those who are suffering. Job knew God intimately: favorite titles include God (Elohim), Lord (Jehovah), The Almighty (El Shaddai) 48 times in Bible, 31 times in Job, The Holy one, The Preserver of men, Lord (Adonai--master).

---

[2]See the position paper on Paradigm Shift which is also available through Barnabas Publishers. Paradigm Shifts along with ministry structure insights are critical antidotes to plateauing in leadership, a pitfall that all leaders may fall into several times during their development over a life time.

[3]See John Sanders' **No Other Name**, **Eerdmans** Publishing: Grand Rapids, 1992.

BOOK	**Exodus Author:** uncertain, Moses some
Characters	Moses, Aaron, Pharaoh, Tribes of Israel, Joshua
Who To/for	Israelites
Literature Type	Selected Narrative/ vignettes, description of tabernacle-- basically revealed to Moses in a vision; understood only in connection with books which go before and after it. Does not stand alone.
Story Line	*Time-Line*: Exodus traces redemptive history from the time of Israel's slavery (about 400 years after Joseph's death) until Moses has led the people triumphantly out of bondage in Egypt into the desert toward the promised land. *Content-Line*: Exodus highlights the call of Moses as God's leader, the miraculous events, which accompany the release of God's people from slavery in Egypt, the initial formation of Israel into a people of God's law, and the design of the tabernacle--focusing on God's presence among them and their access to Him.

Structure

I. (ch 1)   The Situation--Israel in Bondage
II. (ch 2,3)   God's Solution to the Situation--A Leader
III. (ch 4-14) God' Deliverance of Israel--The Exodus
IV. (ch 15-24) God's Revelation at Sinai--The Law
V. (ch 25-40)   God's Pattern for Worship--The Tabernacle

Theme

GOD'S INITIAL FORMATION OF A PEOPLE
- involved selection of a special leader,
- necessitated a supernatural deliverance,
- required revelation as to His expectations for Holy living,
- concluded by focusing on patterns of worship.

Key Words   redeem (10)

Key Events

The preservation of Moses, call of Moses, authoritative power encounters on the gods of Egypt--10 Plagues, The Exodus/supernatural release and preservation at Red Sea, the initial trials of the desert, Sinai disclosures (destiny fulfillment for Moses), the revelation of the tabernacle (patterns of worship--see typological explanation in Hebrews).

Exodus continued

Purposes
- to show God's continued fulfillment of His promise to Abraham,
- to record the law and the context in which given.
- to record the celebration of the Passover and heighten its memorial importance in focusing on God,
- to reveal numerous essentials of leadership; this book is filled with information on leadership.

Why Important
It traces the **emergence of the nation**. It shows how critical leadership is in the early stages of an effort. As Morgan indicates Exodus teaches us about God's sovereignty. His righteousness is revealed in purpose and plan and His judgment is seen to be with wisdom and power. And Exodus teaches us about the salvation of man. Worship must have God at center and life concentric around that. **Obedience must be simple and complete even against opposition.** See Morgan (Handbook...), 1st 3 paragraphs, page 5ff.

Where It Fits
In the redemptive drama Exodus occurs early in Chapter 1, The Making of A Nation. A nation needs leadership, people, a land and a unifying culture or value system. At the beginning of Exodus, a leader is chosen by God, Moses. There are people. It is the Exodus that unites them into a nation of people with its own culture and value system. Their crisis experiences in leaving Egypt, crossing the Red Sea, and desert wanderings unite them under a leader. Their revelation from God concerning values and proscriptions on living bind them further together as a budding nation. All they lack is permanence--which a land would bring them. This they miss in the Exodus. That will come later in Joshua. In terms of the leadership time line, Exodus describes the beginning of Pre-Kingdom Leadership, A. The Desert Phase. Moses will exert strong leadership as these people become disciplined for entrance into the land and the warfare it will bring. His leadership was combined: religious, some military, and political. His dominant authority was spiritual.

Exodus continued

Leadership Lessons

1. **ESSENTIAL INGREDIENT.** The presence of God is the essential ingredient of desert leadership (Exodus 33:15).
2. **GIFTED POWER.** Miraculous intervention by God is the major manifestation of His presence in desert leadership. A leader must be able to invoke powerful intervention by God in crisis times. (Exodus 4-12; 14,15, 16,17 etc.).
3. **DEATH OF A VISION.** Sometimes God must break a self-driven ambitious leader (kill his vision) before He can later resurrect that same vision through the same person, now pliable (Exodus 2,3).
4. **SPIRITUAL AUTHORITY POWER BASE.** Great visions require great experiences with God in order to authenticate them. Moses, call, power encounters with Pharaoh, revelation on mountain, etc. (Exodus 3, 4-12).
5. **INSTITUTIONALIZED REMEMBRANCE.** God's miraculous interventions are to be reminders to all generations and hence should be institutionalized to preserve their memory. Word of mouth is good enough for Patriarchs/ small followership--but larger followership needs repeated public reminders (see Exodus 13:14; this is repeated in Deuteronomy and Joshua).
6. **CREATIVITY AND REMEMBRANCE.** Songs, poems, and other creative efforts are excellent communication vehicles for *remembrance* events, interventions, etc.
7. **APPROPRIATE STEPS OF PROGRESS.** Followership limitations must be recognized by leaders and appropriate steps taken to let them progress little by little (Exodus 13:17,18).
8. **HEROES AND MODELING.** Historic heroes are needed to remind followers of God's past workings--promises must be kept for integrity sake (Exodus 13:19).
9. **DEEP EXPERIENCES AND SPIRITUAL AUTHORITY.** A deep faith challenge experience with God, inspired by a leader and shared by leaders and followers instills spiritual authority in the leader (Exodus 14:31, see also Joshua 3:7, 4:14).
10. **WOMAN LEADER.** Miriam is a prophetess--dominantly an inspirational leader. She does not hold an official position (neither did Moses) as Aaron did (Exodus 15:20,21). Supernatural power gifting can not be denied in a woman even in a male dominated culture.
11. **ESSENCE OF REBELLION.** Followership rebellion (unwillingness to be satisfied with God's sovereign working in their lives) is essentially against God's authority (Exodus 16:8) not against the leader.

Exodus continued

12. **MINORITY WILL MISS.** Some followership will always miss the essence of God's revelation and requirements (Exodus 16:20,27).
13. **CORPORATE TESTING A NECESSITY.** Repeated trials and deliverance are needed in order for followership to really know and trust God (Exodus 17:1ff).
14. **SPIRITUALITY AUTHORITY BASICS.** Revelatory experiences of a leader, when seen by followers, like deep faith challenges and interventions by God, build spiritual authority in a leader (Exodus 19:9).
15. **WRITTEN BACKUP.** Oral law must be written down to preserve it for generations to come (Exodus 20, 21, 22, 23).
16. **GOD'S TIMING.** God has purposes in delays that are strategic (long range)--can't be necessarily perceived in our tactical (immediate or short range) interpretation (Exodus 23:28, 29, 30).
17. **SPIRITUAL AUTHORITY SPEEDUP.** Deep shared experiences of God with fellow leaders enhances spiritual authority (Exodus 24:9-18).
18. **PARTICIPATION A MEANS OF GROWTH.** Followership participating in God's activity is one of the motivational keys to leadership (Exodus 25:1,2 They give to provides resources for building the tabernacle in which God's presence will be known).
19. **INTERCESSORY BASICS.** Aaron's intercessory ministry in the tabernacle is a foreshadowing of the New Testament Philosophical Intercessory Model (Exodus 28:29-30; Jesus high priestly ministry in Hebrews).
20. **ANOINTING PROTOTYPES.** Bezalel and Oholiab and others illustrate Spirit anointing of natural abilities and acquired skills--a foreshadowing of the New Testament Stewardship model. Note especially endowed for God-chosen work (Exodus 31:1ff).
21. **CALL TESTED.** Leadership is often tested (integrity check for leadership responsibility) in its loyalty to followership and its willingness to sacrifice to bring that reluctant followership to development (Exodus 32:9ff).
22. **INTERCESSORY BASICS.** Moses demonstrates intercessory ministry of leadership (Exodus 32:11ff). He uses the character and purposes of God as intercessory levers with God. To do this requires *intimacy* with God.
23. **NECESSARY LEADERSHIP INGREDIENT.** The presence of God is the necessary and sufficient ingredient for leadership. Moses will not proceed to lead God's people without it (Exodus 33:15).
24. **TANDEM TRAINING AS TRANSITION MEANS.** Tandem training--deliberate shared experiences, close observation--has been a major development process for Joshua who is to transition into

Exodus continued

      leadership (See Exodus 17:8 Rephidim, 24:13 Mountain, 32:17 law/
      Mountain; 33:11 tabernacle).
25. **INTIMACY**. Intimacy with God should be a motivating force for a
      leader (Exodus 33:15-23).
26. **ALLEGIANCE**. Absolute allegiance is required of desert followership.
      Those who have received much have much responsibility (Exodus
      34:14).
27. **MOTIVATIONAL GIVING**. Willingness is at the heart of any appeal
      for financial resources from followership (Exodus 35:21ff See also
      36:6,7).

For Further Leadership Study

1. Exodus along with Numbers should be studied to systematically identify
   followership principles. Exodus and Numbers contain many individual
   leadership acts which can be studied to shed light on Desert Leadership.
2. The tabernacle should be studied typologically (using Hebrews for
   suggestions).

Special Comments
See Morgan (Handbook...), last 4 paragraphs, pages 8,9

BOOK	Leviticus	**Author:** uncertain, Moses some

Characters   Moses, Aaron

Who To/for   Israelites

Literature Type   Narrative description of things revealed to Moses about the priesthood, sin, requirements for the people; can not be understood apart from the book (Exodus) just previous to it.

Story Line   Having set up the tabernacle in the last part of the book of Exodus, God now speaks from it to reveal more of Himself (Ex 25:22). The Israelites go nowhere, do nothing except to listen to what God has to say.

Structure

I. (ch 1-10)   A Sinful Peoples' Approach To God--The Offerings
II. (ch 11-22)   A Separated People--Avoiding Sin
III. (ch 23-24)   A Consecrated People--The Feasts
IV. (ch 25-27)   A Responsive People--obligatory and voluntary Signs

Theme ·   **THE HOLINESS OF GOD**
  • demands perfection in approach to God,
  • requires perfection in daily living,
  • results in benefits of God's blessing, and
  • has long term lasting implications.

Key Words   holiness (and other cognates) (131), sacrifice (several hundred), clean and unclean (several hundred), atonement (36);

Key Events   Priests are consecrated, Nadab and Abihu disciplined,

Purposes
  • to instruct Israel in holiness and sin,
  • to instruct the priesthood of its sacred task,
  • to prefigure in types the coming ministry of Christ,
  • to point out the necessity of religious leadership.

Why Important   First, it makes the people **conscious of sin and its nature.** The fact of sin is throughout the book. Because of it, there is need for sacrifice to atone for it, mediation between God and sinful humanity to account for it, separation from it, and

Leviticus continued

celebration for escape from it. The nature of sin is such that it separates man and God. Sin is seen from the human viewpoint as exclusion from nearness to God, from knowledge of God, and from communion with God. It is the holiness of God, stressed in Leviticus, which necessitates this separation. Second, it makes the **people aware of redemption and its nature.** God is teaching what worship is in its most elemental forms; it is approach to a Holy God via His solution to the sin problem which prevents it. The book and its requirements are a form of corporate negative preparation. Its demands leave us gasping for help. We are unable to worship in the way in which it wants us to. This will point us forward to the true way of worship which will come via Christ.

Where It Fits   In the redemptive drama Leviticus occurs early in Chapter 1, The Making of A Nation. It stresses revelation concerning religious life. Leviticus describes the beginning of Pre-Kingdom Leadership, A. The Desert Phase. Moses repeatedly receives revelation concerning sin and relationship with God. The role of the priesthood is given in Leviticus.

Leadership Lessons

1. **RELIGIOUS RITES**. Religious leadership must explain the meaning of religious rites--their purposes, meaning, and necessity (burnt offering, grain offering, fellowship offering, etc.).
2. **CENTRALITY OF COMMUNITY**. Religious leadership points out the need for community--the central place to unify religious life (Leviticus 3:2 offerings done here, judgment done here, petitions done here, guidance sought here).
3. **CORPORATE SIN**. Religious leadership must recognize the whole community may sin--corporate sin as well as individual sin. The need for vicarious confession and atonement is a function of leadership (Leviticus 4:13, 5:27).
4. **NATURE OF SIN**. Religious leadership must understand the nature of sin--its seriousness, its pervasiveness in life, its effect upon relationship with God, need for repentance, confession, and atonement.
5. **PROVISION**. God repeatedly makes provision for full time religious workers.

Leviticus continued

6. **DISCERNMENT**. Discernment between good and evil (right and wrong) is a major function of religious leadership. (Leviticus 10:10).
7. **REVELATORY SENSITIVITY**. A leader must be able to hear from God for his/her people. "The Lord said to Moses" or "The Lord said to Moses and Aaron" repeatedly occurs in Leviticus. Our times will change. Our needs will change. But our source of answer is consistent and will reveal details that we need in our lives.
8. **SACREDNESS OF MINISTRY**. Ministry is a sacred thing and must be done carefully before the Lord in His way.
9. **GOD'S CHARACTER--BASIC.** The character of God is the essential basis for laws and standards (Leviticus 19:2).
10. **SECULAR IMPORTANT**. Details of life are important to God and have bearing on our relationships with God.
11. **LEADERSHIP STANDARDS.** *The Moses Principle*--higher standards for leaders--is re-enforced in Leviticus (in the marriage standards-- defects, etc. see Leviticus 21:7ff, 13 ff).
12. **CORPORATE REMEMBRANCES.** The Sabbath, Passover, Firstfruits, Feast of Weeks, Feast of Trumpets, Day of Atonement, Feast of Tabernacles all point out the importance of corporate remembrance of God. Religious leadership must keep these remembrance events alive before followers (Leviticus 23).
13. **WAITING AND GUIDANCE.** Crises situations in which the Lord's will is not clear demand that leadership wait upon and hear from God (Leviticus 24:12-16).

For Further Leadership Study
1. Why was Aaron anointed and ordained publicly for ministry and not Moses ?
2. What leadership implications, if any, are seen in the year of Jubilee or sabbatical years for the land?
3. Leviticus puts forth prohibitions that are later abrogated or altered in later revelation of God's demands--compare especially with New Testament truth. This highlights the notion of progress of doctrine in the Scriptures in general and the starting point plus process model in particular.

Special Comments
Key verses Leviticus 17:11; 19:2. This is a book that must be explored typologically in order to see the beauty of Christ and what he has done for us on the Cross. (See also a clincher verse, 1 Chronicles 16:29)

BOOK	**Numbers** **Author:** uncertain, Moses some
Characters	Moses, Aaron, Miriam, Joshua, Caleb, Balaam, the twelve spies
Who To/for	Israelites
Literature Type	Historical narrative; selected vignettes of desert years.
Story Line	About a year after the Exodus, the events of the book of Numbers commences. It spans a period of about 40 years. The Israelites travel across the desert and are on the edge of the land that God promised to Abraham. They spy out the land. A negative report frightens the people. A minority report by two of the spies, Joshua and Caleb, urges entrance into the land and faith in God to do it. The majority report holds sway. They fail to enter in and are disciplined by God who asserts that none of the doubting people will ever go in. It will be a new generation who will go into the land. The Israelites then become a desert people for 40 years. Numbers records many of the incidents which happened--intentionally selecting those which show disobedience by a faithless people and God's intervention to those who are faithful--especially Moses in crisis moments.

Structure

    I. (ch 1-10)   God's People Prepared to Enter The Land
   II. (ch 11-25) God's People Excluded From the Land
 III. (ch 26-36) God's New People Prepared to Enter the Land

Theme

GOD'S DISCIPLINING OF HIS PEOPLE
- followed His preparation of them to enter the land,
- was necessitated by their lack of faith and obedience,
- required 40 years of wandering in the desert to rigorously train them for hardships, and
- resulted in their avid readiness to conquer the land.

Key Words   wilderness (45), murmuring and cognates (11)

Key Events   numbering of tribes; organization of camp, cleansing of Levites; Passover celebrated; Miriam and Aaron rebel; spies go into land, people refuse to go; rebellion of

Numbers continued

> Korah; Moses pivotal point (strikes rock), judgment--
> fiery serpents, brass serpent; Balaam's prophecies;
> wickedness with Moabite women; victory over
> Midianites.

Purposes
- to show how God sovereignly works out His plans in spite of responses of His people,
- to teach many lessons about discipline,
- to teach many lessons about leadership and followership.

Why Important   Numbers is a book about **obedience**. It illustrates the
folly of disobedience and the necessity of discipline for
obedience. This basic pattern will be repeated throughout
the Scriptures. Numbers (see Morgan Handbook, pages
15,16) warns us of the results of doubting God yet
displays His patience to persist in His plans. **God can not
be defeated; His methods are perfect and His
provision is sufficient**. We recognize that crises such as
Kadesh-Barnea will come to test all of us. Our **view of
God** determines what will happen. Our **attitude toward
the opportunity** reveals our real view of God. Failure
comes from impure motives and compromise.

Where It Fits   The book of Numbers parallels events in Exodus and
Leviticus which means it occurs early in the redemptive
drama, Chapter 1, The Making of a Nation. But it lasts
forty years so goes beyond the Exodus time table. In
terms of the leadership time line, Numbers describes the
beginning of Pre-Kingdom Leadership, A. The Desert
Phase. This book more than others contains leadership
acts and shows how followership affects leadership.
Moses' critical pivotal point is graphically detailed in
Numbers. Leadership backlash, a process item that many
leaders go through is illustrated in this book. This book
is imminently about leadership and followership. A
major issue is the corporate rejection of the sovereignty
of God, seen in the many murmuring passages. This is a
great book of warnings for leaders and followers.

Numbers continued

Leadership Lessons

1. **SEE EXODUS LESSONS.** This book contains many of the lessons of Exodus so I will not repeat them here. Where passages are duplicated in both books, the leadership lessons drawn from Exodus will apply also. Either book may however give details that do not occur in the narrative of the other. So examine each of the lessons from Exodus that occur also in Numbers for additional details.
2. **COSTLY RESPONSES.** Both obedience and disobedience are costly. Numbers paints this vividly. But of the two, disobedience has long range implications that continue to be costly.
3. **ORDER.** There is a proper place for order and administration. There is a proper time for Numbering and a reason for it. Later, God shows in David's case the improper use of numbering (for pride's sake).
4. **LEADERSHIP LEVELS.** Numbers highlights the need for intermediate and lower levels of leadership. Where the sphere of influence of a major leader is great in extensiveness there must be adequate intermediate and lower levels of leadership.
5. **LEADERSHIP AND JEALOUSY.** Jealousy in leadership should be expected by a successful or powerful leader.
6. **CORPORATE FAITH CHECK.** The sending of the twelve is indicated in Numbers (ch 13) to be a corporate faith check--a testing of the entire followership.
7. **MINORITY.** Seldom is the majority (followership) right where faith issues are dominant. It is the minority (2 of the 12) who can hear God and believe Him who are frequently right at critical times. This is a simple illustration of the oft repeated historic occurrence of change coming from the peripheral and not the center.
8. **TESTING PATTERN.** The testing pattern for individual leaders is seen to hold for corporate groups (see Numbers 14:36-38 where the ten receive the ultimate of remedial treatment via the plague).
9. **PIVOTAL POINT.** Moses major pivotal point which altered his ultimate destiny is given in more detail and offers a phrase which says why this is important (20:12 because you did not trust in me enough to honor me as holy in the sight of the Israelites). It will probably take a paradigm shift concerning what holiness is to understand this perplexing discipline in Moses life.
10. **SUBTLE DEFEAT.** Followership can be subtly seduced by surrounding cultural pressures (see ch 25). the New Testament seems to indicate that Balaam gave advice to the King of the Moabites

Numbers continued

concerning this way to defeat Israel even though the narrative in
Numbers seems to indicate that Balaam is pretty clean.
11. **WOMEN LEADERSHIP.** Women can exert powerful influence even
in a male dominated culture if leadership is open to hear from God (see
Zelophehad's daughters and Moses response, ch 27).
12. **COSTLY OBEDIENCE.** Moses last major act (vengeance on
Midianites) even though successful must have been costly personally
(he was married to a Midianite and had good relationships with his
father-in-law, a Midianite priest).
13. **PREPARATION--A GOAL.** The essential goal of desert leadership
was preparation of followership for the task of conquering the land.
Corporate development of one's followership is both for the present and
for the future.

For Further Leadership Study

1. Numbers is a gold mine of leadership acts. Each can be studied
profitably to understand about Desert Leadership. All the leadership acts
in Numbers need to be identified, catalogued, and annotated for potential
leadership findings.
2. Hundreds of leaders are mentioned in Numbers. These highlight the
importance of intermediate and lower levels of leadership. Numbers
should be studied to identify and catalogue these leaders. In fact, all the
leaders mentioned in the Bible should be identified, catalogued, and
annotated.
3. Comparative study of the lessons of Exodus should be studied to see if
they hold for Numbers. Further details which may add to these lessons
should be studied.

Special Comments
See Morgan (Handbook page 16) for an excellent running summary of the
contribution of Genesis through Deuteronomy to the onward flow of God's
redemptive history. Key verse, Numbers 14:28-30

BOOK	**Deuteronomy** **Author:** uncertain, Moses some

Characters   Moses, Aaron, Joshua and others seen in Exodus, Numbers, Leviticus

Who To/for   Israel

Literature Type   Record of Discourses by Moses

Story Line   The book of Deuteronomy takes place in about a month. It just precedes entry into the land--see Joshua. This is the last month in the life of Moses. He has reflected back on his leadership and the Israeli followership. From those reflections he encourages the people and warns them. There is a tremendous sense in all of the discourses of an **expectation that they will go in and conquer the land.** This is a corporate application of Goodwin's expectation principle. [4]

Structure

I. (1-4:43)	Words of Historical Reflections
II. (4:44-27:10)	Final Words on Living standards
III. (29-31:13)	Final Words on the Covenant
IV. (31:14-33)	Final Words For Moses and From Moses--The Two Songs

Theme   **MOSES FINAL WORDS** (as leader)
- involve <u>reflective warnings</u> drawn from their short desert experience,
- remind them of <u>standards of obedience</u> reflecting God's desires for them,
- give <u>encouraging expectations</u> looking forward to their entering the land,
- close with songs of <u>warning</u> and <u>blessing</u> that prophesy the future.

Key Words   hear (50), do, keep, observe, obey (177), love (21)

Key Events   Major discourses by Moses

---

[4]Goodwin's expectation principle states that *A potential leader tends to live up to the expectations of a leader that he/she respects.* Moses uses this social dynamic in a corporate way.

Deuteronomy continued

Purposes
- to prepare the followership for transition to new leadership,
- to exhort the people to profit from God's lessons of the past,
- to insure continuance of his leadership goals for the future,
- to create a sense of destiny (expectancy) concerning entrance into and conquering of the land.

Why Important	This book is particularly important in terms of leadership lessons. An old leader, perhaps the greatest in the Old Testament, is moving off the scene. What will happen to that which he began? At least 10 major leadership lessons are seen or modeled in this great book. Leadership transition is in focus. This is a book which brings **closure to Moses' leadership ministry and projects an anticipation of God's future working in the land.** If Moses had been able to project the kind of spiritual authority he radiates with in Deuteronomy when they first arrived at Kadesh-Barnea (Numbers) they would have probably entered in then instead of 40 years later. What we see is a mature leader who has been processed along with the followership in the desert years.
Where It Fits	In the redemptive story, Deuteronomy occurs in the early part of Chapter 1, The Making of A Nation. This is the pre-kingdom leadership era, the Desert Leadership. Moses gives his farewell messages as a leader. The people have become a disciplined followership. The situation for the past 40 years has been one of order, discipline, learning to trust God. Moses has groomed Joshua to take over as the new leader over a period of years. Deuteronomy records the final efforts from Moses for smoothing out the transition and giving Joshua the very best start in leadership.

Leadership Lessons

1. **LEADERSHIP TRANSITION.** In a time of leadership transition the new leader and followers need to be reminded of the *heritage* they have.
2. **ROOTED.** *Dynamic reflection on the past* encourages faith expectations for the future.

Deuteronomy continued

3. **HISTORY**. Lessons from the past need to be *recorded* and retaught from generation to generation.
4. **NEW CHALLENGE**. The new leader and followers need a new challenge in order to insure the new leader's success. (Otherwise, they will be constantly compared to the old leader since they are only maintaining his/her work.)
5. **AWESOME PRESENCE**. The *presence* of God with a leader and followers is *the key* to leadership effectiveness.
6. **CREATE EXPECTATIONS**. The future perfect mode, *detailing expectations*, is one of the single most powerful motivating factors an old leader can use to insure on-going leadership effectiveness beyond his/her extent of leadership.
7. **INFLUENCE CENTER**. The place where God has chosen to place His name--There needs to be a *centralized location* of God's blessing that rallies the followers in terms of covenant, heritage, and renewal.
8. **PURGING**. Purging out must be a central value of institutions and movements, since they are always susceptible to *degenerative influences* of surrounding culture and must carefully guard against them.
9. **RENEWAL OF COVENANT**. At critical junctures in the life history of a people there should be a renewal of a *covenant* with God.
10. **LEADERSHIP SUCCESSION**. *Aptness to lead* and not nepotism is the basic principle of leadership succession: a. God's selection, b. tried character, c. proven giftedness. The nepotistic approach leading to failure (see Kings and Chronicles) is similarly repeated by charismatic leaders who begin churches and parachurches over and over in our day.

For Further Leadership Study

1. Trace the phrases which create future expectations on the part of the followership (go in and take possession, when you go in the land, etc.)
2. See Deut 1:26ff which gives Moses' interpretation of a *corporate pivotal point* in the life of the nation. Pivotal points which usually refer to marker events in the life of an individual can also occur to groups.
3. Deut 4:23ff gives Moses' own interpretation of his personal pivotal point which kept him out of the land--shows one of the ramifications of leadership backlash. See also Num 12ff.
4. Deut 8:2 gives the concept of corporate testing.
5. Deut 9:23-29 (see also Exodus 32) is another illustration of the leadership prayer principle--If God calls you to a ministry then He calls you to pray for that ministry. Moses was one of the great intercessors

Deuteronomy continued

of the Old Testament. His intercessory ministry is worth a continued detailed study.

6. Study Deut 17:14-20 for its implications of the future kingdom that is coming. Study it also for its warnings and safeguards to protect kings. These standards were violated by almost every king. Notice the place of the Word of God in a king's life.

7. Deut 31:17 validates the cross-book major essential ingredient leadership lesson: The essential ingredient of Biblical leadership is the **powerful presence of God in the life and ministry of the leader**.

8. See in Deut 32,33 major purposes for hymnody—reflective warnings and blessings.

9. Study the two closing songs of Moses for leadership lessons.

Special Comments
This book breaks new ground in introducing the motivating factor of love. God's love of His people is his motive for His ruling of them. His people's love for God should be the motive of their obedience. Key Verse, Deuteronomy 10:12,13. Note Deuteronomy 18:15 which most likely refers to Christ.

BOOK **Joshua**   **Author:** uncertain, perhaps Joshua some

Characters   Joshua, Achan, Caleb

Who To/for   for the Israelis

Literature Type   Historical narrative, selected vignettes taken from the approximately 30 years time of the conquest of the land by Joshua

Story Line   Moses has died. He has publicly chosen his successor as leader. Surprisingly it is not one of his sons. It is Joshua the son of Nun, one of the two spies who more than 40 years ago had opted for going in to the land. Over the 40 years in the desert Moses had trained Joshua--in modern terms, mentored him and groomed him for this top leadership role. Now he is to lead the Israelites into the land. They are paused outside the swollen Jordon river. God gives Joshua (3:7, 4:14) **spiritual authority** with the people by supernaturally enabling them to cross the river. They consecrate themselves anew, by circumcising all the males. Then they are ready to begin the conquest of the land. Joshua seeks personal assurance and a plan from God to take Jericho, a fortified city that blocks control of the center of the north/south axis of the country. God meets him in a preincarnate theophany (or Christophany) and reveals to him the plan for taking Jericho. The methodology is clearly God-given and its results finalize the transition of Joshua's leadership. Jericho falls in a mighty sweeping supernatural victory. One thing remains to establish Joshua's on-going leadership. After a great success there is often pride and a tendency to become self-sufficient. Ai, a surprising loss to a weaker force reveals God's intervening presence, points out obedience to Him is crucial for victory, and takes away any self-confidence. Having split the north/south communication lines Joshua then begins campaigns to subdue the northern and southern halves of the country. The land is allotted to the tribes. Each must mop up its section of land. Some did; some did not totally. Caleb, the other spy who had stood with Joshua many years ago stands out as an inspirational hero in the battles. Joshua

Joshua continued

closes his leadership with inspirational words to encourage the Israelites to go on with God.

Structure
I. (1-5)   Entering The Land
II. (6-12)   Conquering The Land
III. (13-3-22) Settling The Land
IV. (23,24)   Joshua's Final Exhortations From the Land

Theme
THE LAND PROMISED BY GOD
- is entered supernaturally with God's reminder of His holiness and leading,
- is conquered strategically with a series of battles indicating God's presence and blessing,
- is distributed according to Moses' intentions for tactical warfare (the mopping up campaign), and
- after being conquered offers special challenges to maintaining a relationship with God.

Key Words
inheritance and cognates (60+), possess and cognates (22)

Key Events
Joshua's call, the two spies, crossing the Jordan, the memorial stones, circumcision at Gilgal, supernatural encounter with the Captain of the Lord's Army, the fall of Jericho, the defeat at Ai and Achan's sin, Ai destroyed, covenant renewed at Mount Ebal, The Gibeonite deception, The miraculous intervention in the victory at Gibeon--sun stands still, southern cites conquered, northern cities conquered, land distributed (each portion described), Levites given towns, Joshua's two farewell addresses.

Purposes
- to show generally the faithfulness of God,
- to show specifically God's continuing fulfillment of His promise to Abraham (23:14)
- to show how God intervenes in a leader's life and ministry,
- to point out the importance of complete obedience to God's revelation and the consequences of partial obedience.

Joshua continued

Why Important   In the redemptive drama, God has made significant
progress in spite of His people's lack of total obedience.
He has fulfilled portions of His promise to Abraham.
There are many descendants. He has claimed them for
Himself in delivering them from Egyptian bondage. He
formed these people into a disciplined people in the desert
experiences. He is now going to lead them into the land.
Joshua tells of this stage of the redemptive drama. Their
obedience is not complete. All the land was not totally
conquered though generally it was. But they are not yet a
unified nation under a centralized leadership. They are a
commonwealth of tribes spread out. They have just gone
through a 40 year period of tight centralized authoritarian
rule. Now they need some breathing room. They must
move from dependence (the centralized authoritarian desert
years under Moses and war years under Joshua) to
independence (the commonwealth time seen in the Judges)
before they can properly be ready for interdependence (the
kingdom years). They will need a time of independence
and crises before they will be ready to submit their
autonomy to a centralized Kingdom. They will need a
time of corporate negative preparation before they will
willingly follow a kingdom over which God providentially
superintends. If Joshua were missing from the canon we
would not understand the Kingdom books which are to
come. We would have missed a great leader who finished
well. So few finish well that we need these examples. We
would miss seeing a great leader follow a great leader.
Generally, the next leader after a great leader is almost
doomed to failure. We would miss out on understanding
the justice of God. **Joshua, along with Deuteronomy, is a
great book on leadership and highlights what spiritual
authority is.**

Where It Fits   In the redemptive drama, Joshua occurs in Chapter 1, the
Making of a Nation. The last of the items for the making
of a nation is a permanent place, a land that is their own.
Joshua will fulfill that necessity. This great desert leader
is poised to sweep in and take the land. In the leadership
time-line, Joshua occurs in Phase B, Conquering the
Land, in the Stage II. Pre-Kingdom Leadership.

Joshua continued

Leadership Lessons

1. **LEADERSHIP TRANSITION**. Leadership transitions are very difficult. Most leadership transitions in the Scriptures are negative at best. This transition from Moses to Joshua is the best Old Testament illustration of a good leadership transition.[5] Elijah to Elisha (though not many details given), Jesus own preparation of the disciples, and Barnabas' mentoring of Paul are the other positive examples.
2. **SPIRITUAL AUTHORITY**. Spiritual Authority, in a leader is highlighted in this book. Joshua has as hard a task as any leader in the Bible. He is following one of the greatest, if not the greatest leaders of Old Testament history. Successors to great leaders traditionally fail to measure up. Four things pave the way: a. Moses has publicly transitioned Joshua into leadership. b. Joshua needs a personal confirmation from God and receives it (1:1ff, note especially 1:3, 6, 8). Especially is the presence of God promised, the essential ingredient of leadership. c. Joshua needs spiritual authority in order to succeed Moses as a leader. God promises that to him (3:7) and does it (4:14). d. Joshua faces a new and challenging task in a different locale than was Moses desert leadership. This will keep comparisons between his leadership and Moses to a minimum.
3. **CROSS GENERATIONAL LEADERSHIP**. Joshua and Caleb were able to inspire a younger generation and lead them to victory. All of Joshua and Caleb's generation (with the possible exception of Levites) died in the desert. And a new emerging leadership, hardened by the desert were ready for the challenge of the land. This new generation needed to be set apart to God (were circumcised after crossing the Jordan; evidently Moses had lapsed on this in the desert).
4. **VISION**. Joshua's encounter with the Captain of the Lord's army illustrates several important issues in leadership. One, God must give vision for large tasks. Two, a leader needs at least some personal, intimate, awe inspiring experiences to validate his/her own sense of destiny and to build spiritual authority. The plan for the attack of Jericho (a fortified city which would normally be sieged over a prolonged number of months) brought immediate victory and confirmed that God was with the Israelites. This news spread throughout the

---

[5]I identify 10 events or stages that mark this leadership transition. See Appendix D of **The Joshua Portrait: A Study in Leadership Development, Leadership Transition, and Destiny Fulfillment.** Available through Barnabas Publishers.

Joshua continued

    promised land to all the peoples. They were rightly fearful of the Israelites and the coming attacks they would finish.

5. **EARLY VICTORY.** An early success for a leader does much to insure his leadership. Jericho did this for Joshua.

6. **EARLY DEFEAT.** Just as an early success is necessary for a leader to gain followership, an early defeat insures that dependence upon God is a necessity and will keep pride from getting the upper hand. Ai did this for Joshua.

7. **FLESH ACT.** Guidance requires knowing *what, when*, and *how* of God's will. To go ahead knowing one and assuming the others can lead to ramifications that are unpleasant. Such a decision concerning some major guidance is called a flesh act in leadership emergence theory. Joshua, though a good leader, made such a decision concerning the request by the Gibeonites. Joshua provides a warning to all leaders concerning this guidance process item. Note the telltale phrase, 9:14, "but did not inquire of the Lord. All leaders will be faced with situations where decisions could easily be made without inquiring of the Lord.

8. **FINISHING WELL.** Joshua illustrates several of the characteristics of a leader who finished well.[6] (1)He had a <u>personal vibrant relationship</u> with God right up to the end. (4) Truth was lived out in his life so that <u>convictions</u> and promises of God were seen to be real. (5) He left behind an <u>ultimate contributions</u> as a pioneer and writer. (6) He fulfilled his sense of destiny by conquering the land. See footnote below for other characteristics some of which were also probably part of Joshua's life. Particularly in his two final speeches (Joshua 23, 24) to the nation, did he illustrate the value of *by faith claiming and holding on to the promises of God*. See especially 23:14.

9. **FINAL CHALLENGE.** Joshua sought to move the nation forward after his own leadership, with a challenge to walk with God (see Joseph and Moses had also demonstrated the importance of challenging people after a life time of ministry. Joshua's challenge is pointedly given in 24:14.15.

---

[6]Comparative study of leaders who have finishing well have identified 6 descriptors: (1).They maintain a <u>personal vibrant relationship</u> with God right up to the end. (2) They maintain a <u>learning posture</u> and can learn from various kinds of sources--life especially. (3) They evidence <u>Christ likeness in character</u>. (4) T⁻ ·th is lived out in their lives so that <u>convictions</u> and promises of God are seen to be real. (5) They leave behind one or more <u>ultimate contributions</u> (saint, stylistic practitioners, mentors, public rhetoricians, pioneers, crusaders, artists, founder, stabilizers, researchers, writers, promoters). (6) They walk with a growing awareness of a sense of destiny and see some or all of it fulfilled. See position paper on Ultimate Contribution available from Barnabas Publishers for explanation of these types.

Joshua continued

10. **CENTRALITY LACK.** For all of Joshua's good points he did not establish with vigor a central place of worship nor establish Moses' national celebrations which would have served to help unify the nation after their dispersal into their various provinces. This lack shows up abundantly.
11. **GENERATIONAL HERITAGE.** The remembrances and celebrations failed to vicariously pass on to the coming generations the reality and power of God. The Judges makes it clear that as long as those who had led during the conquest were alive the nation followed God (Judges 2:10). Somehow the form only and not the function of these remembrances were passed on. Was Joshua lacking in this?
12. **LEADERSHIP TRANSITION.** Joshua did not transition in a leader to replace himself. His own transition in by Moses was a sterling example of what should be done. The Scripture is silent on this. So it is hard to condemn Joshua. But the lack of centralized leadership creates a vacuum as given in the Judges.

For Further Leadership Study
1. Identify, categorize, and annotate the many leadership acts in Joshua. This book is a seed plot for leadership lessons via the *leadership acts* genre.
2. See also the biographical analysis of Joshua with its many lessons.

Special Comments
Key Verse Joshua 1:2,3. Morgan (see Handbook pages 26-29) points out how two major truths are presented about God in this book. God is a God of justice. This is not contrasted with New Testament revelation of God as love. It heightens it. God can not be a God of love if He does not justly deal with sin which destroys a people. And that is what happens in Joshua. Sin which has been growing like a cancer in the land (over 400 years worth) must be surgically removed. There has been plenty of treatment over the years to arrest it. And now the time has come for it to be removed in order that others may know and follow God fully. That God is perpetually at war with sin is graphically displayed in the book. The second great truth points out the response of a people to God. Earlier in Genesis we were introduced in its initial stages to the great truth that a godly person must walk by faith (Genesis 15:6). Now we see that great truth highlighted. The just shall walk by faith. Faith as an on-going response is highlighted throughout the book.

BOOK	**JUDGES** **Author:** uncertain
Characters	Othniel, Ehud, Shamgar, Deborah (Barak), Gideon, Abimelech, Tola, Jair, Jephthah, Ibzan, Elon, Abdon, and Samson are the major characters. There are others.
Who To/for	Israelites, chronicling their history and getting ready for the kingdom
Literature Type	Historical narrative of selected vignettes covering a period of time stretching from the death of Joshua to the judgeship of Samuel--covering maybe 300 years.
Story Line	For a long period of time, longer than we have been a nation, the twelve tribes lived scattered. There is frequent civil war in specific locales and much fighting with various surrounding nations and peoples who were not totally destroyed when the land was taken. In short, there is an oft repeated 6 stage cycle: 1. People serving God, 2. People turn away from God 3. God brings a crisis 4. People turn to God 5. He raises up and sends along leaders (the Judges) 6. The people are delivered. The degeneration starts again and the cycle is repeated. There are 7 cycles and at least 13 of these charismatic leaders who usually lead a volunteer army to deliver in the crisis, including: Othniel, Ehud, Shamgar, Deborah (Barak), Gideon, Abimelech, Tola, Jair, Jephthah, Ibzan, Elon, Abdon, and Samson. Some of these are more well known than others. Intentional selection is worth noting, especially with regard to information on each. For example, note the extended coverage of Deborah/Barak, Gideon, Jephthah and Samson. These are evil times and few there are who follow God. In the opening section of the Judges, the writer sums it up well, (Judges 2:7) "After Joshua had dismissed the Israelites, they went to take possession of the land, each to his own inheritance. The people served the Lord through out the lifetime of Joshua and of the elders who outlived him and who had seen all the great things the Lord had done for Israel." And then again in the closing portion a repeated phrase haunts us--Judges 21:25, "In those days Israel had no king; everyone did as he saw fit." These are the pre-kingdom years.

JUDGES continued

Corporately the people are negatively prepared for the kingdom which will come.

Structure

I. (ch 1-3:6) Setting the Times of the Judges
II. (ch 3:7-16) 7 Degenerative Cycles of the Judges
III. (ch 17-21) Three Illustrations Enforcing a
Concluding Reason for the Evil Times

Theme

The Degenerative Times of the Judges
- began after Joshua and the immediate generation which had seen God's work in conquering the land passed off the scene,
- were usually instigated by compromising loyalty to God and by worshipping the gods of the surrounding people,
- followed a cyclical pattern (see story line),
- were inherently evil and lacked a unified leadership to stem the tide.

Key Words

evil (14), judge & cognates (22), a repeated phrase is important: In those days Israel had no king; everyone did as he saw fit. (Judges 17:6, 18:1, 21:25)

Key Events many crises

Purposes
- to rationalize the need for the kingdom,
- to show that each new generation must embrace God for themselves,
- to warn others how easy it is for succeeding generations not to own the ideals of previous ones,
- to point out the need for continual leadership,
- to show the moral depravity of human beings who operate without God's standards.

Why Important

This book shows us what happens **when people are left to themselves to manage their affairs and standards of life. It also shows how God steps in to preserve what He can in order to move toward His purposes.**
Morgan summarizes the living values of this book (see Morgan Handbook pages 30-33) by stating this book serves as a warning to the nation (and people of God in

JUDGES continued

general) of the process of deterioration and the process of
restoration as well as giving us a message of hope. God
forever moves towards his purposes and His methods are
still the same: discipline (punishment), mercy, and
deliverance. Without this book we would not understand
the need for the kingdom which so upset Samuel (see 1
Samuel).

Where It Fits   The Judges occur in the redemptive drama in Chapter 1,
The Making Of A Nation. This period of time in which
each of the tribes associates with the others from a
decentralized base in a commonwealth arrangement lasts
from250 to 300 or so years. It is a long period of time
more nearly equal to the time in Egypt than the Desert
years. This period of time is preliminary to the final
completion stage of the nation--that is getting a united
government. In terms of the leadership time-line, the
times of the Judges takes place as the final phase of Stage
III Pre-Kingdom leadership, entitled Conquered by the
Land. It is a time when revelatory information from God
is sparse. There are few who are following hard after
God (see Ruth for exceptions). It is a time of extreme
decentralization in leadership--both religious, military,
and political. It is a time of crisis leadership in
degenerate times. It shows that *maintenance leadership*
(times of the Judges, Desert Leadership) is much tougher
than *Great challenge* leadership (Joshua's time). When
there are no major goals around which people can be
united there will be deterioration and fragmentation and
minor goals. It is a time of negative preparation which
will lead to a unifying movement toward the kingdom.
Most of the lessons on leadership from this period are
negative. There are a few positive examples of faith
being exercised (see Hebrews 11:32 This book contains
excellent leadership source material for two genres--mini-
biographies of leaders and for leadership acts. These
leaders must be judged in the light of the times in which
they lived and of the revelation they had rather than in
terms of our present understanding.

JUDGES continued

Leadership Lessons

1. **CONTINUITY OF LEADERSHIP.** Joshua did not train nor install a successor to his leadership. As the tribes spread no one person was the central clearing house for leadership among them.
2. **DECENTRALIZATION PROBLEM.** In movements and organizations there is an ebb and flow between over centralization, like the Desert leadership under Moses or Challenge leadership under Joshua and decentralization like the times of the Judges. Neither extreme is healthy. Both are necessary. While decentralization allows for autonomous development of leadership at lower levels it also makes for a non-unified, lack of overall control. The Judges illustrate the extreme swing of decentralization. See Greiner's article on this concerning modern organizations. [7]
3. **COMMUNICATION PROBLEMS.** Leadership needs good communications. The scattered tribes had very poor communications with each other.
4. **LACK OF MINISTRY STRUCTURES.** In the Desert Leadership era there were clear ways which God used to reveal Himself and bring His people to worship Him. During the Challenge era these were lost. They are practically non-existent. Knowledge of God was probably by word of mouth only. There is no mention of any structures or regularizing of religious requirements during the period of the Judges-- Conquered by the land.
5. **WOMEN IN MINISTRY.** Deborah seems to be the first instance of prophetic office in this leadership era. God will develop this leadership role/function and use it greatly during the kingdom era to come. Again Deborah demonstrates that a woman with gifted power will be respected even in a heavily dominated male society.
6. **ABUSE OF POWER.** A major hindrance to finishing well throughout the scriptures is the abuse of power. In degenerative times this will almost be the norm. So it is with a number of the Judges and even local leadership.
7. **REALITY OF GOD.** There is always the need for generational leadership--that is, the passing on of solid truth/experiential to the up and coming generations (2:10). Remembrances are one way. But they frequently degenerate to meaningless rites. It is the experiential that is primary. This was lacking in the Judges.

---

[7]Larry Greiner, *Evolution and Revolution As Organizations Grow* in **Harvard Business Review**, August 1972.

JUDGES continued

8. **REVELATORY VACUUM.** (See 6:7) During degenerative times there is usually a lack of revelation or a sensitivity to it or obedience to it. During the Judges, a new office, the prophetic is being generated. In general revelation is at a minimum. This points out the need of leaders to get vision from God.

9. **SUPREME LOYALTY TO GOD.** In the seven degenerative cycles the key issue is supreme loyalty to God. The first commandment was violated repeatedly. God can be patient with many things and deal with them over time--but supreme loyalty to God is a must in order for Him to deal with issues. This is missing during the times of the Judges.

10. **PATTERNS OF DEGENERATION.** Leaders should get perspective on their situation by taking a longer look and identifying patterns. Broader perspective allows for the identification of patterns and hence potential for prediction and correction. The times of the Judges followed a six stage pattern: 1. People serving God, 2. People turn away from God 3. God brings a crisis 4. People turn to God 5. He raises up and sends along leaders (the Judges) 6. The people are delivered. The degeneration starts again and the cycle is repeated.

11. **CORPORATE TESTING.** (3:1) Corporate groups are tested and developed just as individuals are. Here the surrounding nations were part of God's testing for Israel in order to produce the same kind of discipline that was learned in the Desert and under Joshua.

12. **RAMIFICATIONS.** Midianites (6:1 ff) not fully destroyed (one of Moses last acts). Incomplete obedience usually carries with it ramifications which will protract hindrances in the future.

13. **COSMIC LEVEL WARFARE.** In a book which relegates the supernatural to natural causes there is a mention (Song of Deborah) of a possible cosmic level warfare going on--see 5:20 From the heavens the stars fought, from their courses they fought against Sisera.

14. **PUBLIC COMMITMENT.** Jephthah forced the elders who approached him and promised to make him leader to publicly announce this in front of people (11:9-11). This "get it in writing principle" needs to be heeded today. Getting promises and important information in writing is not necessarily an expression of distrust but is a careful procedure which allows for clarification and better understanding between parties. Later if things do fall apart it may prove to be the salvation of a thoughtful leader. Word of mouth agreements are fraught with misunderstanding and room for abuse of power.

15. **CERTAINTY GUIDANCE.** When leaders are faced with crisis leadership they must be certain that God has spoken to them clearly

JUDGES continued

about it. See Gideon's two examples (6:36-40 and 7:7-16). See
Samson's birth (13:8ff).
16. **INTEGRITY AND OATHS.** The book of Judges makes clear that the
making and then keeping of oaths is a prime indicator of integrity.
Integrity in leadership is necessary if followers are to trust their leaders.

For Further Leadership Study

1. Two power encounters are worthy of special study: Gideon's with Baal in
6:31ff and Jephthah's with Chemosh in 11:23.
2. There are some excellent examples of the Double Confirmation guidance
process item in the Judges. Study Gideon's two examples (6:36-40 and
7:7-16). See Samson's birth (13:8ff). God is especially patient with
Gideon. Note the timing of second double confirmation.
3. There are numerous leadership acts which can be studied with profit in
the Judges.
4. This book closes with some incidents which point out the extent of
degeneration. These should be studied in order to see how pervasive evil
was in the society and in turn how difficult the situation was into which
leadership had to work.

Special Comments
This is a book full of leadership lessons. One major one concerns leadership
selection, God always finds the providential leader at the right moment. And
close observation usually shows that the leader was processed by God to
prepare for the crisis. Key verse: Judges 2:12-14

BOOK	**Ruth** **Author:** uncertain
Characters	Ruth, Naomi, Boaz
Who To/for	Israel people--authenticates the genealogy of David
Literature Type	Historical narrative containing a series of short vignettes ranging over a time of perhaps 10 years.

Story Line

During a famine in the latter part of the time of the Judges, an Israeli family-- Elimelech, Naomi and two sons, Mahlon and Kilion--from Bethlehem moves to Moab in other to survive in the harsh times. While there, Elimelech dies and Naomi is left to raise her two boys. They grow up and marry two Moabite women. After they had lived there about ten years both the sons also die. Naomi hears that times are now better back in Israel. So she decided to go back. One of the young widows opts to stay and remarry. The other, Ruth, makes a decision to go back with Naomi. She will serve Naomi's God and become a part of Naomi's people. Back in Bethlehem it is harvest time. According to the Levitical law owners should leave some of the harvest for poor people. Ruth goes to one of the fields to get some grain. There she meets a man, Boaz--the owner of the field. They fall in love. As a kinsman he has the right to purchase land from Naomi and to marry Ruth and raise up children to fulfill the family. He does this after a moment of apprehension in which they discover there is a kinsman closer who has the right. This kinsman gives over his right. The book closes with the birth of a child-- Obed, who is the grandfather of David, the second king.

Structure

   I.   (ch 1)   Ruth's Choice of Faith
  II.   (ch 2)   Ruth's Faithful Labors
 III.   (ch 3)   Ruth's Venture of Faith
 IV.   (ch 4)   Ruth's Reward of Faith

Theme

RUTH'S MODEL OF GODLINESS IN CRISIS TIMES
- involved a life changing committal to serve God,
- met with God's approval and provision,
- providentially led to marriage to Boaz,
- and resulted in a child who was in the redemptive line.

RUTH continued

Key Words   kinsman (14), redeem & cognates (9)

Key Events   Famine, migration of family to Moab, deaths of men of
                     family, Naomi's decision to return, Ruth's decision to
                     return, Ruth's labors in Boaz's field, Boaz's decision to be
                     the kinsman redeemer, the public acceptance of the
                     Kinsman redeemer obligation by Boaz, the birth of the
                     child Obed

Purposes
- to show that there was godliness in the times of the judges,
- to show how God's provision follows when His standards are followed,
- to show that God's mercy was broader than just Jewish people,
- to foreshadow the Kinsman Redeemer, a Lucan portrait of Christ as the
  Son of Man, the near kinsman who can redeem the human race,
- to authenticate and explain David's lineage particularly why a gentile is
  included in it.

Why Important: The book of Ruth takes place during the latter part of the
                     Judges. Yet it contrasts so in moral tone with that era. It
                     shows that in the midst of times of spiritual declension
                     there are those who do follow God in integrity. It further
                     shows incorporation of a gentile woman, Ruth, in God's
                     plan. It also shows how a gentile can have Biblical faith
                     and come to trust in the living God. God provides for
                     Ruth in every way. The book also prefigures Christ.
                     Boaz is a type of Christ, the kinsman redeemer. Luke
                     will portray Christ as an ideal human who has every right
                     to redeem the human race. **Apart from this little book,
                     we would not know of a remnant of godly people in
                     the times of the Judges.** God has His people in the most
                     trying of times. They follow His ways and see his
                     provision for life. The genealogy of Christ in Matthew
                     includes Ruth's name, one of three women mentioned.
                     The book of Ruth is one of two books named after
                     women--both heroines and models in trying times.

RUTH continued

Where It Fits   This book fits in the latter times of the Judges and hence occurs in Chapter 1, The Making of a Nation.   This is in the latter stages of the pre-kingdom leadership era.

Leadership Lessons

1. **LOCAL LEADERSHIP.** Ruth shows how when God's statutes are followed there will be provision (2:1,2; 4:1ff). The local leadership followed God's ways including the concept of leaving some of the harvest for the poor and the kinsman redeemer (Levirate custom).
2. **GODLY LEADERSHIP MODELED.** Both Ruth and Boaz are positive models of lay leadership and especially so in that they live in such degenerate times. Saintly lives will have impact.

For Further Leadership Study
1. Study the kinsman redeemer custom. See its fulfillment in Jesus, the Son of Man, as portrayed in Luke.
2. Here is an example of an ultimate contribution which is the preservation of the line of David (and eventually Christ). See 4:16ff.

Special Comments
Key Verse: Ruth 1:16. Morgan identifies two major permanent values in the book (see Morgan Handbook, pages 33-36). The book opens up the idea of what a saintly person is. A saintly person is one separated to do God's will. God is the sufficiency of trusting souls. Both Ruth and Boaz modeled saintly lives. Circumstances neither make nor mar saints but are used by God to process them to trust. The book also teaches the values of saintship. It is such people that God uses as His instruments. The value of one individual can not be underestimated in God's economy. Only heaven will reveal the value of single individual's lives to God's redemptive purpose.

BOOK	*1 Samuel* **Author:** uncertain
Characters	Eli, Hannah, Samuel, Saul, Jonathan, David
Who To/for	Israel
Literature Type	Historical narrative; vignettes ranging over a period of perhaps as much as a hundred years from the time of Samuel's birth to Saul's death.
Story Line	The book of Samuel in time immediately follows the times of the Judges. It picks up with the narrative time-line of Judges 16. In these times of the Judges God wants to move toward some permanent solution of the temporary *crisis leadership syndrome.* So His first step is to move to a judge who is not a crisis leader only and who can serve to unify the people. The first thirteen chapters show how Samuel was providentially raised up as a leader. It is a beautiful story in which a woman, Hannah has a need. She wants a child. God has a need. He wants a leader. God intertwines His purposes with hers. Samuel is given by God to Hannah. Hannah gives him back to God. She is blessed with other children. And God is blessed with an unusual leader of integrity who will be the transition leader that will link up to the kingdom. Samuel's ministry as judge was not just a momentary deliverance but a continual one. He visited the different tribes and judged them--that is, established law and justice for them. Samuel paves the way for a centralized kingdom. Crises around the people spur the need; Samuel's own sons are not able to replace him. The people demand a king--showing their need for one but also showing that they basically did not trust the unseen King. God gives them one king, Saul, who outwardly is what they would expect. But he fails repeatedly to follow God. His kingdom is spiritually bankrupt. God replaces him with David, whom God describes as *a man after my own heart.* The last part of 1 Samuel describes Saul's fall and David's early pre-kingdom years, in which David is gaining military expertise as a guerrilla warfare leader with a para-military band. Samuel is a transition book tracing the evolution of the kingdom.

1 SAMUEL continued

Structure
    I. (ch 1-7)   Samuel's Leadership as Last Judge
    II. (ch 8-15)   Saul's Leadership as King--Rejected
    III. (ch 16-31)   David's Preparation to Lead As King

Theme
THE TRANSITION TO CENTRALIZED LEADERSHIP
- involved Samuel, the last of the Judges and a widely accepted leader, whose efforts were central to unifying Israel around one leader,
- initially rested upon Saul, whose failure before God taught the people what government by man really meant, and
- finally rested upon David, a man prepared by God, to establish it.

Key Words
none common to all three lives

Key Events
Hannah's crisis and dedication of Samuel, Prophesy against Eli's house, Double confirmation of the prophesy through Samuel's first word, Ark captured, death of Eli, Ark returned to Israel, Samuel's victory over the Philistines at Mizpah, Israel asks for a king, Samuel anoints Saul, Saul made king, Saul brings deliverance to Jabesh, Samuel's farewell address, Samuel rebukes Saul, Jonathan attacks Philistines, Israel routs Philistines, Jonathan violates Saul's Oath, the Lord rejects Saul as King, Samuel anoints David, David serves with Saul, David and Goliath, Saul's jealous actions against David, Saul tries to kill David, David and Jonathan's friendship, David on the run--many incidents including two in which he spares Saul's life, David's run in with Nabal and marriage to Abigail, Saul and the Witch of Endor, numerous military vignettes of David while on the run, Philistines defeat Israel--Saul and Jonathan slain.

1 SAMUEL continued

Purposes
- to show the transition of leadership from judges to kings,
- to illustrate that a godly judge could rule in troublesome times with divine wisdom,
- to more fully point out God's movement to fulfill the Abrahamic promise (the nation now established as a unified nation of people in the land under a stable government),
- to fundamentally illustrate by three differing leaders the essentials of successful and unsuccessful leadership.

Why Important   1 Samuel and 2 Samuel need to be taken together to understand three principles of God's selection of leaders to do His work. Three leaders are highlighted in 1 Samuel. Their selection illustrates well this first major umbrella principle which will be reflected over and over again in the kings. *The ultimate victory of God is independent of the attitude of individuals or peoples towards Him.* God selects, gives opportunity, and works through a leader who responds to Him or rejects a leader who will not respond. The other two principles are given in 2 Samuel. The books of 1, 2 Kings and 1,2 Chronicles which follow are not understood apart from *this fundamental book which shows the transition of government to a kingdom and gives God's sovereign principle of selection of leadership.*

Where It Fits   1 Samuel covers the boundary time from Pre-Kingdom to Kingdom Leadership and the boundary from chapter 1 The Making of A Nation to chapter 2 The Destruction of a Nation.

Leadership Lessons

1. **LEADERSHIP MODELS.** Three leadership models, Samuel, Saul, and David are compared and contrasted. There are many lessons [8] that could be given for 1 Samuel. but most of them will be given in the

---

[8]1 Samuel is a book filled with leadership lessons. I can not do justice in two or three pages hence I prefer to give here just the major high level observations and reserve detailed leadership lessons for the genres of literature of leadership acts and biographical presentations--subjects of two other Leadership handbooks.

1 SAMUEL continued

biographical studies on Samuel, Saul, and David. Several leadership acts including 1 Samuel 12, Samuel's final public farewell which give valuable lessons. The major lesson to be learned in comparing and contrasting these three models is that LEADERSHIP THAT RESPONDS TO GOD WITH INTEGRITY WILL BE BLESSED WHILE LEADERSHIP WHICH DOES NOT WILL BE BYPASSED IN GOD'S ON-GOING PROGRAM.

2. **SELECTION PROCESSES.** The ultimate victory of God is independent of the attitude of individuals or peoples towards Him. God selects, gives opportunity, and works through a leader who responds to Him or rejects a leader who will not respond. This principle needs to be balanced with the major overall principle of 2 Samuel.

3. **LEADERSHIP TRANSITION.** Several important leadership principles found in Samuel's transition experience with Saul should be listed. These are given in more detail in the analysis of the leadership act of 1 Samuel 12.

    a. **COMPLEXITY**. Leaders should be forewarned that leadership transition is a difficult problem for leaders and followers.

    b. **TIMING.** Leaders must learn how and when to personally transition out of a leadership role or function.

    c. **CONTINUITY**. Leaders should be responsible for affirming continuity of leadership.

    d. **LEADERSHIP PUBLIC CONFIRMATION** . In a time of leadership transition new leadership must be publicly confirmed and backed by the old leadership in order to point out God's continuity

For Further Leadership Study

1. Study the biographical studies of Samuel, Saul, and David.
2. Study again the failure of nepotism as Samuel sought to install his sons as leaders succeeding himself.
3. Study social base processing. Samuel's family failure is rooted in the modeling he saw in Eli's family. Be aware of the fact that it is difficult for a Godly leader to pass on a heart for God to his/her children who grow up in religious situations.
4. Abuse of power, one of the major pitfalls of leaders is illustrated in Eli's sons and Samuel's sons. Positional privilege led to abuse of power.
5. Why is God so hard on Saul? He removes Himself so quickly over issues so seemingly small (though at the heart they are dealing with integrity) when later on in kingdom leadership He does not seem to deal

1 SAMUEL continued

so harshly with kings who on the surface seem much more disobedience and unresponsive to God.

6. Study the concept of sense of destiny with regards to Samuel and Hannah. His destiny was more or less sealed by an act of his mother before his birth. This is one of the special categories of destiny preparation.
7. Samuel's learning to discern God's Word is a classical Word Check in the Scriptures.
8. Samuel's rejection by the people gives valuable lessons on Spiritual Authority.
9. Saul's two repeated failures (integrity and obedience checks) highlight the importance of pivotal points[9] in a leader's life.
10. Jonathan and David illustrate lateral (peer) mentoring and highlight its importance.
12. David illustrates the importance of submission to authority in his repeated incidents with Saul when he could have killed him.
13. Abigail's leadership act in 1 Samuel 25 is priceless and shows sensitivity and tremendous influence skills. She is a woman who exercises important leadership skills in a male dominated culture. She is probably typical of many women in the culture.

Special Comments
This book is filled with leadership information. Key verse: 1 Kings 8:19,20.
1 Samuel 12 is a major leadership act in which Samuel models good leadership transitional characteristics.

---

[9] A pivotal point in a leader's life is a critical process item(s)which : 1. can curtail further use or expansion of the leader, 2. can limit the eventual use of the leader's ultimate contribution, or 3. can enhance the leader toward ultimate purposes.

BOOK	2 Samuel **Author:** uncertain
Characters	David is the central character. Others include: Abner, Joab, Mephibosheth, Uriah, Bathsheba, Nathan, Ammon, Tamar, Absalom, Ahithopel, Hushai, Ziba, Shimei, 37 mighty men of David (2 Samuel 23)
Who To/for	Israel
Literature Type	Historical vignettes all related to David's rise, fall and restoration as King during a period of 40 years.
Story Line	The book commences with news of Saul and Jonathan's death. David is anointed king of Judah and his first act is to inquire of God what he is to do. This sets the tone for David's reign and is generally followed throughout his years as king. Over a period of seven years there is warfare off and on between Saul's descendants (still reigning over most of Israel) and David's followers. David's kingly qualities are eventually recognized by all and he is crowned king over all Israel. David's reliance upon God in his kingship is underlined by his return of the Ark, the symbol of the presence of God with the nation and his desire to build a temple. David gains victories over Israel's nations, expands the kingdom, and establishes it. Then David sins by taking another man's (Uriah) wife (Bathsheba) and having that man killed in battle. Nathan, a faithful friend and prophet rebukes David with one of the most effective exhortive passages in all of scripture. David repents but must live through the ramifications of his sin which eventuates in his own son Absalom's rebellion and deposing of David as king. David's army finally defeats Absalom's and he is returned to his kingship. The last section of the book contains two Psalms which reveal the character of David and display why he was a man after God's own heart. His attitude toward God is given in the first. His secret of success is given in the second.
Structure	I. (ch 1-10) David's Rise As King II. (ch 11-20) David's Fall and Restoration As King III. (ch 21-24) Aftermath Summary--Selected Issues

2 Samuel continued

Theme   **DAVID'S KINGSHIP OVER ALL ISRAEL**
- first involved a lengthy transition of 7 years over Judah and military skirmishes with Israel,
- lasted 33 years over all Israel, of which the first years are the glory years,
- reaches its turning point in David's sin against Uriah (the Bathsheba incident),
- was marred by weaknesses in David's family and administration of the Kingdom which led to Absalom's rebellion (part of God's punishment for the Bathsheba incident),
- included a time of restoration following a major victory over Absalom.

Key Words   David (several hundred times)

Key Events   God's covenant with David, David's Sin against Uriah, Nathan's rebuke, Ammon's rape of Tamar, Absalom's revenge of Tamar, overthrow of David, and death.

Purposes
- to continue illustrating principles of leadership (those of success and those bringing failure),
- to give insights into David's heart toward God, since his is the standard for measuring the kings to come, (though imperfect, David's basic attitude was a high view of God including worship, trust, belief in God's greatness and his own destiny with God),
- to foreshadow the role of prophetical leadership in its correctional function (Nathan and David) which role will be expanded to the writing prophets during the years of the declining kingships.

Why Important   Two major principles of God's working with leadership are seen in this development of David as king. In terms of a leader's cooperation with God and being used by God, it is clear **that a leader's view of (attitude toward) God is the major limiting or expansive factor in his/her leadership.** It is equally clear that **God is involved in the process to shape a leader's attitude.** Or to say it in other words--**God's opportunity to work through a leader is created by the attitude of that leader towards God.**

2 Samuel continued

Abandonment to God is a key. How do leaders get their attitude toward God? A leader's opportunity is created by the attitude of God towards him. In the end, the leader does not persuade God to do something, but allows himself/ herself to be persuaded by God to be something. The conforming attitude--willingness to know, to be and to do God's will is the attitude that God looks for and through that attitude acts with the leader. But these principles must be taken in the context of the overriding one of 1 Samuel; the ultimate victory of God is independent of the attitude of individuals or peoples toward Him. The **covenant with David given in 2 Samuel 7:1-17 and David's response 7:18-29 not only gives God's intents for David and his descendants which will explain much of what happens in the books of the Kings and Chronicles but also points out God's leadership selection principles** (leader's attitude toward God and God's shaping of the attitude).

Where It Fits   2 Samuel covers the initial time in Kingdom Leadership, the United Kingdom, and just precedes the boundary from chapter 1 The Making of A Nation to chapter 2 The Destruction of a Nation.

Leadership Lessons

1. **BIOGRAPHICAL GENRE.** 2 Samuel is biographical genre. As such its major lessons are depicted in detail in the study of David which is included in another handbook. The lessons are much too detailed to include on the one or two pages allocated to this overview. A few important ones that affect an overall macro approach to leadership lessons will be given.
2. **SELECTION PROCESSES.** 1 Samuel shows us from the Godward side that the ultimate victory of God is independent of the attitude of individuals or peoples toward Him. He will work through leaders or not depending on their response to Him until He accomplishes His purposes. 2 Samuel shows us selection from the Manward side. It is clear **that a leader's view of (attitude toward) God is the major limiting or expansive factor in his/her leadership.** It is equally clear that **God is involved in the process to shape a leader's attitude.** Or to

2 Samuel continued

say it in other words--**God's opportunity to work through a leader is created by the attitude of that leader towards God.**

3. **SOCIAL BASE PROCESSING.** One of the 6 major barriers[10] to a leader's continuance and thus finishing well over a lifetime includes family processing. Throughout 2 Samuel it is clear that family problems are critical to the development of David as a leader reaching his top potential. Deuteronomy forbade a king to entangle himself with many wives. David violated this. Jealousies between potential heirs to the kingdom and sexual abuse within the family all contribute to the eventual overthrow of David.

4. **PLATEAU BARRIER.** Another of the 6 major barriers to finishing well is that of plateauing, a common occurrence in leader's lives. David was not adequately taking care of the kingdom. His affair with Bathsheba seems to begin with his inattention to his duties as king. Absalom's ability to persuade the people (at the city gate) that they needed representation at court for their problems to be heard and taken care of are a strong indication that David has plateaued.

5. **SEXUAL BARRIER.** Another of the 6 major barriers to finishing well is that of illicit sexual relationships. David's affair with Bathsheba illustrates this problem. Nathan's prophecy, when correcting David, came true and shows that the ramifications of sin happen even though forgiveness is experienced.

6. **PRIDE BARRIER.** Another major barrier to finishing well includes pride. 2 Samuel 24 and (and 1 Chronicles 21) detail the affair of David's numbering of Israel's fighting men. The heart of this was pride as indicated in the Chronicles' version. Improper pride (that is, pride which is self-centered and egoistic denying God's rightful accomplishments) is often the beginning of the downfall of a leader.

7. **ABUSE OF POWER BARRIER.** Another of the six major barriers to finishing well include improper use of power which is available to a leader. While for the most part David was good on this issue (2 Samuel gives specific focus on showing David's innocence in many issues) he failed in this in the Uriah murder.

8. **GOD'S STANDARDS.** The Moses' principle which states that *leaders may be held to higher standards than followers because they are such influential models before followers* is shown to hold even among leaders. God has high standards even among leaders for accomplishing some of His purposes. For example, when David desires to build the

---

[10]These six barriers include: family problems, illicit sexual relationships, incorrect handling of finances or greed for finances, abuse of power, pride (inappropriate and self-centered), plateauing.

2 Samuel continued

temple, God forbids him because of his warlike track record. The
temple must be built by a peaceful person.

9. **POOR FINISH.** David, especially as seen so positively in the Psalms
   which depict a heart that is warm toward God, dependent upon God in
   crises, and one that repents of sin, never-the-less fails to finish well.
   The leadership transition to Solomon is fraught with political intrigue
   and manipulation by all concerned. His last words to Solomon are of
   vengeance. The major barriers to finishing well kept David from
   finishing well. But even so he accomplished much and was greatly
   used of God (see Acts 13:22, 36). David's life serves as a warning to us
   both positively and negatively. Positively we are to have a passion for
   God as he did and to worship God and turn to God in all our life
   experiences. Negatively we are to avoid those major pitfalls which kept
   him from being all he could be.

10. **GOD'S PATIENT DEALING.** David's life illustrates the grace,
    mercy, and patience of God in shaping a leader. God seems to go to
    every extreme to meet a leader whose heart has a bent toward God, even
    though he/she fails in many aspects to reach the potential possible. That
    we have a God who so lovingly deals with us to shape us over a lifetime
    should encourage us as leaders to attempt leadership with its ever
    increasing complexities and opportunity for failure.

For Further Leadership Study

1. There are numerous leadership acts in 2 Samuel which can be studied with
   great profit.
2. Study 2 Samuel comparatively with 1 Chronicles in order to see the
   change of perspective when viewing David's life via the court recorder
   versus a religious scribe's viewpoint.
3. Study 2 Samuel to identify the major leadership roles that control a
   kingdom. Note especially the place of the historians, advisers, and
   prophets.
4. Study Nathan's carefully thought out rebuke to David regarding his sin
   with Bathsheba (2 Samuel 12). This leadership act is well done and
   should be noted for two major reasons: upholding the adviser/ prophetic
   function and communicating with impact.
5. Absalom's conspiracy is a beautiful example of Sower's change dynamics
   model. Four of the five stages were completed.[11]

---

[11]Sowers' model is a social dynamics model for bringing about change in a societal situation. His model
includes 5 stages: Convergence of Interest, Establishing an Initiating Set, Developing a Support Group,
Establishing an Execution set, and Freezing the Change. See **Bridging Strategies--Leadership
Perspectives for Introducing Change** available through Barnabas Publishers.

2 Samuel continued

6. Ahithopel's leadership should be studied for its important lessons on change dynamics.
7. David's Psalms must be studied to give a **balancing viewpoint of David.** The lessons mentioned above seem harsh and negative concerning David. To balance this, study the Psalms attributed to David to see his heart for God, his passion to worship God, his desire to do God's will, his utter dependence upon God in the crisis experiences of his life, his willingness to be transparent and go to God with his sins, his repentance, and his acceptance of God's forgiveness, etc.

Special Comments
While we might lament David's fall and generally poor track record during his latter reign, we do have to recognize as the New Testament does, the bent of his life, something worthy of emulation. Two passages in Acts highlight this bent. In Acts 13:22 God calls David a man after His own heart, who will do everything I want him to do. And in 13:36 Paul asserts that David served God's purpose in his generation. He was a man of passion--sometimes controlled, used by God and directed toward God, and sometimes not.

BOOK 1 **Chronicles** **Author**: unknown; Jewish Tradition--Ezra

Characters   The first nine chapters list chronologies of leaders from Adam to Saul of Kish. After that David is the central character.

Who To/For   Israel

Literature Type   Lists of genealogies; highly selected vignettes and interpreted comments about David's reign

Story Line   1 Chronicles focuses on leadership. It lists more leaders by name than any other single book in the Scriptures (including Numbers). Following an initial listing of patriarchal, tribal, and clan leadership, the book of 1 Chronicles focuses on David's kingly line and then the tribes of Judah, Simeon, Reuben, Gad, Manasseh, and Levi. It next lists the Temple musicians which is in keeping with the Priestly view of David's accomplishments. Other Levites are then listed. The tribes of Issachar, Benjamin, Naphtali, Mannasseh (the previous listing was of the 1/2 tribe of Manasseh), Ephraim, and Asher. The special genealogy of Saul the Benjaminite is given in detail. All of this is preliminary to the focus of David's leadership. Indirectly, the book is saying that leadership is crucial to the ongoing spirituality of a nation. From chapter 9 on, the focus is on David--chapters 9 and 10 introduce the background of David's kingdom (brief overview of Saul's reign). David's reign is given in a post-reflective evaluation from a Priestly viewpoint which will highlight the necessity of God's centrality in the life of the nation (or its lack thereof). Again the remaining chapters are filled with names of leaders. There is much detail given in 1 Chronicles that supplements that already given about David in 2 Samuel. Comparative study, with the view of intentional selection in mind, will yield added information and lessons about David's leadership.

Structure   I. (ch 1-10) Genealogies Leading to David's Kingship
               II. (ch 11-29) David's Reign from a Priest Centered Perspective

1 Chronicles continued

Theme   **DAVID'S REIGN FROM A RELIGOUS PERSPECTIVE**
- is legitimated by a God given heritage,
- is described in glowing terms beginning with Hebron and continuing with events such as the story of the Ark and others which focus on religious impact in the life of the nation.

Key Words   Again, as in 2 Samuel, David is repeated many times.

Key Events   Saul's tragic end, David's crowing at Hebron, the Ark and its return, David's desire to build the temple, God's response to David, victories over Ammonites, Syrians, Philistines, David's Sin in numbering the people, preparation for building the temple and organization of its workers, David's civil exploits, David's closing message and intent for Solomon to build the temple, Solomon's enthronement from the bright side.

Purposes
- to highlight the importance of God in the history of the nation,
- to point out the importance of the priesthood during David's reign,
- to show that that Israel under David reached its greatest strength (though not material splendor),
- to impart hope that if God will be put central Israel will yet be blessed,
- to point out how moral standards, moral character of individuals and of the nation as a whole relate directly to the centrality of God in the nation.

Why Important   The intentional selection of content which emphasizes the place of religion in affecting government and national life highlights a most important principle. **It is the presence and power of God in Israel's history (or removal of His blessing) which makes the difference in the rise and fall of the nation**. When God is honored, He blesses the nation. When He is forgotten or disobeyed the nations falls into crisis. 1 Chronicles gives a second view of David's reign, clarifies some details of 2 Samuel and adds others. It **highlights dependence upon God and God's blessing as a major secret of David's reign**.

1 Chronicles continued

Where It Fits   1 Chronicles in its main focus covers the initial time in
Kingdom Leadership, the United Kingdom, and just
precedes the boundary from chapter 1 The Making of A
Nation to chapter 2 The Destruction of a Nation. Though
it deals with this period of history it is written much later
with a view toward explaining why Israel fell and with a
purpose of encouraging a return to dependence upon
God.

Leadership Lessons

1. **BIOGRAPHICAL GENRE.** The major focus of 2 Chronicles, apart
from lists of leaders, is biographical in nature. As such its major
lessons are depicted in detail in the study of David which is included in
another handbook. The lessons are much too detailed to include on the
one or two pages allocated to this overview. A few important ones that
affect an overall macro approach to leadership lessons will be given.
2. **COMPLEXITY OF LEADERSHIP.** The book as a whole points out
the complexity and difficulties of leadership. In almost an aside it adds
a dimension of complexity not found in any of the other historical
accounts (1 Samuel, 2 Samuel, 1 Kings, 2 Kings, 2 Chronicles). That
dimension involves spiritual warfare. In 1 Chronicles 21:1 there is an
indication of spiritual warfare involved in leadership. Satan is
mentioned by name (one of the very few times this label is used in the
entire Old Testament) as being the prime cause for a major failure on
David's part. This emphasis is, of course, given much more detail in the
Pre-Church Leadership and New Testament Church leadership eras.
3. **LEADERSHIP REPERCUSSIONS.** The same chapter depicts one of
the hazards of leadership. Failure in leadership will bring repercussions
to followers (who may be quite innocent in the matter). Leadership has
its rewards but it also has its responsibilities. Whereas Hebrews 13:17
admonishes followers to submit to leaders in order to make their
leadership productive, pleasant, and desirable because of responsibility
before God for leadership, 1 Chronicles 21 gives the other side of the
coin and shows what will happen to followership should leaders go
astray. This is a great warning for leaders.
4. **ESSENTIAL INGREDIENT OF LEADERSHIP.** 1 Chronicles
emphatically affirms the basic principle of leadership first given by
Moses and highlighted in Joshua's ministry, as well as the successful
judges. IT IS THE POWERFUL PRESENCE OF GOD IN THE LIFE
AND MINISTRY OF A LEADER WHICH IS THE NECESSARY

1 Chronicles continued

AND SUFFICIENT CONDITION FOR EFFECTIVE LEADERSHIP.
Where this is missing whether in part or whole there will be failure in
leadership.

For Further Leadership Study

1. Notice the way 1 Chronicles depicts the transition from David to
   Solomon in a much more positive light (Solomon will build the temple--
   the central force in unifying Israel religiously) than does 2 Samuel (the
   political view of what happened).
2. The leadership act depicted in 1 Chronicles 21 with its great warnings to
   leadership should be studied by every Christian leader and its lessons
   continuously applied to present leadership responsibilities and decisions.
   Pride is at the heart of much of leadership failure in our times. Satan will
   use this as a wedge to enter and destroy our leadership. This is especially
   true of successful leaders.

Special Comments
The 2 books of Chronicles cover the period of history seen already in 2
Samuel, and in 1, 2 Kings. But two different foci should be pointed out.
First, whereas the focus in Samuel and the Kings is from a courtly
perspective that of 1 Chronicles is from a priestly perspective highlighting
the importance of the temple. Most likely written after the exile and during
the era of the rebuilding of the temple it is natural that it should highlight
historically those things in David's reign which focused on his interest in the
temple and preparation for it. A second focus different in the Chronicles is
that they almost exclusively confine their selections to Judah, only referring
to Israel where necessary to explain something in Judah. And within the
tribe of Judah, it is David's descendants who are in focus. In 1 Chronicles
the genealogies are selected and lead up to David and then follow him. The
distinctive note (as Morgan emphasizes) is that of religion and its effect
upon national life.

BOOK: **PSALMS** **Authors:** many; attributed to: David, Asaph, Sons of Korah, Solomon, Heman, Ethan, Moses according to early inscriptions

Characters none highlighted as such, several mentioned, David, Moses,

Who To/For Israel in general, some are to the Lord, some are for the righteous, some to all humankind in general

Literature Type A Psalm, i.e. units of Hebrew Poetry usually grouping several stanzas to make a larger unit. Inscriptions apparently added later indicate authorship of about 100 of the 150 psalms. These come from a time period of about 900 or more years. Much figurative language.

Story Line These are individual Psalms, the earliest of which probably came from Moses. The latest probably came from the time of exile in Babylon. There is no story line but each represents either individual worship to God in the varying times of life or corporate worship to God when in a congregational setting.

Structure The person (unknown) who collected the psalms together indicates a fivefold structure. However, the structure does not seem to be helpful in learning the Psalms.

    I.   Book I. Psalms 1-41
    II.   Book II. Psalms 42-72
    III. Book III. Psalms 73-89
    IV. Book IV. Psalms 90-106
    V. Book V. Psalms 107-150

Theme **INTIMACY WITH GOD** (meaning a worshipful , dependent transparency)

- should be a normal part of life--public and private.
- will be necessary in the ups and downs of life.
- demonstrates the reality of God to others.

Key Words Bless & cognates (90+), Praise, & cognates (170+) various names of God

PSALMS   continued

Key Events   none except where alluded to in the Psalm as a stimulus for
writing it

Purposes
- to indicate how an individual can worship God,
- to give a songbook for use in public worship,
- to indicates the ingredients of worship,
- to give prophetic indications of Messianic prophecy in a context of
  worship.

Why Important   These show us the inner responses of people to God
during the times in which they lived. The other books
(Genesis through Esther) give us historical data and
interpretation of those times. These give us the feelings
of God's people and show their need of and dependence
upon him. This is particularly true of leaders. We
see various leaders, some known, some unknown and
their view of God and His actions in their lives.
        This is the third of the great bodies of revelation
from God (1. Promise, 2. Law). The first is an oral
promise (what God will do). The second is a set of
outward written standards (how humankind is to respond
externally). This third one is written and yet very
transferrable orally. It represents **internal affective
response to God**. Morgan (see Handbook page 83)
indicates that the permanent values of the Psalms (that is,
what we would miss if they were absent) are :*the
conceptions of God that produce worship:* his essence,
eternality, essential might, intervening power, lordship,
and sovereignty; *the response of humankind in worship*:
submission, trust, and joy; *the activities of worship:*
God's call to worship, man's response--transparency
before God, acknowledgment of God's gifts, offering of
praise and thanks, God's becoming to the worshipper
what he/she needs.

Where It Fits   In the redemptive time-line, the Psalms span chapters 1
and 2, the Making of a Nation and the Destruction of a
Nation. The highest acme of the nation is reached as well

PSALMS   continued

as the lowest of lows. You will get some highs and lows in the Psalms as individuals celebrate God's goodness and as they face crises. In the leadership time line, the Psalms span three leadership eras, Pre-Kingdom Leadership, Kingdom Leadership, and Post-Kingdom leadership.

Leadership Lessons

1.   **INTIMACY.** Leaders need intimacy with God on a regular and on-going basis as well as unusual times of God's affirmation.
2.   **NON-IDEAL SITUATIONS.** Expect ups and downs, leadership is rarely ideal.
3.   **THE GREAT SURPRISE.** All leaders will usually come under attack via slander from within from Christians. (see Psalms 27:12, 31:12,13,18 35:4,11,12,15,16,20 37:12,13 38:12 41:5-9 52 whole thing, 55:9,12,13,20 56:1,2,5 57:4, 59:3,9,12 62:4 64 whole thing 71:10 maybe not David 109:4 140:3) Expect conflict in leadership especially slander. Expect to be hurt (sometimes intentional, sometimes not.) One would normally expect this kind of treatment in a secular situation but it usually catches you by surprise in a Christian situation.
4.   **WORD FROM GOD.** In crisis situations you must be able to hear from God (and learn to wait to hear). David expected God to speak to him in crises. He used God's past revelation to guide him. He had standards based on what he knew of God's revelation.
5.   **PRIVATE AND PUBLIC WORSHIP.** Leaders should initiate and model worship in appropriate cultural forms so that followers can know what intimacy is.
6.   **RECOGNIZE A NEED FOR BALANCE IN INPUT.**   A leader needs both an emotional/intuitive (affect) and an analytical (cognitive) approach to hearing from God. The Psalms by and large are speaking to the affect and use an emotional/ intuitive sensing of God. The Proverb s use an analytical approach. You need both to keep from crashing (going to an extreme) in one or the other.
7.   **ULTIMATE SOURCE OF DELIVERANCE.**   God is the ultimate source of deliverance in crises for leaders. David always turns to God as the ultimate source of his deliverance. (Psa 60:11,12, Psa 62 God only psalm). This along with David's repentant attitude and his desire to worship God are at least part of the explanation for what it means to be a person after God's own heart (Acts 13:22).

PSALMS   continued

For Further Leadership Study

1. Many of the Psalms written by David give tremendous insights into the processing he was experiencing. These should be correlated to the historical incidents and give added data for processing analysis.
2. Two historical Psalms (77,78) conclude with a reference to leaders (Moses, Aaron, David) and are obviously saying something about leadership and the place of modeling and God's working with his people through leaders. These should be studied carefully for leadership implications.
3. Psalms should be studied with a focus of what do they teach about God. If Morgan's double assertions (held in dynamic tension) are true that *God's opportunity for a leader is created by the attitude of a leader towards Him* and that a leader's opportunity is created by the attitude of God toward that leader (from comparative study of Saul, David, and Samuel) then Tozer's comment (adapted slightly) is super significant. *What a leader thinks about God is the most important thing about that leader.* The Psalms are full of what leader's think about God. These should be studied, imbibed, and should shape us as leaders to expand our view of God.

Special Comments
The word Psalm is from the Greek and comes probably from the Septuagint. It means a poem set to music. Some commentators indicate that almost one quarter of the New Testament quotes from the Old Testament come from the Psalms. There are many ways of looking at the Psalms including groupings into the following categories: *Messianic* (2, 8, 16, 22, 31, 40, 45, 69, 72, 110, 118), *Nature* (8, 19, 29, 65, 104), *Penitential* (32, 38, 51, 130), *Historical* (78, 105, 106, 136), *Imprecatory* (1 out of every 10 contain imprecation but especially 5, 7, 10, 35, 36, 52, 58, 109), *Companion* (3/4, 14/15, 20/21, 22/23, 32/33, 42/43, 90/91, 105/106), *Royal* (93-100), *Egyptian/Hallel* (113-118), *Songs of Ascent* (120-134), and *Hallelujah* (146-150). The Psalms are not basically analytical in essence but are affective and conative--that is, they impact upon our feelings and our wills more than our knowledge--though there is much teaching in them. The Psalms focus on the inner life (i.e. true devotion from the heart, both individual and corporate). They show that the inner life must reflect total dependence upon God, should be filled with adoration for God, and is expressed in all the changing experiences of life.

| *BOOK* | Proverbs | **Authors:** | probably many; some attributed to editorial efforts of Solomon, Agur, Lemuel |

Characters   none

Who To/For   Israel

Literature Type   Hebrew poetry, chapters 1-10 in stanzas or contextual groupings of stanzas--extended parallelism; chapters 11-31 generally in couplets or short extended parallelism. Much figurative language.

Story Line   *none*

Structure

    I. (ch 1-9) Wisdom Contrasted with Foolishness (in Contextual Units)
    II. (ch 10-24) Individual Pearls of Wisdom Edited by Solomon (mostly couplets)
    III. (ch 25-29) Individual Pearls of Wisdom Edited by Hezekiah (mostly couplets)
    IV. (ch 30) Sayings of Agur (couplets and units)
    V. (ch 31) Sayings of King Lemuel (units)

Theme   **WISDOM FROM GOD**
- is drawn from all of life,
- applies to all kinds of life situations and relationships, and
- distinguishes between wise people (those who accept it and use it) or foolish people (those who do not accept it or use it).

Key Words   wise & cognates (100+), instruction & cognates (26)

Key Events   none

Purposes
- to show how God reveals truth out of life,
- to give instruction on how to comport oneself in a number of life situations: life and death, family, use of the tongue, friendship, laziness, general wisdom--100s of issues, God and man, etc.
- to shows that a wise person is one rightly related to God and obedient to His truth,
- to show, in general, that following the Lord is a very practical everyday reality.

Proverbs continued

Why Important   In addition, to the written law, the Proverbs show that God
revealed detailed instruction in terms of the many practical
aspects of life. This book is important not only in the social
truth it gives but also in showing how God reveals truth in
daily life. This is a horizontal book--deals with social life
and human relationships. Psalms is a vertical book--dealing
with a person's relationship to God. Both are needed to
make a balanced follower of God. Philosophically the book
begins by affirming God. It asserts therefore that there can
be no discovery of ultimate truth save upon the basis of
revelation and the fundamental revelation is that of the
existence of God. How man relates to God is then seen to be
crucial. In the progress of redemption, this book is
important because it shows **God's provisional revelation
for everyday life**. Life itself is meant to teach us God's truth
if we are willing to hear Him in and through it (see Proverbs
1:20-33).

Where It Fits   The Proverbs come dominantly from the Kingdom
leadership era and from Chapter 1 The Making of A
Nation and Chapter 2 The Destruction of a Nation. It
shows how God gave truth to the common folk who were
neither literate nor had access to a central storehouse of
revealed truth as did the Priests.

Leadership Lessons
     While the Proverbs (except for a selected few items) are not directed
toward leaders in particular, their thrust on horizontal relationships with
others and their emphasis on character make them especially applicable to
leaders who must develop relational skills and must have character as
foundational to their leadership. This is an example of the leadership genre,
Indirect --passages dealing with Christian character or behavior which also
apply to Christian leadership as well. While there are many items from
Proverbs which deal with relational skills and character I have limited my
choices only to the ones most applicable to leadership issues.

   1. **FOUNDATIONAL RELATIONSHIP.** It is a vertical relationship
      that is given as foundational for understanding wisdom. Leaders first

Proverbs continued

need to have a proper respect for God as the giver of wisdom before
they can truly learn from life. Leaders need the wisdom of God in their
ministries. The Proverbs assert that a proper relationship with God is
the foundational access to that wisdom from God (Prov 1:7, 1:29, 3:7,
2:5, 8:13, 9:10, 10:27, 14:26, 14:27, 15:16, 15:33, 16:6, 19:23, 22:4,
23:17, 24:21)

2. **LEARNING POSTURE.** One of the findings concerning effective
   leaders states that Effective Leaders maintain a learning posture all their
   lives. The Proverbs certainly assert the validity of this finding.
   Wisdom does not come automatically. There must be proactive
   learning posture if a leader is to learn from God via life. (1:20-33,
   2:1ff, 19:8 and many others).

3. **RESPONSE TO CORRECTION.** One way a learning posture is
   expressed is by a person who can learn from criticism. (9:8, 10:8, 10:17,
   11:3, 12:1 and many others).

4. **DISCIPLINE.** Another way a learning posture is expressed is by a
   proper response to the discipline of the Lord. Processing in life is
   ultimately from the Lord and is meant to teach lessons of life.
   Particularly is this so where it is clear that the Lord is bringing
   discipline upon our lives. (3:11,12, 17:3, 17:10, 27:21 and others).

5. **CRISES.** It is the crises experiences in life which are particularly
   instructive. These tend to test us and shape us like no other
   experiences. A person with a learning posture will respond to crises
   expecting to go deep with God and to learn much about personality and
   character (24:10,11).

6. **USE OF WORDS.** A leader must be extremely careful in the use of
   the tongue even more than is indicated in the Proverbs which treats this
   as a major topic. This is so because people in influential positions are
   listened to with much more emphasis. That is, their words carry added
   weight (even if not intended) with followers who look to them (6:2,
   6:16-19, 10:11, 10:19, 12:14, 12:19, 15:1, 15:4, 15:23, 15:28, 12:19,
   16:24, 16:27, 28, 17:9, 17:27, 28, 18:13, 25:11, 26:18,19, 27:2, and
   many others).

7. **PRIDE.** Pride can lead to failure. It is one of the six major barriers
   which hinder leaders from finishing well. Proverbs warns against it and
   its dangers (13:10, 16:18, 18:12, 27:2).

8. **CORPORATE WISDOM.** Wise leaders need counsel from peers and
   upward mentors in their decision making. Major leadership decisions
   should never be made just unilaterally (11:14, 15:22, 20:18 , 24:6, and
   others)

Proverbs continued

9. **ULTIMATE CONTRIBUTION.** A leader's good reputation, both in character and achievement should be a major determining factor in living out life, since it will be a major legacy left behind (10:7, 11:3, 19:1, 19:22, 20:17, 22:1).
10. **INTEGRITY.** In leadership, character, and especially integrity and honesty, are necessary if followers are to trust leaders (4:23, 10:9, 11:1, 11:3, 16:11, 17:15, 20:10)
11. **GENEROSITY.** Generosity is especially esteemed as a characteristic of a wise person. Even more so, does it stand out in leadership (11:24, 25, 26, 14:21, 19:17, 21:13, 22:9,)
12. **ACCOUNTABILITY.** Leaders are people who must be accountable for their ministries (12:27, 18:9, 22:12, 27:23-27, 28:19, 31:1ff).
13. **OPPORTUNITIES.** Proverbs exhorts to make the most of opportunities. One of the positive signs of growing leadership is its ability to recognize and exploit opportunities. One of the signs of plateauing is the inability to sense opportunity or the inability to follow up on it (12:27, 14:4, 28:19, 31:1ff)
14. **STRATEGIC PLANNING.** Leaders must give foresight to their leadership. Planning is good but it must always be held in perspective of God's sovereignty (14:15, 16:1, 16:4, 16:9, 16:33, 19:21, 21:1, 21:30, 21:31, 22:13, 27:12).

For Further Leadership Study
1. Study the phrase *fear of the Lord* and its parallel phrase which explains it to see the many ways of relating to the Lord in order to receive wisdom.
2. Study the concept of justice as a leadership responsibility.
3. Study the concept of righteousness as a corporate standard in order to determine a major goal of leadership.
4. Because of intentional selection ,the vertical verses dealing with God's sovereignty in a book devoted almost wholly to horizontal relationships take on added emphasis. Study these verses for their implication to leadership.

Special Comments
Key verse: Proverbs 1:7. The first part of the parallelism is repeated twice more in the book with progression in the second member of the parallelism. Note also the vertical verses (sovereignty of God, e.g. 5:21, 15:3, 16:1,2,4, 7, 9, 11, 17:3, 15, 18:22, 21, 20:10, 21:1, 30, 31, 22:12) in this horizontal book. They especially stand out.

BOOK	**ECCLESIASTES**	**Author:** traditionally, Solomon

Characters   none

Who To/For   Israel

Literature Type   Hebrew Poetry, units, figurative language

Story Line   There is no story line.

Structure
    I.   (ch 1:1-11)   The Theme Stated--Emptiness of Materialistic Pursuits
    II.   (ch 1:12-8)   Solomon's Empirical Evidence of the Emptiness of Materialistic Pursuits
    III.   (ch 9-11:8)   The Effects of Pursuing Materialistic Things
    IV.   (ch 11:9-12)   Corrective Thoughts

Theme   **THE EMPTINESS OF LIFE BASED ON MATERIALISTIC PURSUITS**
- is seen in many specifics including: accumulation of knowledge, pleasure, wealth, intellectual ability, religious life and the fact that death ends it all and is inescapable,
- results in a hopelessness and a *live for the moment attitude* since nothing will matter in the end when death conquers, but
- should drive a person to seek God.

Key Words   wisdom and cognates (almost 50), vanity (emptiness) (37), under the sun (human Perspective--31)

Key Events   *none*

Purposes
- to show that true satisfaction with life will not come from pursuing life apart from God,
- to point out the importance of death,

Why Important   This book warns us of what happens when we become cynical about life. It also shows us that even with the best of starts, we do not have a guarantee to finish well. See Morgan (Handbook, page 94 and 95). He postulates

ECCLESIASTES continued

two permanent values. He says **to forget God** is to enter into life and fail to see its profound value and will result finally in an affirmation that it is empty. **To see God**, relate to Him and obey Him in life is to enter into life in the most profoundest sense and to finally admit it has been worth it all.

Where It Fits   If Solomon did write this or caused it to be written, then this book belongs to Chapter 1, The Making of A Nation, just prior to the entering of Chapter 2, The Destruction of A Nation.   It would belong in the first phase of the Kingdom leadership era. If Solomon did not author it and it was written later, which is a possibility then it would be difficult to locate.

Leadership Lessons

1. **GENRE.** At best this is an example of an indirect leadership source. While there are a number of individual lessons that may be given the nature of the book is best suited to drawing out higher level abstractions based on the message of the book as a whole. Several are given.
2. **WARNING 1.** Assuming that Solomon did write this a major lesson that needs to be discerned concerns the starting point for leadership. Solomon had wealth, power, a consolidated kingdom and wisdom from God to run his kingdom. Yet he did not finish well. Lesson: **A good start does not guarantee a good finish.** Leadership is a life long process which requires development all along the way. Very frequently talented people who have so much going for them, do not finish will. A faithful plodder who follows hard after God may do much better than a very qualified and able person who does not follow hard after God. In Solomon's own words the race is not always to the swift or the battle to the strong (9:11).   Do not be too quick to lay hands on some talented person who is converted for leadership. Let them first prove their character.
3. **WARNING 2.** Assuming that Solomon did write this a second major lesson needs to be observed. It is clear it is written from someone far along in their life experience. The book reeks with cynicism. There is a tendency in leadership, so aptly illustrated here that needs to be pointed out. Leaders tend to become cynical toward the latter stages of their ministry. Lesson: **Avoid a cynical attitude which tends to put down**

ECCLESIASTES continued

    emerging leaders and their ideas. Recognize that they may be able to pull off some of the things you know won't work for a variety of reasons.
4. **ULTIMATE CONTRIBUTION.** Live so as to leave behind an ultimate contribution set which pleases God and has potential to live beyond you. That is, live with eternity in view and not just your lifetime here on earth.
5. **REVELATION.** Nowhere do we find that Solomon had a hunger for the written word of God nor did he apparently study it as his father David did. It is clear that he did receive wisdom via natural life learning. Leader's who do not base their ministry around the written word of God may run dry when experience runs out.

For Further Leadership Study

1. What difference does the resurrection make to the perspectives given in Ecclesiastes? Death seems to be a heavy and foreboding topic that lurks behind the whole book.
2. What does Ecclesiastes tell us about a focused life?

Special Comments
In the latter part of his reign Solomon simply gives a reflection back on what he has learned in life. The book is cynical and carries heavily humanistic reasoning. It is clear that Solomon did not receive much revelation from God in the latter part of his reign. And nowhere do we find that Solomon was a hungry student of God's word. The Kings and Chronicles make it clear that he did not finish well. Key verses 1:12-14, 2:11, 12:13,14.

BOOK	**SONG OF SONGS** **Author:** traditionally, Solomon
Characters	Solomon, a Shulamite maiden, a chorus of maidens
Who To/For	Israel
Literature Type	Poetry, idyllic vignettes
Story Line	These songs are idylls and behind them is the actual story of a romantic story--the winning of a bride. Idylls do not necessarily proceed in consecutive form. The actual order must be constructed. There are flashbacks. The following is an adapted story line constructed by Ironsides.

King Solomon owned a vineyard some distance away in the hill country of Ephraim (8:11). He leased it out to vineyard workers. The head of the household was probably dead. There was a mother and two sons (1:6) and two daughters, one of whom is the Shulamite (6:13) and a little sister (8:8). The Shulamite had natural beauty but was basically unnoticed by the family (1:5) as such. The brothers demanded hard work from her (1:6). She had few privileges and little opportunity to care for her personal appearance as the work was demanding. She pruned vines (2:15) and set traps for the little foxes (2:15) who raided the vineyard. She also shepherded a herd (1:8). She was deeply sun-tanned. One day a tall handsome stranger came to the vineyard. Solomon was traveling incognito. He showed an interest in her. She wished she could do something about her personal appearance which obviously bothered her. She thinks he is a shepherd from a nearby location. She asks him about his flocks. He avoids a direct answer and speaks loving words to her (1:8,9,10). He promises rich gifts for the future (1:11). He wins her heart and leaves with the promise that some day he will return. She dreams of him at night and sometimes imagines him to be nearby. She even looks for him at least in her mind. Finally he does return in all his kingly splendor to make her this bride (3:6,7). There are flashbacks of remembering and love scenes.

SONG OF SONGS continued

Structure
    I. (ch 1-2:7) The Marriage Event
    II. (ch 2-8-7:9) Flashback Memories of Courtship
    III. (ch 7:10-8) Wedded Life

Theme
    THE TENDER LOVE OF A MAN AND WOMAN
- is worthy of a public celebration--the banquet,
- will have endearing memories worth reflecting on, and
- should be known in her setting.

Key Words
    beloved (30+)

Key Events
    See story line.

Purposes
- to value marriage and wedded love,

Why Important
    Human love is important and is the basis for a lasting relationship between a man and a woman. By its inclusion in the canon, we sense God's affirmation of love between a man and woman. It is a thing to be enjoyed and remembered and celebrated. It is a pure relationship that brings joy to both man and woman.

Where It Fits
    If Solomon did right this or caused it to be written, then this book belongs to Chapter 1, The Making of A Nation, just prior to the entering of Chapter 2, The Destruction of A Nation. It would belong in the first phase of the Kingdom leadership era.

Leadership Lessons

1. **GENRE.** This does fit any of the six leadership source genre except very remotely, the indirect. It is therefore difficult to draw out lessons. I see no specific leadership lessons. But an abstract one based on the overall thrust of the book can be suggested.
2. **SOCIAL BASE PROCESSING.** While there are a few dedicated leaders who will be eunuch-like by choice in order to do a difficulty ministry without the complications of a family, most will normally operate out of a married context. The deterioration of the family (part of social base processing) is one of the major hindrances to finishing well.

SONG OF SONGS continued

The Song of Songs exhorts us to recognize the importance of the physical side of marriage and the emotional side of it. Leaders operating out of a married context must be prepared to give a heavy priority to satisfying their mate's emotional and physical needs—two of the most important social base needs. The illicit sexual barrier which also is a major hindrance to finishing well usually starts with an unsatisfactory sexual relationship in the home. This book, taken as a whole, then while presenting a happy prospect of marriage is also a major warning to leaders.

For Further Leadership Study
1. There is a mystical interpretation of the Song of Songs. Perhaps it could be studied for implications for leadership. I have not done this.
2. Providing you are married, study the Song of Songs to be challenged about your own sexual and emotional relationship to your spouse.

Special Comments
Historically, this love song has been interpreted literally or mystically. A literal interpretation highlights what I have said above. Two mystical interpretations see this as representative of love on a higher spiritual plain: 1. love of God for Israel, the Jewish view, 2. Love of Christ for His church, a Christian view. I tend to move with the more literal but recognize along with Morgan that human love certainly illustrates something of the ultimate love as suggested by Ephesians.

BOOK	**1,2 KINGS Author:** uncertain
Characters	Many kings of Israel and Judah. Two important oral prophets, very powerful ones, are also reviewed--Elijah and Elisha.
Who To/For	Israel
Literature Type	Historical narrative, selected descriptions of reigns of kings and several prophets.
Story Line	The narrative begins with a united kingdom. It gives Solomon's story. Then after the split it gives the stories of the kings of the northern (Israel) and southern (Judah) kings are given. Usually they follow a consecutive order, swapping back and forth from northern to southern kings and giving some appraisal of each king's reign using David as a positive standard and Jereboam as a negative standard. Highlights of each reign are selectively presented. The dominant focus is from a court perspective.

Structure

I.	(1 Kings ch 1-11)	Solomon's Reign--A United Kingdom
II.	(1 Kings ch 12-16)	A Divided Kingdom
III.	(1 Kings ch 17-22)	God's Corrective Intervention--Elijah's Prophetic Ministry
IV.	(2 Kings ch 1-9)	God's Corrective Intervention--Elisha's Prophetic Ministry
V.	(2 Kings ch 10-25)	Downhill--With Few Exceptions

Theme

THE HISTORY OF THE KINGS
- after David, included Solomon's united reign, tragically involved a split of the kingdom into northern and southern,
- traces each from north and south evaluating them in terms of their following God or not,
- was punctuated by God's attempts to correct through prophetical leaders such as Elijah and Elisha, and
- resulted in a downward trend with occasional brief episodes of turning to God which ended in the early capture and deportation of the northern kingdom and later the same result for the southern kingdom.

1,2 KINGS continued

Key Words   kings (almost 600 times in the two books), prophets
                    (about 75 times in the two books)

Key Events   Many, too numerous to list. Usually there are three to
                    four incidents given per king (Solomon has many more).
                    Elijah and Elisha have many and as such deserve special
                    study due to the notion of intentional selection.

Purposes
- to give historical background for understanding the writing prophets,
- to emphasize the importance of history and reflection upon it for lessons,
- to trace the decline of the kingdoms and underline the spiritual causes
  behind the declines,
- to show the weakness of nepotism as a leadership selection methodology,
- to show the rise of the prophetic ministry and its more important role as
  the kings declined,
- to point out that spiritual leadership does make a difference.

Why Important   God's plans called for a strong nation sensitive to Him
                    and obeying Him. Such a nation He could use to bless
                    the whole world and reveal Himself to that world. The
                    Kings show how leaders can easily miss their way and
                    miss God's purposes. And God will patiently try to
                    correct the situation. But there comes a time when God,
                    in order to be true to His nature, must call a halt to the
                    rebellious leaders and followers. Apparently God's plans
                    have been thwarted. If this is all the record we had we
                    would have to conclude failure. But our story goes on
                    and we see a sovereign God working out His plans in
                    spite of imperfect people who will not follow Him.

Where It Fits   The books of 1,2 Kings occur in the Redemptive Drama
                    in Chapter 1, The Destruction of A Nation. Sad to say
                    leadership and followership were basically on a
                    downward trend away from God. God made His
                    attempts repeatedly to call them back. But in the end
                    they chose to self-destruct. And God continued His plans
                    anyway. In terms of the leadership time-line, 1,2 Kings
                    describe the breakup of the united kingdom and trace the
                    divided kingdom until the northern kingdom is gone.
                    The southern kingdom is then traced until its destruction.

1,2 KINGS continued

Leadership Lessons

1. **GENRE.** The books 1, 2 Kings are almost entirely made up of the biographical source of leadership material and as such provide a gold mine for leadership lessons. For most of the kings only partial time lines can be constructed. Only pivotal points in the life of the king or marker events[12] in the life of the nation are given. The principle of intentional selection is important to recognize in scanning these records. Then too, one must look for summary passages or interpretive passages given by the historian. Usually there is some assessment by the writer of the overall effectiveness of the leader using either David for a positive standard or Jereboam for a negative standard. I will leave detailed specifics of these studies to Handbook II which displays biographic information. I will point out one or two specific details from a king's biographical sketch where the value has wide application but for the most part I will point out only important overall lessons from these two books.

2. **HISTORY.** One of the leaders at court was the historian or court recorder (1 Kings 11:41, 14:19, 14:29, 15:7, 15:31, 16:20 and many others). These Biblical reminders usually given after the biographical sketch of the king point out the importance of having a recorded history. Greiner has pointed out something of why the history for an organization[13] is important. Para-church and church organizations are usually lax in this. Change dynamics studies and organizational culture studies rely heavily on linear historical records. In addition, items should be noted historically in order to celebrate God's past dealing and to note eliteness and uniqueness thus motivating for present and future efforts. In addition, one motivational approach used by leaders in key leadership acts almost always is to give historical perspective leading up to the situation pointing out God's intervention or warnings. History is important. Leaders should insure that it is kept for their organizations.

---

[12]A marker event is a given incident in the history of an organization or movement which in retrospect is seen to have been a turning point which introduced some significant aspect of organizational culture or affirmed and stabilized some yet to be established norm or value. Organizational values are important to identify and know for management of organizational culture is one of the major functions of top leadership.

[13]Larry Greiner, *Evolution and Revolution As Organizations Grow* in **Harvard Business Review**, August 1972. In this article Greiner postulates that an organization is much more determined by its past than it is by the opportunities around it. He is speaking primarily from an organizational structure and organizational culture perspective.

1,2 KINGS continued

3. **JUSTICE.** Justice is the central ethic of kingdom leadership. (1 Kings 3:1-15, 7:7 and others). See especially the illustration which follows concerning the two women and the child, 3:16-28).

4. **PIVOTAL POINT.** A major pivotal point is noted for Solomon prophetically (1 Kings 9:4-9, note especially verse 6,7). This warning was given at the high point of Solomon's yet young reign, the dedication of the Temple. Solomon who had everything going for him is a major cause for bringing about the exile. Word checks in particular and Word processing in general must be heeded by leaders if they are to develop to full potential.

5. **ALTERNATE FORMS/ PROPHETIC ROLE.** (See also 1 Kings 14:1 and other such indications of a school of the prophets--where some could be trained). God develops this role during the times of the kings to warn them of problems or their lack of fulfilling the kingly role or to challenge them to opportunities. This word processing function when heeded by the king brought God's blessing. When ignored His wrath. Note that many of the kings had a personal prophet on staff (David had Nathan and Gad). Implications for present leadership include the need for lateral or peer mentoring relationships for accountability sake as well as upward mentors. See especially 2 Kings 17:13, where the phrase My Servants the Prophets appears. This phrase will reappear in other Old Testament books. This hints of the larger umbrella principle-- God will alter His program to by-pass people or means or whatever to carry out His purposes. See also Romans 11:20,21 for a warning along similar lines of this lesson to us who live in the Church Leadership era.

6. **AUTHORITY COVERING.** The incident with Joab (1 Kings 2:31-35) points out the principle of covering, when you act under the authority of leadership and its orders that leadership carries a major responsibility for actions and ramifications. When you act under your own auspices without the knowledge of your superiors or their approval you will carry the major responsibility for its ramifications.[14]

7. **HOLY AMBITION.** God is pleased when we partner with him on grand endeavors of leadership (1 Kings 3:4-15). Effective leadership at its heart is leadership which demonstrates self-initiative, courage, and response to challenges, on the one hand, and yet sees God's vision for the situation, on the other hand. It is not self-ambition unchecked, just ambition. It is not waiting for God to somehow break in and hand the

---

[14]This does not alleviate moral responsibility for carrying out orders while under cover contrary to conscience nor does it relieve total responsibility for leaders in responsibility for those acts done by leaders under them. Where issues are a-ethical and deal with methodology, planning, and other such over which there can be differences the basic notion of covering holds.

1,2 KINGS continued

vision on a platter (Holy). It is a combination, **Holy Ambition.** With such an attitude and discernment, God is pleased and will enable. This affirms Morgan's value of God working in response to the attitude of the leader.

8. **COMPLEX LEADERSHIP.** Larger complex organizations will require a variety of leadership to handle its many structures, problems, and opportunities. 1 Kings 4:1-19 details the kind of leadership Solomon needed for administration of the kingdom. Other kings following his lead developed court leadership in much the same manner.

9. **NATIONAL CELEBRATIONS.** The completion of the temple was heralded by a national celebration. Large celebration events are necessary for affirming organizational culture values, for unifying diverse portions of organizations and for serving as a rallying point for all out commitment or recommitment to God and His purposes. 1 Kings 8:1-21 details just such an event. Celebrations should be used more frequently than they are in order to manage organizational culture.

10. **LEADERSHIP TRANSITIONS.** There are two basic approaches to leadership transition as depicted in the books of 1,2 Kings. Nepotism (the usual transition)[15] or revolution (1 Kings 11:21-40). Neither guarantee anything. God will bless both forms if the parties are willing to trust Him and follow Him. Leadership transitions are complex, should be planned for, and rarely are done well in Christian organizations. The records of the kings certainly affirm this to be true.

11. **FEW FINISH WELL.** Of the biographical sketches given in 1,2 Kings it is clear that leaders at high levels have many barriers to keep them from finishing well. About 1 in 5 of the leaders given in 1, 2 Kings and 2 Chronicles finished well. Barriers include sexual sin, abuse of power, wrongful pride, plateauing (in their experience with God or falling away), family relationships, greed or misuse of finances. Categories of finishes include cut off early, finish poorly, finished so-so, finished well, and can't be sure.[16] The characteristics of a good finish include six (most leaders who finish well have good marks on 4-6

---

[15]A particularly poor one is the transition from Solomon to Rehoboam (1 Kings 12:1ff)

[16]The Scriptures use several phrases to indicate different gradations of finishing poorly or well. **Best,** e.g. Hezekiah, 2 Kings 18:3, he did what was right in the eyes of the Lord, just as his Father David did--he removed the high places. **Next Best** (limited good), e.g. Amaziah, 2 Kings 14:3, he did what was right but the high places were not removed. David may or may not be mentioned (see 2 Kings 12:2 concerning Joash.) **Poor,** e.g. Azariah, 2 Kings 15:27, he did evil in the eyes of the Lord. He did not turn away from the sins of Jeroboam, son of Nebat. See also Menaham 2 Kings 15:17,18 for the same evaluation. **Worst,** He did evil...and was not buried with the Kings (i.e. was not honored with a state funeral, a major insult).

1,2 KINGS continued

of these characteristics--outstanding leaders, like Daniel or Paul, have all six): (1) a <u>personal vibrant relationship</u> with God right up to the end. (2) a <u>learning posture</u>. (3) <u>Christ likeness in character</u>. (4) Truth is lived out in their lives so that <u>convictions</u> and promises of God are seen to be real. (5) <u>ultimate contributions</u> to God's on-going work. (6) a sense of destiny.

12. **OWNERSHIP.** In change dynamics, planned bridging strategies emphasize the necessity for ownership of impending changes by the followership. Effective leaders know this and seek to build attitudes of ownership in their followers. A particularly inept (negative) illustration of this is given by Rehoboah (1 Kings 12:1-24).

13. **CENTRALITY IN WORSHIP.** Jereboam rightly recognized the place of centrality in worship as a major means of unifying a large and diverse people. Unfortunately he chose not to follow God and provided centralized worship of other gods (see 1 Kings 12:26-33). Never-the-less the principle is valid and can be applied in a variety of ways (like Urbana which illustrates this centrality function as well as the large national celebration function) by high level leadership. This principle is indirectly supported by the references of assessment of the kings by the historians--one of the qualifying phrases has to do with whether or not they removed the high places (decentralized places of worship, which were frequently animistic in nature).

14. **GUIDANCE.** While leaders must seek the wisdom of others in their decision making, it is clear where ultimate responsibility lies. They can not depend on someone else's guidance for their own lives (see the strange incident of the young prophet, 1 Kings 13).

15. **SPIRITUAL LEADERSHIP.** It is clear from the differences in the time of duration of the northern kingdom and the duration of the southern kingdom, that spiritual leadership makes a difference in the life of a nation. Both kingdoms initially had God's blessing. The northern kingdom never responded to God's corrective prompting through the prophets. There was not one leader who followed God in the northern kingdom during its entire life. The southern kingdom had several leaders who followed after God in varying degrees of faithfulness. There was some response to God's prophetic promptings. The southern kingdom outlasted the northern by many years. The major difference was spiritual leadership. Spiritual leadership can make a difference even in the midst of major deterioration. This is one of the major overall lessons of 1,2 Kings and 2 Chronicles.

16. **MENTORING.** Jehoiada illustrates the importance of an upward mentor. He carried out this function from a priestly role. As long as he

1,2 KINGS continued

was alive he was able to mentor Joash there was a positive following of God.[17]

For Further Leadership Study
1. One of the longest prayers in the Bible is Solomon's given in 1 Kings 8:22-53. It is worthy of study as are all of the prayers of the Bible.
2. The concept of covering (and the whole idea of accountability and responsibility for leadership) should be studied in depth throughout the entire Bible. It should be done from an ethical expertise perspective as well as a pragmatic one.
3. See also the biographical sketches and lessons learned from them in Handbook II which displays biographical genre and findings. By far the large majority of lessons for the books of 1,2 Kings and 2 Chronicles are contained in Handbook II. Here is given only larger macro lessons.

Special Comments
These historical records remind us of the importance of keeping historical accounts, reflecting on them, and learning lessons from them. Christian churches and organizations today are very lax on this. These histories do for the prophets what the Acts do for the Pauline epistles. They give historical data which helps us interpret the prophets times and messages.

---

[17]Comparative study on leaders indicates that as well as barriers to finishing well there are aids to finishing well. Five major aids to finishing well include: (1) Perspective, (2) repeated renewal experiences, (3) use of spiritual disciplines, (4) learning posture, (5) mentoring. See position paper, Listen Up, Leaders! which reflects on this comparative study. Available through Barnabas Publishers.

BOOK 2 CHRONICLES   Author: uncertain, Jewish Tradition--Ezra

Characters	Covers the same time period as 1,2 Kings but focuses on the Davidic line.
Who To/For	Israel
Literature Type	Historical narrative, summaries of the kings with a few critical incidents highlighted. There is a distinct focus on religious issues.
Story Line	The reign of Solomon is treated in depth and then there is a tracing of the Kings of Judah until the Babylon captivity.
Structure	I. (ch 1-9) Solomon's Reign--His Building of The Temple II. (ch 10-26) Cycles of Degeneracy and Religious Reform And the Final Trend Leading to Captivity.

Theme   **THE HISTORY OF THE KINGS OF JUDAH**
- begins with a glorious start in Solomon's construction of the temple of God,
- follows a pattern of degeneracy with occasional religious reforms,
- with each of the reforms usually getting smaller and less penetrating until degeneracy prevailed and led to captivity.

Key Words	house (148) referring to temple or house of God and priest(s) (80); these carry the religious focus of the book.
Key Events	many

Purposes
- to present the history of the Davidic line,
- to trace the importance of the temple as a focus for religious life,
- to show how the priesthood and religious life are important to the nation,
- to highlight the importance of God in the history of the nation,
- to show that Israel under Solomon reached its apex in terms of material splendor but not in terms of spiritual strength,
- to warn against formalism,
- to impart hope that if God will be put central Israel will yet be blessed,
- to point out how moral standards, moral character of individuals and of the nation as a whole relate directly to the centrality of God in the nation.

2 CHRONICLES continued

Why Important   Focuses on the importance of vital religion to a nation. No nation can long endure without God and His purposes central to their existence. Formalism without life will prove empty.

Where It Fits   Like the books of 1,2 Kings, the time portrayed in 2 Chronicles occurs in the Redemptive Drama in Chapter 1, The Destruction of A Nation. But it is written long after with a view toward reflecting on causation of the destruction of the nation. It focuses on the importance of the central function of religion in the life of the nation. Where the function is emphasized and followed there is life. Where omitted death follows. Sad to say leadership and followership were basically on a downward trend away from God. God made His attempts repeatedly to call them back. But in the end they chose to self-destruct. And God continued His plans anyway. In terms of the leadership time-line, 1,2 Kings describe the breakup of the united kingdom and trace the divided kingdom until the northern kingdom is gone. The southern kingdom is then traced until its destruction.

Leadership Lessons
1. **GENRE.** The book of 2 Chronicles like 1, 2 Kings is almost entirely made up of the biographical source of leadership material and as such provides a gold mine for leadership lessons. Again for most of the kings only partial time lines can be constructed. Only pivotal points in the life of the king or marker events in the life of the nation are given. The principle of intentional selection is very important since this is a post-period reflection which focuses on a religious perspective. Then too, one must look for summary passages or interpretive passages given by the historian. I will leave detailed specifics of the biographical studies to Handbook II which displays biographic information. Many of the macro lessons of 1,2 Kings applies to 2 Chronicles as well. I will point out only one or two important overall lessons from this book which may differ or add to what was previously given for the two books, 1,2 Kings.
2. **PRESENCE OF GOD.** 2 Chronicles with its emphasis on religious influence in the nation makes much of the presence of God or His absence in the affairs of the kings and the nation. This affirms from a broader perspective the already identified essential ingredient of

2 CHRONICLES continued

leadership, that which is both necessary and sufficient, the presence of God in power in the life and activities of leadership.

3. **WOMEN IN MINISTRY.** In times of crisis, gifted women exert considerable leadership influence regardless of the male dominated structures of the society. Hilkiah, a priest leader, did not hesitate to go to Huldah, the prophetess, when a word from God was needed (2 Chronicles 34:22ff).

For Further Leadership Study
1. Since both 1,2 Kings and 2 Chronicles cover common ground, comparative study should be made to see added detail or emphasis.
2. What part does spiritual leadership play in a nation (even if that leadership is not perfect and even in the majority of the nation does not heed that leadership)? Does it extend the life of the nation? Does it give further opportunity for the nation to come back to God?
3. Study the kings of the reforms (Jehoshaphat, Joash, Hezekiah, Josiah) for special lessons about recrudescence and renewal and how God uses it in the life of organizations, movements, and nations.

Special Comments
This book highlights that spiritual leadership can make a difference. The cycles of degeneracy were halted by reforms. The kings of these reforms, Jehoshaphat, Joash, Hezekiah, Josiah made a difference. Life was prolonged for the nation as a whole. In comparison, the northern kingdom had no such leaders or spiritual reforms in its history and degeneration moved rapidly until its termination. The southern kingdom lasted several hundred years longer though they were not population wise nor militarily stronger than the northern kingdom.

BOOK   **JONAH**   Author: Jonah

Characters   Jonah

Who To/For   Israel (northern kingdom) but applicable to both.

Literature Type   narrative; select incidents focused on a crisis time in
                    Jonah's life

Story Line   Jonah, a prophet (2 Kings 14:25), received a commission
                    from the Lord to go and preach to the Assyrians in
                    Nineveh. This great warlike nation was an enemy of
                    Israel (and eventually defeated them and took them into
                    captivity). Jonah did not want to obey this word from the
                    Lord. So he determined to run away--go somewhere
                    where he was not known. He took passage on a ship. The
                    Lord brought a storm. The crew determined that
                    someone on the ship was the cause of their trouble. They
                    cast lots and it fell on Jonah. When questioned he
                    admitted he was running away from God. He and they
                    determined that to save the ship the best thing to do
                    would be to throw Jonah overboard. This they did. God
                    sent a large fish which swallowed Jonah whole. During
                    the three days Jonah was in the fishes stomach he
                    desperately called on the Lord for deliverance. The fish
                    vomited Jonah onto dry land. Again the Lord gives the
                    command. This time Jonah obeys (with some reluctance
                    in his heart). His message is well received. The
                    Assyrians repent. Jonah is displeased because he had
                    hoped they wouldn't and that God would destroy them.
                    Jonah waits to see if anything will happen to the
                    Assyrians. God shows Jonah that He is sovereign and
                    has concern for the Assyrians as well as the Jewish
                    people. The narration ends here but it is clear Jonah got
                    the message since he actually wrote up the testimony
                    which certainly puts himself in a bad light.

Structure   I.   (ch1:1-17) Jonah's Disobedience and Discipline
                    II. (ch 2:1-10) Jonah's Deliverance
                    III. (ch 3:1-10) Jonah's Obedience
                    IV. (ch 4:1-11) Jonah's Reaction

JONAH continued

Theme   **JONAH'S RELUCTANT OBEDIENCE**
- was prefaced by initial disobedience,
- was necessitated by God's discipline,
- brought about timely deliverance for Nineveh and was used by God to show His concern for non-Jewish peoples.

Key Words   prepared (4 times) this indicates the sovereign control behind the things happening to Jonah

Key Events   *see the story line*

Purposes
- to illustrate God's missionary purpose, i.e. to show Israel's true purpose as typified by Jonah,
- to show God's concern for individuals and His intervention in their lives for their good: the sailors, the Assyrians, Jonah.
- to cause a major shift in thinking about God being exclusively just for Jewish people,
- to demonstrate God's processes for bringing about a major shift in thinking,

Why Important   This book more clearly than any other portrays God's missionary concern in the Old Testament. His purpose, all the way from Abraham on, was to bless the nations through Israel. The book is intended to teach His people the lesson of the inclusiveness of God's government, and to rebuke the exclusiveness of their attitude toward surrounding peoples. This is a book which teaches us much about God and how He deals with leaders.

Where It Fits   It is not exactly certain where Jonah fits specifically but generally it fits leadership wise in Phase B, the Divided time of Kingdom Leadership and in God's redemptive drama it fits in Chapter 2, The Destruction of A Nation. It occurs a good number of years before the actual destruction of the northern kingdom by Assyria.

JONAH continued

Leadership Lessons

1. **GENRE.** This is biographical genre and as such its many detailed lessons are covered in the biographical sketch of Jonah. The detailed explanation of these lessons is given in Handbook II which presents biographical findings. However, I will repeat some of them here as they have macro implications for leadership across books. The actual events from Jonah's life are concentrated in a relatively small time frame-- perhaps as much as six months of his life or as little as two or three months. However, the period taken as a whole forms a pivotal point in his life with a major change in his perspective as the eventual outcome of God's shaping processes.

2. **GOD'S SHAPING PROCESSES.** The central shaping process is that of a paradigm shift, a major change in Jonah's thinking about the Assyrians and God's concern for non-Jewish people. Before the paradigm shift Jonah held a fairly typical Jewish view of non-Jewish people. God exclusively deals only with Israel in order to bless. God is basically against non-Israelites. After the shift Jonah saw that God is not exclusively for Israel. He has concerns for all nations--to show His mercy and grace to all who repent. The means for getting at the paradigm shift included a series of processes: (1) a ministry task, that is, a special assignment from God, (2) an obedience check, which was failed, (3) followed by remedial action which included a life crisis, (4) a repeated obedience check, which was passed, and brought with it God's blessing in ministry. Finally, the end result of the process was reflection on what had happened and a challenge to see it from God's perspective which led to the paradigm shift. For Jonah the pattern that took him through to the paradigm shift included: apparent obedience (misperceived), initial disobedience, reluctant obedience, willful acquiescence (seen long after the fact in the transparency involved in writing the book as a testimony of what happened).

3. **BROKENNESS.** Sometimes in order for God to get the attention of a leader, He has to take the leader through a brokenness experience.[18] Such was the case with Jonah. The prayer/song from the midst of his life crisis shows that Jonah had gone through a brokenness experience and was committed afresh to God for His deliverance and aftermath.

---

[18]**Brokenness** is a state of mind in which a person recognizes that he/she is helpless in a situation or life process unless **God alone** works. It is a state of mind in which a person acknowledges a deep dependence upon God and is open for God to break through in new ways, thoughts, directions, and revelation of Himself that was not the case before the brokenness experience.

JONAH continued

4. **SOVEREIGNTY.** The book clearly shows that God is behind the scenes in the shaping of a leader. Numerous sovereign interventions are pointed out: there was a boat ready, a storm comes up, Jonah is chosen by the lots, there is a fish ready, there is an overwhelming response by the Assyrians, there is the sun, the vine. All leaders must learn to see God in the experiences of their life and to believe that He is using them to shape his/her leadership.
5. **FOCUS/ BEINGNESS.** God's ministry to a leader is often more important than God's ministry through the leader. What we are is fundamental to what we do. If a typical missionary were to report back to the sending group concerning the events of Jonah, they would report on what happened in Assyria, the great revival, the turning to God. But God's emphasis is on what is happening to Jonah.

For Further Leadership Study
1. Study in depth the biographical sketch on Jonah given in Handbook II which details kinds of processes, their purposes and lessons. Notice especially the testing patterns.
2. Notice the repeated pattern, *the way up is down* which is often how God must lead in order to get a person where He wants him/her (location wise, attitude wise, and guidance wise--see Joseph, Moses and others).
3. Recognize the problem of inflexibility [19]in most strong leaders. One of their strengths is convictions and a strong will. The other side of the coin of this strength is inflexibility. Paradigm shifts are a major way God breaks through inflexibility to take a leader own in development. Study Jonah to learn vicariously about inflexibility in your own life. Ask, if God were to come into my own life with a Jonah-like experience, what is the inflexibility that He would deal with? If you can't answer this, get some of your followers or peers to help you see some of your inflexible ways and thinking that God may want to deal with.

Special Comments
Key verses 3:10 and 4:1-3. From a leadership standpoint the illustration of how a paradigm shift takes place is very instructive since much of leadership influence is doing that, bringing about major perspective changes in people's thinking.

---

[19]Inflexible leaders: 1. have a tendency to plateau. 2. tend not to be life-long learners, 3. tend to be naive realists, 4. do not perceive paradigm shifts very easily, 5. tend not to finish well. God frequently uses brokenness experiences to take them through paradigm shifts which overcome these tendencies.

BOOK   **JOEL**   **Author:** Joel

Characters	Joel, a prophet
Who To/For	probably the southern kingdom
Literature Type	Extended Hebrew poetry; a vision and its application
Story Line	Joel is prophesying during a time of a plague of locusts in the land (threatening famine) and seeks to understand what God is saying through this time of trouble. He sees it as a present judgment and indicative of future judgments and a final one.
Structure	I. (ch 1:1-20) The Present Day of the Lord II. (ch 2:1-31) The Coming Day of the Lord III. (ch 3:1-21) The Dreadful Day of the Lord
Theme	**THE DAY OF THE LORD** • is near and demands response, • is coming soon and demands response, • is ultimately certain and restorative for Judah.
Key Words	day of the Lord (5 times)
Key Events	The locust plague

Purposes
* to show how God brings judgment via *natural catastrophes*,
* to introduce a concept of a future judgment of God in which God will judge Gentile nations,
* to show that disasters of all kinds bear analysis of God's intent in them for our response.

Why Important   This book defines the day of the Lord as the on-going method and activity of God which will culminate in God's accomplishment of all His purposes in the affairs of humanity. It illustrates principles of divine government. God is ruling behind the scenes to accomplish His purposes. He graciously warns and appeals to His people to return. Disasters are His calls to

JOEL   continued

His people, forewarning them of worse future disasters if they do not respond. The book also sketches the main points of God's plan for the ages . Future judgments are followed in the far distant future by a major judgment. But before it comes there will be a special time, indefinite in length, of blessing in which God pours out His Spirit. The New Testament identifies it as the age of the Spirit-- our time. Beyond the age of the Spirit, Judah and Jerusalem will be restored--becoming very influential. God will bring back scattered Jewish people. And there will be a final judgment the basis of which will be the nations attitude toward Israel.

Where It Fits   Joel takes place in the divided kingdom on the leadership time-line and during Chapter 2, The Destruction of A Nation. These were critical times. Much of our leadership literature comes from this period of time. This serves to point out a major reason for leadership-- conflict, problems, crises. If there were no problems there probably would be little need for leadership. Leaders must embrace this major function as necessary to their existence and see these negative issues as challenges and part of their raison d'être.

Leadership Lessons

1. **MACRO CONTEXT--SENSITIVITY.** Joel highlights God's sovereign working in circumstances in order to correct His people. This points out the need for leaders of any era to be sensitive to what is happening around them in society in order to see God's working through it. How do we do this? Apart from some special revelatory gifting which some leaders have we can improve our sensitivity by studying books like Joel and many other of the prophets which do just this sort of thing--they interpret the circumstances of the times in order to perceive God's working through them. And of course we can listen to those special few through whom God is speaking about our times--with discernment (1 Thessalonians 5:20,21). The ability to sense God in circumstances around him/her whether macro (regional, national, international) or micro (local, district) is one of the important skill (or trait) of a leader who is getting vision from God for his/her people.

JOEL   continued

2. **FUTURE PERFECT**. Davis[20] in the secular field has re-emphasized for us what is a major Biblical perspective for leaders. And that is the concept of the future perfect. We must use future perfect thinking in our strategic planning. Joel illustrates this. He deals both with *this day* (our present response to God's prompting) and with *that day* (a coming reality). His pronouncements of that day leave no doubt that it will happen. And he lives in light of that future reality as if it were true today.

3. **ACCOUNTABILITY**. It is clear that leadership in our day will be accountable to God in a yet to happen major event in the future. Leaders must know that there is a final accountability in which there will be justice. Without this hope, present, negative, and unjust situations will overwhelm. Joel emphasizes this. We may think we get away with something but there will be a final reckoning.

4. **COMMUNICATION STRATEGIES**. Joel's appeal for change in the society is given at local levels (elders, people themselves). Leaders must use varied communication strategies when opting for change. This is a *grass roots* approach. Essentially it uses a Sower's model of bringing about change.[21] Frequently, the way to bring about change is to get a mass movement at the lowest levels which will surge upward to controlling leadership. Other prophets will take another communication approach, appealing to the few who are the opinion leaders and power brokers.

For Further Leadership Study
1. Study Joel to note the proper responses to God's testing in major circumstances (priests, farmers, everybody). Basic pattern?
2. What should be the impact of far distant future on present actions?

Special Comments
Key verse: 2:28-32 which points forward to the Age of the Spirit in which we live. The three fold testing pattern for individuals (test, response, expansion) holds for corporate groups also. See 2:25ff for the promised expansion if the test is responded to positively.

---

[20]Davis' article, *Transforming Organizations* in **Organizational Dynamics**, Winter 1982 and his book **Future Perfect: A Startling View of the Future We Should Be Managing Now**, a 1987 Addison-Wesley Publication describe the future perfect paradigm. It posits that strategic thinking should not be incremental seeking to extrapolate the past and improve it piece by piece but should be future perfect--that is, taking a quantum leap in vision to the future ideal that should be there. Present managerial decisions should then be made in light of beforemath thinking--implications from the future perfect ideal.

[21]Sower was a social scientist who identified a five stage model for bringing about large societal change: 1. Convergence of Interest, 2. Establishing an Initiating Set, 3. Developing a Support Group, 4. Establishing An Execution Set, and 5. Freezing the Change. The three early stages have this mass grass roots appeal.

BOOK	**AMOS**	**Author:** Amos

Characters   Amos, a shepherd turned prophet

Who To/For   Israel, the northern kingdom; surrounding nations: Syria, Gaza, Edom, Ammon including Judah

Literature Type   Extended Hebrew Poetry, visions, and application of the visions to current situation in Israel

Story Line   During the time of Uzziah, King of Judah, and Jeroboam, King of Israel, Amos who was a shepherd by trade, received a series of visions about Israel (and surrounding nations) which he gives in an authoritative manner including announcement, explanation with exhortation, and in descriptions of major visions which he received.

Structure   I. (ch 1,2)   Announcement of God's Judgment on Six Nations, Israel and Judah

                 II. (ch 3-6)   Explanation of God's Judgment on Israel

                 III. (ch 7-9:10)   Six Vivid Visions Portraying God's Judgment

                 IV. (ch 9:11-15)   Future Restoration

Theme   **GOD'S JUST JUDGMENT**
- on six surrounding nations and on Israel and Judah is announced with authoritative certainty, and further,
- for Israel is explained and justified, and
- is asserted as certain because of 6 graphic visions, and
- includes a future restoration after the judgment.

Key Words   transgress and cognates (12), punishment (8)

Key Events   none specific

Purposes
- to warn about material prosperity and its tendency
- to turn people away from idolatry and material pursuits toward God,
- to show that God is the God of all the nations as well as of the Israelites-- all answer to Him,
- to point out the sins for which the nation of Israel is being held accountable: idolatry, self-indulgent luxury, partying, debauchery, oppression, extortion, bribery, injustice.

AMOS continued

Why Important   This book shows that God's Divine government extends
to more than just Israel. Principles of judgment on
nations as a whole are given. The standards by which the
nations are judged is based on the fact that they have
harmed other nations. Attitudes of nations toward one
another forms a major basis of judgment. A major
principle of judgment deals with truth. Nations that have
received more truth from God will be held more
responsible. Privilege means responsibility. If truth is
refused then judgment is more severe. The patience of
God in bringing judgment is also seen. The figure of
speech introducing each announcement of judgment to
each of the eight nations in chapters 1 and 2 shows that
God does not act immediately in judgment but allows
time for repentance and response to Him. But when that
response is not coming and sins pile up, judgment will be
certain. And so the northern kingdom eventually fell, for
it did not respond to the voice of God through *His
Servants the Prophets*, of whom Amos is one.

Where It Fits   Amos like Joel takes place in the divided kingdom on the
leadership time-line and during Chapter 2, The
Destruction of A Nation. This was a critical time for the
northern kingdom. Response to Amos' message could
have prolonged the life of the northern kingdom.

Leadership Lessons
1. **MACRO CONTEXT--PROSPERITY**. Poverty has its special
problems and leadership must deal with those. But Amos shows that
prosperity also has its problems. Frequently in times of prosperity
people trust in their security and their religion is nominal. Amos is a
leader in a time of material prosperity and religious weakness. In fact,
decisions were made which denied religion in order to make money.
2. **SPECIAL LEADERSHIP**. When dealing with a problem like lack of
religious reality and material issues dominating a society a special kind
of leadership is needed. This is so, because leaders growing up in that
society are enculturated into those corrupt values. Two characteristics
stand out in the kind of leadership that is needed to address such a
situation: 1. the leadership must come from without the normal stream,
2. it must be strong leadership backed by spiritual authority. Amos was
just such a person. Prophets in general were one of God's answers to

AMOS continued

address kingly leadership. But even prophets (coming out of the schools of prophets) can be nominal. So God raises up one who is even outside the normal stream of the prophets--a shepherd. And He backs him with spiritual authority--heavy revelatory information. God will not hesitate after making appeals to leadership to go to an alternative form of leadership to continue His purposes. So today. Expect God to raise up leaders from the periphery who challenge the status quo.

3. **FOLLOWERSHIP INFLUENCE.** Leaders are supposed to influence followers toward God's purposes. But 2:11,12 shows that the reverse effect is also often true. Followers can corrupt leaders. They can pressure leaders toward conformity to roles they want, rather than that which God intended.

4. **PROMISE OF VISION.** Leaders are people who are influencing God's people toward God's purposes. 3:7 contains an underlying principle of God concerning vision. Leaders, sensitive to God, can expect God to reveal His purposes. By faith, this principle needs to be applied in critical situations today. Will not the Sovereign Lord reveal His plans to his servants, that is, His leaders?

5. **PRIVILEGE AND RESPONSIBILITY.** 3:2 carries with it an underlying principle of how God works and views His people. *Special privileges require special responsibility and will therefore have special judgment.* What was true for Israel, then God's people through whom He was working is ever more true today of His church, which has even more truth and clarity about God and His purposes.

6. **PRINCIPLES OF JUDGMENT.** Principles of judgment on nations as a whole are given in Amos.

   a. There will be justice. God will eventually judge all nations. These nations surrounding Israel are typical of all nations.

   b. The standards by which the nations are judged is based on their actions and judgments of other nations.

   c. A major principle of judgment deals with truth. Nations that have received more truth from God will be held more responsible. Privilege means responsibility. If truth is refused then judgment is more severe.

   d. The patience of God in bringing judgment is also seen. The figure of speech introducing each announcement of judgment to each of the eight nations in chapters 1 and 2 shows that God does not act immediately in judgment but allows time for repentance and response to Him. But when that response is not coming and sins pile up, judgment will be certain.

AMOS continued

These principles of Judgment for nations contain within them God's ways and views and can be applied to smaller units such as the diverse manifestations of His Works today: local churches, denominations, para-church organizations. Relationships between them, revelation of truth, privilege and responsibility, all will apply.

8. **BI-VOCATIONAL MINISTRIES.** Amos should be an encouragement to both lay people and those who are proactively ministering via bi-vocational ministries. Amos makes it clear (1:1 shepherd of Tekoa, 7:14 neither a prophet nor a prophet's son) that he is not a usual run of the mill leader. He is special and has special anointing and power from God. The secret lies in his call. Coming from such a different perspective, he will be able to provide leadership that a typical leader would not have. God can greatly empower lay leaders and bi-vocational leaders who see their role and calling as offering unique perspective.

9. **LACK OF REVELATION**. When judgment is continually refused, then God will withhold revelation (8:11,12) This is frightening-- especially to leaders who must have God's vision to lead.

10. **HOPE.** One of the major inspirational functions of Biblical leaders is to provide hope. Amos while not pulling any punches about judgment always holds out hope both to present response by followers and to a future time (see especially 9:11-15).

11. **SUCCESS OR FAILURE**. Amos shows us that we can not always expect success in ministry (in his case, mass repentance and correcting of unjust issues in the society). We must on the one hand lead expecting success but on the other hand must recognize faithfulness in our gifted ministry. Both success and faithfulness ought to be high values for leaders. If both are high values, then we can deal with results as they happen.

For Further Leadership Study
1. What is the importance of a call in giving a leader confidence and spiritual authority? What happens if there is lack of call?
2. Study Amos, like Joel, for sensitivity to God's sovereign working in macro contextual circumstances.

Special Comments
Amos was a lay person not trained in the School of the Prophets. Yet he exercises a very powerful ministry. Essentially there was no response to his forthright appeals. The judgment fell on Israel as Amos predicted--though God gave them further time for repentance.

BOOK	**HOSEA** **Author:** Hosea
Characters	Hosea, Gomer (his wife)
Who To/For	primarily Israel, the northern Kingdom
Literature Type	A strange mix of personal historical narrative and extended Hebrew poetry.
Story Line	Hosea married a woman named Gomer. Three children were born to them all having names with special prophetic meaning--*Jezreel* (God will scatter), *Lo-ruhamah* (not loved), and *Lo-ammi* (not my people). Gomer proved unfaithful and left Hosea. Eventually He divorced her. She went to the depths of degradation finally becoming a slave. Hosea sought her out in her awful state and bought her back and restored her to his side. God uses this as a means of illustrating His own relationship to Israel. Israel, in a spiritual sense, is Jehovah's wife. He is going to chasten His unfaithful wife but will eventually buy her back and restore her to the place of blessing.

Structure

  I. (ch 1-3)   Israel's Unfaithfulness--Illustrated in Hosea's Own Married Life

 II. (ch 4-13)   Israel's Unfaithfulness Described, Deplored, Condemned

III. (ch 14)   Israel's Ultimate Restoration

Theme   **ISRAEL'S UNFAITHFULNESS TO GOD**
- is tragically and empathetically illustrated in Hosea's own personal situation with Gomer,
- is described in terms of Israel's breaking of their covenant with God just like Gomer with Hosea,
- is in spite of God's tender love for her and His ultimate plans for her.

Key Words   whoredom and cognates (14)

Key Events   See story line

HOSEA continued

Purposes
- to announce Israel's destruction which is to come,
- to show God's tender love for Israel in spite of her unfaithfulness,
- to show God's holiness for He can not tolerate the deep sin running rampant in Israel forever,
- to give hope by showing that God will eventually restore Israel.

Why Important   Israel had gone beyond the limits which God could tolerate. The long ministry of Hosea was during one of the darkest periods of the northern kingdom's history. Anarchy reigned in political life. Rulers murdered to obtain the throne. Foreign alliances compromised Israel's situation and introduced idolatry. Conditions of everyday life involved murder, robbery, untruthfulness, self-indulgent luxury. And yet God loved Israel. But His holiness demands justice. Hosea shows the interplay between these wonderful attributes of God. Morgan (see Handbook page 123) describes three permanent values of this BOOK. Sin is revealed for what it is at its deepest and worst (the rejection of God's love and faithfulness); the ultimate result of sin is judgment (God could not be loving and faithful without dealing with it); God's love will conquer in the end.

Where It Fits   Hosea like Amos and Joel takes place in the divided kingdom on the leadership time-line and during Chapter 2, The Destruction of A Nation. This was a critical time for the northern kingdom. Whereas Amos' ministry duration was relatively short and specific to a given moment in the northern kingdom's history, Hosea's ministry was prolonged over a long dark time for the northern kingdom. His long ministry models God's patient loving beckoning to His people who refused to return to Him.

Leadership Lessons
1. **MODELING**. God uniquely goes out of His way to point out how important it is for a leader to recognize that he/she is modeling God and God's attitudes and God's values when ministering. Both God's tender love and His holiness are demonstrated through Hosea's life and ministry.

HOSEA continued

He is the classic Old Testament illustration of speaking the *truth* in *love*. Both are needed in ministry. It is not truth alone for that is justice without mercy. Nor is it love alone which is mercy without justice. It not an either/or but a complex both/and perspective. The negative side of modeling is emphasized also. 4:9 like people, like priests. Leaders model both good and bad whether they want to or not. It is not enough to say do as I say not as I do. They will do as you do anyway.

2. **SOVEREIGNTY/EVENTS OF LIFE.** The book of Hosea especially by using Hosea's personal life is calling attention to the need for acknowledging God in the events of life. Not only is this demonstrated in Hosea's life but in his appeals to Israel (2:8-13). Sensitivity to God's sovereignty extends to practical issues in everyday life. Effective leaders recognize this and count on it.

3. **LEADERSHIP FUNCTION.** A major religious leadership function categorized under the inspirational function is to make God, His ways, and His purposes known. My people are destroyed for lack of knowledge (4:6--given in a context addressing Priests and Prophets and pointing out this lack in their leadership).

4. **JUSTICE.** The opening reference to the naming of Jezreel (1:4) is a reminder that God ever holds unjust situations in mind and will eventually judge them and bring about correction. This characteristic of God with His followers highlights a trait that all leaders need--that of demonstrating justice in their ministries with their fellow leaders, followers, and those over whom they have influence outside their own situation.

5. **COMMUNICATION/AFFECT.** God's use of a marriage relationship to demonstrate His own views and feelings toward His people shows the importance of affect learning as well as cognitive. Abstract truth alone will not usually be enough to change lives. Followers need to feel truth. Leaders need to be aware of this in their communication of truth. The symbolic meaning of the names that Hosea must give his children point out the deep feelings involved. Justive, love, rejection are powerful emotions.

6. **INTEGRITY IN LEADERSHIP.** Integrity is basic to leadership. Hosea reconfirms this repeated emphasis about leadership (5:10).

7. **FUTURE PERFECT PARADIGM.** Hosea like Amos, Joel and other prophets always holds out hope for a future day. In the midst of discouragement, hope for the future, stands out (6:11ff).

8. **DIVINE APPOINTMENT.** It is God who authorizes leadership. Leadership apart from God will disappoint (8:4).

HOSEA continued

For Further Leadership Study
1. Search through and identify the many passages which directly address leadership. Note the issues being highlighted.
2. Most prophets have a strong call to ministry. Note Hosea's different call to leadership (an obedience check which will lead to ministry).
3. Go through the book and note the manifestations of Morgan's three abiding truths for the book: a. Sin is revealed for what it is at its deepest and worst (the rejection of God's love and faithfulness); b. the ultimate result of sin is judgment (God could not be loving and faithful without dealing with it); c. God's love will conquer in the end.
4. How does God feel about our present state of affairs?

Special Comments
Two other prophetic books are unique in that they are not prophecies to anyone but are narratives about the prophets (Jonah and Habakkuk). Hosea is somewhat like them. This book unlike any other book uses a narrative about Hosea, his personal family life, as well as presenting prophetic messages. And it uniquely combines them so that one can **feel** as well as see the result of Israel's sin as God felt it.

BOOK   **MICAH**   **Author:** Micah

Characters	Micah
Who To/For	To both northern and southern kingdoms
Literature Type	Extended Hebrew poetry in terms of narrative messages.
Story Line	none

Structure
    I. (ch 1, 2)   Israel and Judah Judged and Found Lacking/ Promise of Restoration
    II. (ch 3-5)   Leadership Found Lacking/ Promise of Future Leadership And Restoration
    III. (ch 6,7)   Jehovah's Case Against Israel/ Future Restoration Explained

Theme   **FAILURE OF ISRAEL AND JUDAH AND RESPONSIBILITY FOR IT**
- lies in part with its centers of influence, cities, which set the example for the nations,
- lies in part with its leadership whose motivations are improper and lacking,
- is contrasted with a future hope of restoration and a coming leader who will demonstrate God-given motivation.

Key Words   none prominent

Key Events   none

Purposes
- to reveal God's judgment on Israel and Judah at this moment in their history,
- to show the place of responsibility of leadership in allowing the conditions to exist,
- to show that motivation is crucial to leadership,
- to contrast this leadership with a future leadership with proper motivation and its results, that is, to give a Messianic prophecy concerning Jesus.
- to show the importance of cities in influencing national conduct.

MICAH continued

Why Important   While other prophetical books more readily describe the
                       sins of the nation, none place the blame so heavily on the
                       leadership as does Micah. Micah, who evidently
                       ministered in a number of the cities mentioned, also is
                       suggesting how important cities are as centers of
                       influence. Here is a book which is almost entirely
                       dealing with the effects of leadership and with the
                       importance of the urban influence on a nation(s). This
                       book is one of the twenty most important leadership
                       books in the Bible.

Where It Fits   Micah's ministry takes place in Chapter 2, The
                       Destruction of A Nation and in the divided kingdom
                       phase of Kingdom leadership. His ministry overlaps that
                       of Isaiah though it is not as long. And whereas Isaiah
                       mainly ministers to Judah, Micah touches on both
                       kingdoms. His ministry takes place rather late in the
                       divided phase of Kingdom leadership. Time has almost
                       run out for the northern kingdom.

Leadership Lessons
1. **BASIC LEADERSHIP FLAWS POINTED OUT.** Micah in
   denouncing leadership and pointing out its essential responsibility for
   what has happened in the kingdom points out improper leadership values.
   Here are a few:
   a. Might is right (2:1).
   b. Use leadership to gain wealth (2:2, 3:11).
   c. They defraud (that is, promise what they can not produce--2:2).
   d. Use legal means to deprive people of their just due (2:2)
   e. Distort truth because of contextual situation--particularly fear of loss
      of reputation, privilege, and position (2:6, 3:5).
   f. Distort justice to their advantage (3:1-3).
2. **CONTRAST IN LEADERSHIP.** In the midst of this book after
   denouncing leadership Micah by contrast exalts true leadership in giving
   a prophecy of a leader to come. In chapter 5 Micah prophesies of Christ
   who will come and will be all that these present leaders are not.
3. **JUSTICE.** Micah sums up the major traits of good leadership in a well
   known verse. Note the emphasis on justice a repeated theme of most of
   the prophets. Micah 6:8 focuses on justice and mercy and a right
   relationship with God as qualities that leaders (and others need).

MICAH continued

4. **MODELING OF HOPE**. Again a repeated emphasis of leadership is the inspirational function of bringing hope to followers. Note 7:7 *But as for me, I watch in hope for the Lord, I wait for God my Savior. My God will hear me*. About one half of the book speaks to the problems of this day. About one half speaks to the better hope that will come. A neat balance of correction and hope.
5. **GIFTED POWER**. In the midst of weak leadership practicing values such as indicated in item 1 above, spiritual authority is needed. Micah claims that for himself. *But as for me. I am filled with power, with the Spirit of the Lord, and with justice and might* in order to carry out his leadership task. All leaders who follow hard after God will sooner or later run into the need for divine power to operate in their lives or ministry.
6. **BARRIERS TO LEADERSHIP**. Of the six barriers to leaders finishing well noted previously, Micah highlights three: abuse of power, financial greed, and plateauing.[22]
7. **INFLUENCE CENTERS**. Micah stresses the towns and cities and influence centers as a major cause for the state of Israel and Judah. Leaders should recognize the positive good or negative bad that cities and towns have upon nations as a whole. Usually rural peoples migrate to towns and cities (until they get so bad that they want to leave and return back to rural). It is in the cities in the midst of these transitions that people are most readily open for change. They can be influenced in these vulnerable moments for good or bad. Leaders must recognize this important timing period and use it for influencing for good.
8. **COMMUNICATION STRATEGIES**. We have observed in Joel the grass roots approach toward bringing about change. In Micah we see the concept of hitting the decentralized influence centers. In Isaiah we shall see the strategy of hitting the centralized highest power centers. What we see in the Bible is that God uses a diversity of strategies in communicating for change. God uses uneducated people to reach the masses, educated people to reach leaders, and brilliant intellects to reach the highest levels of influence.

---

[22]These ommitted barriers include: family problems, illicit sexual relationships, pride (inappropriate and self-centered). If he were speaking directly to individuals rather than leaders as a group we would probably find these latter three also.

MICAH continued

For Further Leadership Study
1. List the cities and towns that Micah gives specifically.
2. List the kinds of leaders Micah points out.
3. Note how the barriers to leadership finishing well are specifically illustrated. That is, what are the symptoms of these barriers in these leader's lives.
4. What other barriers to leadership finishing well does Micah point out?
5. Micah must be studied of course for its prophetic teaching since half the book is given for that purpose.

Special Comments
Micah was contemporary with Hosea who was prophesying to the northern kingdom and with Isaiah who was prophesying to the southern kingdom. There is a cycle of denunciation followed by a promise of restoration running through all three sections. It is difficult to grasp a major subject of the book. Micah 6:8 should be memorized and be part of the value system of every leader.

BOOK   ISAIAH   **Author:** Isaiah (controversy on this)

Characters	Isaiah, Hezekiah,
Who To/For	Judah, Jerusalem in particular
Literature Type	Extended Hebrew Poetry, Prophetical Revelations, Some historical narrative
Story Line	Isaiah was an upper class educated person who primarily ministered to the court in Judah. He acted as a prophet during the reigns of Uzziah, Jotham, Ahaz and Hezekiah.

Structure
    I. (ch 1-35) Prophecies of Expanding Judgment
       A. First Circle: Judah and Jerusalem (ch 1-12)
       B. Second Circle: The Nations and the World (ch 13-27)
       C. Third Circle: The Chosen and the World (ch 27-35)
   II. (ch 36-39) Historical Interlude Linking Sections
  III. (ch 40-66) Prophecies of Peace

Theme

A HIGH VIEW OF GOD AND HIS WORK
- includes revelations of His judgments which have ultimate purposes including peace, and
- always bears in mind the end results (goal) of God's work--peace which is conditioned by righteousness.

Key Words
Isaiah has such a wonderful understanding of God. His labels and names for God reveal something of his wide range of understanding of God. Consider: The Lord, Holy One of Israel, The Lord Almighty, The Mighty One of Israel, the God of Jacob, the King, Holy One Aflame, Light of Israel, their Maker, God your Savior, the Righteous One, Upright one, Creator, the Holy One of Jacob, the God of Israel, Rock of Israel, the Spirit, the Sovereign Lord, God of Justice, Redeemer, High and Lofty One, Holy Spirit, our Father, the Potter, God of Truth, Our Judge, Our Lawgiver.

Key Events
Isaiah's leadership committal (Isaiah 6), Hezekiah threatened by Sennacherib, Hezekiah's illness and deliverance, Visit of Babylonian envoy

ISAIAH continued

Purposes
- to give us a high view of God,
- to instill a confident trust in God and His purposes,
- to reveal God's governmental principles,
- to give Messianic prophecy, particularly that of the Suffering Servant,

Why Important   Isaiah saw God high and lifted in his leadership committal experience. It is this view of God, one on the throne and ruling that prevails in Isaiah's writing. The principles of His activity in the affairs of humanity is one of the lasting values of the book. Holiness, righteousness, and justice undergird God's ruling activity. He reveals, explains and applies truth to peoples situations. God patiently gives opportunity for people to respond to Him. The inspiration for God's ruling is His love. Grace is thus infused behind the ruling. This is one of the most majestic books in Scripture. It also has deep messianic prophecies.

Where It Fits   Isaiah's ministry like Micah's ministry takes place in Chapter 2, The Destruction of A Nation and in the divided kingdom phase of Kingdom leadership. His ministry overlaps that of Micah and is even longer in extent. Whereas Micah touches on both kingdoms and primarily to the decentralized cities and towns, Isaiah focuses on the centralized ruling elite in Judah. His ministry is taking place rather late in the divided phase of Kingdom leadership. Time has almost run out for the northern kingdom. But Isaiah's ministry helps prolong the southern kingdom. Uzziah, Jotham, and Hezekiah responded favorably to God's words through the prophets especially Isaiah. Ahaz responded reluctantly. All in all Isaiah had a very influential ministry.

Leadership Lessons
1. **GENRE.** Isaiah contains mostly indirect leadership source materials. There are a few passages dealing directly with leadership and a few passages giving biographical information concerning processing but for the most part the material is indirect and hence much more difficult to perceive in terms of leadership issues. There is little biographical information concerning Isaiah himself. This is the second longest book

ISAIAH continued

in the Bible and is filled with numerous complex and diverse prophetical passages. It is not easy to draw leadership lessons from it. I will therefore give some overall leadership observations but will limit them.

2. **RISK TAKER.** Isaiah was a risk taker. Frequently, he would give prophetic words which were very explicit in terms of nations, peoples, and times or dates. He was a bold leader.

3. **INTIMACY AND HIGH VIEW OF GOD.** Tozer has said that the most important thing about a person is what that person thinks about God. If that is true then Isaiah is an important person indeed for he has one of the highest views of God in the Scriptures. He uses more than 40 names or phrases describing God in his writings. He uses the Lord Almighty, probably his favorite term for God numerous times. It is clear that Isaiah saw God as majestic and sovereign and governing this world to bring it to the completion of His purposes. Isaiah can be studied with great profit just reading it and observing Isaiah's thoughts and views about God.

4. **BALANCED VIEW OF GOD.** Isaiah presents one God as both a God of justice and love.

5. **HEART AND MIND.** Isaiah's vocabulary is the most extensive of all the Old Testament writers. It is clear that he was a great intellect. He was gifted mentally to deal in the court scene and with the highest rulers in the land. It is also clear that he had a great heart for God. Frequently one finds a leader with a great intellect but one cool in relationship with God. You can also find leaders with a great heart for God but not very wise. Zeal without knowledge and knowledge without zeal both lead to ineffective ministries. But zeal with knowledge, such as Isaiah had, has potential for a very effective ministry. It seems clear that he was in a place of convergence for who he was.

6. **BARRIERS.** In his leadership passages Isaiah confirms one of the major barriers for leadership failure, that of greed or improper handling of finances (1:23). In addition, he adds one other important barrier--that of hypocrisy (1:11ff and others). Leaders can fool followers concerning depth of religious reality for a period of time--but hypocrisy will sooner or later become evident.

7. **JUSTICE.** Isaiah like most of the prophets strongly emphases justice. In addition, he gives a major reason for justice, that of peace, and not just any peace but peace which is founded in righteousness.

8. **LEADERSHIP SPONSOR FUNCTION.** Isaiah makes it clear that one of the responsibilities of just leaders is to espouse the cause of the helpless and underprivileged. The poor, the widows, the orphans, the

ISAIAH continued

powerless, and those being oppressed should be sponsored and protected by leaders who do have privilege, status, and power.

9. **PERSPECTIVE.** Directly as in 5:13 and 11:9 and others and indirectly by the breadth of his own thinking and prophecies Isaiah shows the importance of the big picture, the broad perspective. Perspective is crucial to leadership. Isaiah always relates prophetic issues to a broad perspective in terms of God's plans and purposes.

10. **SOVEREIGNTY OF GOD.** Isaiah holds one of the highest views of the sovereignty of God (perhaps only exceeded by Ezekiel) of any of the Old Testament writers. Every strong leader in the Old Testament had a high view of the sovereignty of God and sought to be sensitive to God in circumstances around him/her. But Isaiah even goes beyond this to see the overall purposes of God and how present issues fit in with the bigger picture.

11. **HOPE.** A major inspirational function on which Isaiah ranks very high is that of inspiring hope in followers. He does this in several ways. The 40th chapter is one of the highlights in this regard. The entire last 27 chapters (40-66) are in general that which inspires.

For Further Leadership Study

1. There are several direct leadership genre passages that should be analyzed including: 3:1-15 heroes, warriors, judges et al (gives a list of various kinds of leaders) chapter 5, the Song of the Vineyard; chapter 10:1-19 Dealing with Ultimate Justice; chapter 9:8-21 dealing with elders and prominent men.

2. There are numerous references to folk religion, a strong cultural factor, which pervaded God's people (see 1:29, 8:18, 17:8 and others).

3. There are some excellent passages giving processing incidents which should be analyzed in detail including: Isaiah own leadership call in Isaiah 6; Ahaz's faith challenge (a pivot point in his life; he basically failed to respond to the challenge); Hezekiah's faith challenge in chapters 36,37 and his two flesh acts in chapters 38, 39.

4. Isaiah 24:21 may be a reference to cosmic level warfare.

5. Isaiah gives hints of a future resurrection in 25:8 and 26:19. Other than Daniel there is very little Old Testament awareness of a resurrected life.

Special Comments

The structure and theme above were adapted from Morgan. Because of its length it is difficult to assess a theme for Isaiah which is not very generic and rather abstract. Each of the major points themselves could be major themes. Isaiah 43:18,19 and 46:9 provide a beautiful balance. Memorize them.

BOOK   **NAHUM**   **Author:** Nahum

Characters	Nahum, a prophet from Galilee
Who To/For	for Ninevites, also a word for Judah
Literature Type	Extended Hebrew Poetry, prophecies
Story Line	Nothing is known about Nahum. There is nothing personal in the book, just his prophecies for Nineveh.
Structure	I. (ch 1) God's Character and Nineveh's Deserved Punishment II. (ch 2) Nineveh's Certain Judgment, III. (ch 3) Nineveh's Full and Complete Judgment
Theme	**GOD'S WRATH UPON NINEVEH** • flows from His character, • is certain, and • will be completed.
Key Words	Lord Almighty, a repeated name for God
Key Events	none

Purposes
• to announce the coming destruction of Nineveh,
• to vindicate God as a God of justice.

Why Important   God will use this wicked nation, Assyria, to accomplish His purposes, though their motivations may be wrong and their carrying out of the task in violence beyond that necessary. It seems unfair that God will do this. But God is a just God. This book shows that. Because God is a God of love there is then certainty of His wrath. He must do what is right. And what He does must always be interpreted in light of His love. Nahum illustrates these amazing interlocking truths. Assyria was prideful, cruel, and impenitent. These sins must be punished. No other book gives us such insight into the anger of God. Notice: jealous, avenges, wrath, anger, indignation, fierceness, fury. Each of these and the running explanation reveal to us more of who God is. Morgan says it well (see Handbook page 153) when he says that action grows out of passion but is always governed by principle. Since this book does not deal directly with leadership, the leadership

NAHUM continued

principles are drawn from observing the character of God. Leaders should *be and do* in harmony with God's character.

Where It Fits   Nahum's ministry most likely takes place in Chapter 2, The Destruction of A Nation and in the single kingdom phase of Kingdom leadership. It is a special prophecy dealing with Assyria, the nation used by God to destroy the northern kingdom when it had gone beyond the bounds of his patience.

Leadership Lessons
1. **CHARACTER**. Nahum makes it clear that God's actions flow out of His character (see 1:2-3 especially but also all of chapter 1). He thus affirms that observed characteristic of leaders, that *ministry flows out of being*. This should be a major value of leaders. If so, it will enable the continual growth of interiority and exteriority in a leader's spirituality.[23]
2. **CERTAINTY**. God is dependable. This prophecy was fulfilled in its entirety. Leaders must learn to keep their word. Credibility with followership demands that leaders be trustworthy. When they say something they should back it up.
3. **WARNING**. Assyria had turned back to God in response to Jonah's ministry. Yet just one or two generations later they are not following God. This could be for many reasons: no follow-up, basic sin, or whatever. In any case, we should know that unless we build continuity into our ministry (values inculcated, leadership that can perpetuate and inspire on-coming generations) our ministry may also come to naught in the future.

For Further Leadership Study
1. A faith building exercise is to study what was said here about God's judgment upon Assyria and then to read what actually happened in history to Assyria.

Special Comments
This prophecy is more than 150 years after Jonah's message. The repentance to his message was short lived. Now the Assyrians have drifted almost beyond help. If they had repented in response to this message, I think God would have again spared them. This prophecy was utterly fulfilled. The great city and its people are no more. We are always just one generation from going away from God--see Jonah.

---

[23]See my manual, **The Mentor Handbook**, published by Barnabus Publishers for a detailed explanation of spirituality components. My spirituality model has the following components: centrality, interiority, exteriority, spirit sensitivity, uniqueness, fruitfulness (internal), fruitfulness (external), development.

BOOK	**HABAKKUK**	**Author:** Habakkuk

Characters   Habakkuk

Who To/For   For Judah

Literature Type   Extended Hebrew Poetry; dialogue, Habakkuk and God.

Story Line   Habakkuk is in a crisis in his life and ministry. He sees injustice and ungodliness all around him. He is beginning to doubt God, His character and His working. The book exposes his innermost feelings in this faith crisis situation. He voices his honest complaint to God and waits for God's answer. God's answer shocks Him and forces him to ask another question of God. God's next answer is so overwhelming that Habakkuk responds with awe, fear and joy in God's future work.

Structure
   I. (1:1-2:1)   Habakkuk's Honest Struggle With Faith
  II. (2:2-2:20) Habakkuk's Faith-Wait Response
 III. (3:1-19)   Habakkuk's Response of True Faith

Theme   **HABAKKUK'S STRUGGLE OF FAITH**
- involved his honest questioning of God,
- was met by God's own explanation, and
- resulted in a joyous acceptance by faith of that which God was doing.

Key Words   Habakkuk 2:4 the basic answer to the faith crisis.

Key Events   Habakkuk's open challenge to God, God's answer (the Babylonian captivity), Habakkuk's incredulous response to that, God's response (justice for Babylon), Habakkuk's surrender (the faith song).

Purposes
- to teach God's people to trust unconditionally in God's complex workings in history to bring about his just purposes,
- to reveal how God matures a leader in faith,
- to highlight the need always for a person of God to live by faith in God,
- to indicate that when God uses nations in history for His purposes He is still true to His nature.

HABAKKUK continued

Why Important   All leaders must eventually learn to walk by faith, that is, trust in an unseen God's dealings with their own life, ministry, events around them, and the world whether or not they can understand the complexity or see what God is doing. God's people must also learn this lesson. Habakkuk reveals several processes whereby God teaches this valuable Biblical lesson. Like Jonah and Job the book focuses not on ministry to others but on God's dealing with His leader. When there is increasing deterioration in the society, as was the case during Habakkuk's time, ungodliness will abound. And there will be unjust things going on with no apparent repercussions. It is in the midst of these things that we need to see a bigger perspective. We need to see the present happenings in terms of the larger picture, the history leading up to it and that which is to come. God frequently does just that. He meets a leader in a crisis situation by broadening perspective. And we are thankful for just such processing, for otherwise we, like Habakkuk would be ready to give up.

Where It Fits   Habakkuk's ministry most likely takes place in Chapter 2, The Destruction of A Nation and in the single kingdom phase of Kingdom leadership. He probably overlapped with Jeremiah's ministry. And if he did see the prophecy fulfilled (3:16) then he probably ministered in the latter part of the single kingdom era.

Leadership Lessons
1. **BIOGRAPHICAL GENRE.** Habakkuk is a biographical snapshot of a pivotal point, a critical moment in the life of a leader. Its processing includes crisis, isolation, and a faith challenge all of which Habakkuk responds to positively. Lessons include principles on prayer, faith, solitude and a philosophy of God's working in history. See the biographical sketch in Handbook II for the details of this analysis.
2. **FAITH.** Leaders serve an unseen God who has revealed Himself and intervened in history. A basic lesson that all leaders must learn is the one Habakkuk learned here (2:4). Leaders must believe that God is, that He is trustworthy, and that He is a rewarder of them that seek Him (Hebrews 11:6).

HABAKKUK continued

3. **COMPLEX CONTEXTS**. All leaders will at some time or times in their ministry see situations which apparently deny God's existence or love or intervening care (1:2-4). This is particularly true of urban ministries. Their belief in the character and promises of God will be tested. Learn vicariously from Habakkuk's experience. Be forewarned and determine now to go deep in faith in your response to God.
4. **BROADER PERSPECTIVE**. Often God's solution to a perplexed leader is to give that leader a broader perspective, that is a much larger context in which to evaluate the present perplexing situation. The difference in leaders and followers is perspective. Leaders have a broader view on what is happening and what God wants to do. The difference in leaders and effective leaders is better perspective. Sensitivity to God, intimacy with God, and dependence upon God will lead to broader perspective. Leaders who seek God for broader perspective will find Him (2:1; 3:1-15).
5. **TRANSPARENCY**. Honest reflection and transparency with God is the starting point for seeking perspective. Leadership which has learned to be transparent in interiority will be more likely to be transparent in exteriority and thus increase their impact upon followers.
6. **FUTURE PERFECT THINKING**. If we believe God for future happenings, then we should act upon that belief. Habakkuk's response, one of the most beautiful in the scriptures (3:16-19) is an illustration of future perfect thinking. See Davis footnote, Joel.

For Further Leadership Study
1. Study in depth the biographical analysis of Habakkuk's pivotal point.
2. Note the dialogic nature of prayer that develops interiority.

Special Comments
This is one of the special books in the Old Testament which focuses on God's development of a leader (see Job, Jonah). In Seeing the processes-- crisis, isolation, faith challenge-- we learn not only what God was doing with Habakkuk but we can also see how He matures leaders.

BOOK	**ZEPHANIAH**	**Author:** Zephaniah

Characters Zephaniah, a prophet of royal descent (Hezekiah)

Who To/For Judah, Jerusalem-the southern kingdom

Literature Type Extended Hebrew Poetry, prophecies

Story Line Zephaniah lived during the time of Josiah. There is an outward show of revival. Zephaniah's omission of it altogether suggests its superficiality. In the midst of this so called revival Zephaniah tells it as it is, judgment is coming. He indicates the nature of this judgment and its final result--what a real revival should result in.

Structure
    I. (ch 1-2:3)   A Day of Wrath, An Appeal
    II. (ch 2:4-3:8)   The Day of Wrath, Followed by
    III. (ch 3:9-20)   A Day of Restoration

Theme **GOD'S JUDGMENT** (the Day of the Lord)
- will include Judah, foreshadows a greater judgment, and issues in an appeal for repentance,
- is given against Philistia, Moab, Ammon, Cush, Assyria and signals a greater judgment, and
- eventuates in a restoration of His scattered remnant.

Key Words Day of the Lord, Day, that Day (20 or more)

Key Events none except in the prophecies

Purposes
- to down play an outward turning to the Lord,
- to warn of God's impending judgment on Judah,
- to give hope for those who do trust in God,
- to cause a futuristic trust in God's judgment.

Why Important Explains more fully what the day of the Lord means giving as Morgan indicates, content, extent, and intent of it. From Joel we see it as the on-going method and activity of God which will culminate in God's accomplishment of all His purposes in the affairs of humanity. The day of the Lord is the day of man's

ZEPHANIAH   continued

judgment in order for God to accomplish His purposes. It will include direct intervention by God (supernatural) to punish and correct suddenly, swiftly, and irrevocably. In extent judgment will be upon sin. Humanity with all its pollution of all kind will be dealt with. In intent the day of the Lord will climax in God enthroned, a new order in place, a final restoration. The sadness of the day of the Lord will turn to singing after its intents are accomplished.

Where It Fits   Zephaniah's ministry takes place in Chapter 2, The Destruction of A Nation and in the single kingdom phase of Kingdom leadership. He specifically ministers during Josiah's time, so he was concurrent with the beginning of Jeremiah's ministry. His prophetic ministry is at the cutting edge for he does not hesitate to put his finger of the negative issues in the midst of a superficial revival. And too he leans heavily on the judgmental activity of God--pressing the need for accountability.

Leadership Lessons
1. **ACOUNTABILITY**. Zephaniah uses the phrase, the day of the Lord, more frequently than any other prophet. And with it, the judgmental aspect of God's activity. Such an emphasis forces leaders to admit and respond to the need for responsibility before God for their lives and ministries. Leaders who fail to take seriously their responsibility before God for their followers and ministries open themselves up prematurely for the judgment of God, or in terms of leadership emergence theory terminology, for negative (or remedial) processing.
2. **EVALUATION.** Zephaniah forces us to seek a more accurate evaluation of our ministry. In the midst of an apparent revival, he does not mention the limited success but points out the hard things. There is a place for seeing success in ministry and its positive motivational value, but there is also a place for careful evaluation.
3. **FUTURE PERFECT**. Zephaniah's strong emphasis on the day of the Lord, particularly the futuristic aspect gives us confidence (like the Revelation) of a God who has ultimate purposes and is moving toward those purposes inexorably despite lack of human response. As Morgan comments, Joel shows the day of the Lord to be an on-going method and activity in which God is moving toward a culmination of His accomplishments. That is, He is bringing all His purposes in the affairs

ZEPHANIAH   continued

of humanity toward a climax. That future day is seen to be the day of mankind's judgment. It will include direct intervention by God (supernatural) to punish and correct suddenly, swiftly, and irrevocably. In extent it will include judgment upon sin--all the pollution of humankind. Its intent is to see God enthroned, a new order in place, and a final restoration. This book is meant to inspire us. Our sadness should turn to joy as we contemplate things being made right.

For Further Leadership Study
1. Mark the day of the Lord or that day in your bible. It will encourage you to see how firm Zephaniah was in his belief in this future coming event.
2. Study the day of the Lord in 2 Peter 3:10 five characteristics.
3. Study also 1,2 Thessalonians for New Testament clarification on the day of the Lord.

Special Comments
This book is meant to inspire us to rejoice in the hope of the glory of God and to live holy lives as we await it. The New Testament, especially 2 Peter fills us in on the day of the Lord and highlights how we should live in light of that coming day.

BOOK	**JEREMIAH** **Author:** Jeremiah	

Characters Jeremiah, a prophet of priestly descent, Pashhur (20:1ff), Kings Jehoiakim and Zedekiah, Uriah (26:20ff), Zephaniah (29:25ff), the Recabites (35:1ff), Baruch (36:4ff), and others

Who To/For Judah and Jerusalem, the southern kingdom

Literature Type mostly narrative vignettes, visions, prophecies, and some extended Hebrew Poetry

Story Line Jeremiah lived and ministered in the days of Josiah, Jehoiakim, Jehoiachin, and Zedekiah--the last days of the southern kingdom (about 40 years). These were dark days. His message of impending doom was unpopular. He faithfully gave repeated warning in diverse ways over a long period of time. He advocated surrender to the Babylonians--an unpatriotic, unpopular message. He was persecuted, imprisoned, and finally vindicated by God.

Structure I. (ch 1-39) Prophetic Warnings About the Fall of Jerusalem
    A. Ch 1 -20 Undated Prophecies
    B. Ch 21-39 Dated Prophecies
II. (ch 40-44) Aftermath of the Fall of Jerusalem
III. (ch 45-52) Postscripts/ Warnings against the Nations

Theme **GOD'S IMPENDING JUDGMENT ON JERUSALEM**
- was compassionately yet truthfully revealed faithfully over many years (though it was rationalized away and ultimately ignored by its recipients),
- happened as predicted with aftermath results, and
- was extended to surrounding nations so as to reveal divine judgmental standards.

Key Words words dealing with sin (iniquity, sin, sins, sinned, transgression)(more than 50 times),

Key Events Many. Typical include: Jeremiah's call, open air preaching in front of temple, linen belt symbolic act, Potter's House, clay jar smashed, two baskets of figs, letter to the exiles, buying the field, confined in the courtyard, visit to

JEREMIAH continued

Recabites, burning of the Scroll, imprisoned, Put in the Cistern, fall of Jerusalem, freed by Nebuzaradan, Gedaliah assassinated, flight to Egypt

Purposes
- to give a last appeal from God for repentance before the Babylonian captivity,
- to demonstrate what faithfulness is in leadership,
- to have the readers feel the ethos of these times, the heart of God, the ups and downs of Jeremiah, and the continual rejection by the people,
- to give insights on leadership and transparency,
- to give hope in the darkest of times.

Why Important The historical books (2 Kings, 2 Chronicles) give the bare facts of the last forty years of the southern kingdom. But Jeremiah allows us to see the details of what happened--the tremendous appeals by God to bring the people to repentance, the heart of God reaching out to them, Jeremiah's faithful ministry through hardships and sorrow. We feel the situation, not only know its facts. This book, more than any other allows us to see many, many details of God's development of a leader. We have incident after incident which illustrate processes whereby God deals with a leader.

Where It Fits In the redemptive drama, Jeremiah occurs in Chapter 2, The Destruction of a Nation. The nation has already been divided, and the northern kingdom gone. Judah, the southern kingdom stands alone. It is a dark time in which the nation as a whole has rejected God. The times of the book occur about 100 years after Isaiah's ministry. After Hezekiah, the nation, led that way by ungodly leaders, has been on a declining spiral (with one exception-- Josiah's relatively short reign). The ministry of Jeremiah is a last ditch effort to appeal to the nation to return to God and reverse the downward trend. On the leadership time-line, Jeremiah occurs in Phase III, Kingdom Leadership, and phase C, the Single Kingdom. He is a leader, for the most part, outside the power structure.

JEREMIAH continued

> Though the son of a priest, he is serving as a prophet
> (God's corrective force to kingdom leadership).

Leadership Lessons
1. **LEADERSHIP SELECTION.** Leaders are selected by God for tasks.
   Leaders may think that they choose to serve God in their special
   ministries but in the final essence it is God who selects for tasks.
   Jeremiah helps us *understand how* God selects leaders for tasks. See
   names of God and personality of Jeremiah and task called to--contrast
   especially these same items in Ezekiel.
2. **DEEP PROCESSING.** Leaders should expect deep processing in their
   lives and recognize God will have multiple purposes in it (working in
   and working through the leader). Jeremiah illustrates numerous crisis
   and isolation processing incidents. These incidents particularly
   demonstrate Jeremiah's transparency with God and show the *going deep
   with God* aspect of deep processing. The repeated presence and
   affirmation of God was needed by Jeremiah especially in light of
   followership reaction and the deep processing involved.
3. **TRANSPARENCY.** A leader must learn to be transparent before God.
   Jeremiah models transparency before God. Jeremiah is open before God
   concerning his feelings, his faith, his expectancies, his basic reactions to
   his ministry assignments.
4. **SOVEREIGN PROTECTION.** A leader is under God's sovereign
   protection until God's purposes through him/her are fulfilled. Time and
   again it looked as if Jeremiah's life would be ended. But God preserved it
   sovereignly for His own purposes. (See Jeremiah 39, note especially 15ff).
5. **SUCCESS CRITERIA.** Criteria for judging leadership success or
   failure probably varies in terms of leadership types. Jeremiah forces one
   to question the nature of success in ministry at least for prophetical
   types. Perseverance, faithfulness and obedience are important qualities
   with Jeremiah. Yet he does not see success in the sense of people
   positively responding to his message. Followership is least likely to
   respond to negative messages which criticize rather than say positive
   messages which affirm, as in a teacher's ministry.
6. **COMMUNICATIONAL INTENT.** A leader must be willing to use
   varied communication means to get through to followers. God spoke
   through Jeremiah using visions, straight exhortation, prophecies and
   symbolic acts (of varied kinds). God communicated truth but with
   compassion. Notice the several eleventh hour reprieves offered.

JEREMIAH continued

7. **CHANGE STRATEGY.** One strategy for a leader seeking to change a desperate situation is to concentrate his/her ministry on the existing leadership rather than rank and file followership. Jeremiah concentrated his ministry on changing the leadership in the power structures. Change can come by top down effort and bottom up effort. In the end both leaders and followers must buy in. Here Jeremiah knew that the leadership must be reached first if anything lasting was to be accomplished. A leader who is trying to change a desperate situation must recognize the vested interests of leaders in the situation. Expect animated resistance. Their personal concerns and interests in maintaining the system for their own sakes may be more important than doing what is right. They may well be highly resistant to any changes threatening their personal stake in the situation.

8. **POWER BASE.** A leader working from outside a system must depend upon and demonstrate power based on competency, personal charisma, and spiritual authority to even get a hearing. Jeremiah, though from a priestly family, had no positional authority in the hierarchy of leadership in Jerusalem. He was forced to rely upon spiritual authority, force of personality, and his credibility as a prophet who hears from God.

9. **EXPECTATION.** Leaders must believe that God can remedy any situation and proclaim that hope to followers. Though the times were discouraging and Jeremiah felt despair often, he always had that hope that God would meet them if they obeyed.

10. **CONTEMPORARY MODELS.** God frequently has good contemporary models of leadership in dark times just to counter the prevailing scene. The Recabites demonstrate that Godliness is possible even in the terrible times of Jeremiah's ministry.

11. **RISK TAKER.** Leaders, especially in desperate times, must be risk takers if they are to impact with spiritual authority. See symbolic acts, the timed prophecies.

12. **SOVEREIGN PURPOSES.** Nothing will thwart God's activity and ultimate purposes. The nation is destroyed. Seemingly all of God's plans for it gone down the drain. But God moves on. He remakes His work. We are important to God's work but should we fail to respond to God He will move on and by pass us. See Potter incident--see also the great note of hope; He will remake it. See also the prophecy principle involved--response of people to prophecy may condition abrogation of it.

JEREMIAH continued

For Further Leadership Study

1. The numerous process incidents in Jeremiah should be analyzed.
2. The various leadership types in Jeremiah should be catalogued. There are a number of specialized leadership types indicated in the groups that Jeremiah is speaking to.
3. The communication means ought to be catalogued and studied in depth. Particularly in terms of what learning taxonomy is in focus: affect (feelings), cognitive (information), conative (the will), and experiential (experiencing).
4. Jeremiah can be analyzed in terms of change dynamics strategy. His book shows the difficulty of a top down approach. A study of Josiah's life and times also point out the difficulty of a bottom up approach. Both are important in terms of ownership for any lasting change.
5. Jeremiah faithfully ministered during forty years. Yet he does not fit the standard definition of a leader that we use. A leader is a person with God-given capacity and God-given responsibility to influence a specific group of God's people toward God's purposes. He meets all but the last point--he did not move the people toward God's purposes. I think Jeremiah calls us to reevaluate the definition which does hold for almost all leaders in Scripture. Our view of success or what influence is, is probably part of our problem. For Jeremiah evidently was a leader.

Special Comments
Jeremiah is a book difficult to analyze since it is long and chapters do not follow a linear time sequence. There is a reason. Cognitive learning is not in focus. Rather affective and conative learning is. We are meant to sense, feel, and react emotionally to these times. We are meant to commit ourselves to hearing and obeying God. Jeremiah himself is emotional. The intentional selection of so many of the vignettes obviously is intended to move the emotions.

BOOK	**LAMENTATIONS**	**Author:** Jeremiah

Characters   none

Who To/For   Judah, Jerusalem, Edom, thoughtful observers

Literature Type   Five Poems, Extended Hebrew Poetry, uses and Acrostic (not seen in English) as an organizational device

Story Line   An inscription prefacing Lamentations is given in the Septuagint which gives the story line in a short statement. "And it came to pass, that after Israel had been carried away captive, and Jerusalem made desolate, Jeremiah sat weeping, and lamented this lament over Jerusalem, and said..." Jeremiah pours out his heart concerning the sad situation. And it is representative of God's heart and feelings for his people who have disobeyed Him.

Structure

I.   (ch 1)   Jeremiah's Sorrowful Song for Jerusalem-- Solitary and in Ruins

II.   (ch 2)   A Song Explaining the Why of Jerusalem's Destruction--A Judgment from God

III.   (ch 3)   Jeremiah's Song of Identification with Jerusalem In Its Plight

IV.   (ch 4)   A Song of Desolation--Jerusalem remembered and Jerusalem now

V.   (ch 5)   A Song to Jehovah--A Repentant Appeal

Theme   **JERUSALEM'S DESTRUCTION,**
- saddens Jeremiah's heart and must force reflective evaluation,
- was justly deserved and done by God,
- was part of Jeremiah's own personal experience and forced him to the depths of emotions,
- is doubly sad because of remembrances of what it once was and could have been, and
- is a reminder to appeal for the eternal God's mercies from whom alone can come any future hope.

Key Words   Jerusalem and its symbolic name Zion

Key Events   Jerusalem fall, the central event being focused on.

LAMENTATIONS continued

Purposes
- to reveal Jeremiah's sadness at Jerusalem's destruction and hence God's sadness,
- to point out God's continuance, even after disaster,
- to warn against disregarding God's purposes.

Why Important   No judgment of God is without sorrow. How I wish" I didn't have to tell you so" is the attitude, not I told you so." Jeremiah could easily have done this, particularly because his message was rejected for so long and denied as being true.

Where It Fits   This book written by Jeremiah occurs at the end of Chapter 2, The Destruction of a Nation. It is all over. It had been destroyed just as Jeremiah foretold. Jeremiah is one of the refugees with no place to go and not much hope for any ministry. This is the height of testing his leadership heart in the midst of an apparent disaster of all of God's program. He does not live as we do knowing how God went on.

Leadership Lessons
1. **FORM.** The very form of Lamentations is saying something. It is a well thought out and ordered poetic presentation of the aftermath reflection of a great leader. By poetic we know how deeply this leader felt about what happened. By putting it in an acrostic form, the intent would be to make it easily remembered and recalled, stresses just how important an event this was. And it was. It was a pivotal point in the corporate processing of God's chosen people. It is the exact reverse of the Exodus in almost every way. But it is meant to be remembered just as the Exodus was.
2. **CHARACTER OF GOD.** In his post event reflection, Jeremiah makes it clear that God 's dealings with His people were honorable and just and in accord with what they deserved. And it is clear throughout that it was a sovereign God working who brought it about. This defense of God, no matter what, is an outstanding trait of those leaders who know theoretically and yet can also rest practically with the doctrine of the sovereignty of God. See Paul on this (Romans 9-11).
3. **CLOSURE.** Boundary times and/or negative processing (isolation, conflict, crisis, negative preparation) demands closure. Post reflection evaluation is the starting place. The closure may lead to restitution,

LAMENTATIONS continued

reconciliation, and/or vindication of God. It will always lead to awareness of lessons to be learned to make one a better leader for the future. Jeremiah does just this. He brings closure in a most empathetic way to the most tragic and faith shaking event in Old Testament history.

4. **GRIEVING PROCESS.** Tragic events and heavy processing will most likely require a grieving process. Modern Christian counseling has made us aware of this important process for Christians. Jeremiah here goes through that in a healthy way. Its inclusion in the Bible affirms our need for it and models for us a healthy grieving process.

5. **INTIMACY AND TRANSPARENCY.** Jeremiah models for us the importance of sharing our intimate lessons and struggles with others. He is transparent about his feelings and his views on what happened. He shares them in order that others may learn from them. Leaders must learn to do this. It is not the sharing of only our successes which empowers; it is the sharing of our failures as well and the response to God in them as He helps us grow through them that will empower others.

6. **LEADERSHIP HEART TEST.** God frequently tests a leader concerning heart for ministry. Frequently this happens as with Moses, in the midst of the trying situation. But occasionally, as here with Jeremiah, God shows us a more subtle difficult test. This reflective experience and the disaster that happened proved to be a major test of Jeremiah's heart for his ministry and followers. The tendency, and we could well forgive Jeremiah if he did, would be to say, "I told you so! You deserve this. If you had heeded my ministry suggestions you would be all right now. I wash my hands of you. You made your bed; now lay in it!" But instead of I told you so, Jeremiah says with a great sobbing heart in this long love letter, "I wish I didn't have to tell you so!" Many leaders will find themselves separated from a ministry in which there were negative issues dominant. Once out of control of the situation and removed from it, what are the feelings for that former ministry? Jeremiah models for us how we should feel for our former ministries. We should want the best for them and care for them deeply even if our own efforts with them have been undermined. The normal response is the desire for vengeance or something bad to happen to that situation--particularly if there were negative causes that forced a leader out. Learn from Jeremiah.

7. **LEADERSHIP CALL.** Leaders without a strong call will not pass a leadership heart test but will drop out of ministry. Jeremiah had a strong call and over his lifetime saw the intervention of God in his life and ministry. He knew God was trustworthy.

LAMENTATIONS continued

For Further Leadership Study
1. Study Lamentations in order to identify stages of a grieving process. Note also any other observations on grieving.
2. Lamentations is worthy of study just to observe the use of Hebrew Poetry and the use of figures of speech and idioms for emphatic communication.
3. Identify the passages whereby Jeremiah identifies that it was a sovereign God working.
4. What references to Jeremiah's own personal professing are seen in the book?

Special Comments
The inclusion of this book in the Canon says something of God's loving heart for His people. Its o.k. to cry over spilt milk. Sometimes God's love letters come in black envelopes.

BOOK	**OBADIAH Author:** Obadiah

Characters	Obadiah

Who To/For	Edom

Literature Type	Extended Hebrew Poetry, prophecies

Story Line	None

Structure

I.	(1-4)	The Judgment on Edom Announced
II.	(5- 7)	How the Judgment will Happen
III.	(8-14)	Why the Judgment is Necessary
IV.	(15-21)	Further Explanation of the Judgment

Theme **GOD'S JUDGMENT ON EDOM**
- will come through allies,
- is deserved and
- is part of His overall justice.

Key Words	Esau/Edom (9)

Key Events	none

Purposes
- to announce the coming destruction of Edom,
- to point out one of God's principles of judgment for Gentile nations,
- to warn against pride and the tendency to profane the sacred.

Why Important Two major reasons. It clarifies the Esau/Jacob antagonism which is highlighted throughout scripture. See Morgan (Handbook page 138, 139). It does this by pinpointing the essential cause of Esau's sin--pride. It also lays out a major principle that God will use to judge nations--"As you have done it will be done unto you."

Where It Fits Obadiah fits in the Redemptive Drama in Chapter 2, The Destruction of a Nation. It is one of the prophets not directed toward either the Northern or Southern kingdom but to an outside nation, one which had wrongfully treated Israel. Along the leadership time-line this book occurs probably in phase C, the Single Kingdom. It

OBADIAH continued

> could be toward the end of phase B, the Divided
> Kingdom.

Leadership Lessons
1. **JUDGMENT AND JUSTICE.** This book reveals again that God will
   serve justice by bringing retributive judgment to those who deserve it. It
   gives the basic reason for the judgment and also gives the basic principle
   underlying the judgment: (verse 9, 10 and 15). *The day of the Lord is*
   near for all nations. As you have done, it will be done to you. How
   nations treat Israel is a measuring rod that will be used for or against
   them.
2. **DOWNFALL.** God makes it clear that pride was the root cause
   underlying Edom's defiance and actions. This attitude is charged against
   the leadership in particular and populace in general. It again confirms our
   findings about leadership barriers to finishing well. Two types of leaders
   are mentioned, wise men and warriors. Both are judged. This book is
   probably included in the Bible to show us the culmination of pride and
   warn us.

For Further Leadership Study
1. What patriarchal promises were made to Esau? How kept?
2. What warning is given about the patriarch of Edom--Esau? See also
   Hebrews 12:16,17.

Special Comments
One's Pride of heart can easily deceive. Pride of heart belies an attitude
which in effect declares its ability to do without God. A profane person has
no consciousness of the eternal and acts independently of God. This was the
problem of Edom, rooted all the way back to Esau.

BOOK	**EZEKIEL Author:** Ezekiel
Characters	Ezekiel, of the priestly line
Who To/For	to Judah and Jerusalem, those in exile
Literature Type	narrative prophecies, some extended poetry, visions

Story Line   Ezekiel was carried into captivity with the second group of hostages (Daniel went with first). While with the exiles he continually prophesied that Jerusalem would fall. He was shut up to this one vision. Then when it had fallen he was released to speak another message--a message of hope. God is going to restore. From his priestly perspective he sees everything from a high vantage point, the glory of God. In the first half of his message he sees the glory of God departing from Israel. In the latter part of his book he sees the glory of God returning-- the eternal presence of God with His people.

Structure
I. (ch 1-33:20)   Ezekiel--The Glorious God's Watchman
II. (ch 33:21-39)   Ezekiel--The Glorious God's Encourager
III. (ch 40-48)   Ezekiel--The Glorious God's Revealer

Theme   **THE GLORY OF THE SOVEREIGN GOD WHICH WILL BE KNOWN**
- is seen in judgment on Judah and other nations,
- is seen, in his hopeful, future restorative dealings with Israel, and
- is climaxed by His presence in His Temple.

Key Words   Sovereign Lord (NIV 200+); glory of God (20+ times); son of man (at least 92 times); will know (70 times).

Key Events   Ezekiel's several symbolic acts; death of Ezekiel's wife, The fall of Jerusalem.

Purposes
- to highlight the glory of God,
- to affirm the destruction of Jerusalem (temple),
- to give with certainty prophecies whereby people *will know* that God is real and is the Lord,
- to encourage the people in exile by describing a future restoration.

EZEKIEL continued

Why Important   The book closes with a most important phrase, "The Lord is there." Therein lies the secret of Ezekiel's strength and hope. Ezekiel was conscious of the presence of God throughout his ministry. He was the prophet of hope because of His vision of God. Ezekiel had a unique close, mystical, relationship with God. Because of this God revealed much. He in turn reveals to us the essential facts of the nature of God.

Where It Fits   Ezekiel fits in Phase IV. Post-Kingdom Leadership. He is part of the Exile Sub-phase. His leadership was decidedly decentralized as he was an exile isolated in a less well known region of Babylon. The dominant trait of his leadership ministry was that of renewal. His was an inspirational task. Modeling and a direct word ministry (prophetical) were the dominant means of influence.

Leadership Lessons

1. **THE PRESENCE OF GOD IS THE ESSENTIAL INGREDIENT OF LEADERSHIP.** The second and third portions of the book emphasize this positively; the first does so negatively--see especially the final words 48:35 *The Lord is there.* The glory of the Lord departs in part I. His renewing presence is the focus of Parts II, III.
2. **LEADERS SHOULD SEEK TO FOCUS ON REVEALING GOD'S GLORY--THAT IS THEIR MINISTRY SHOULD PRESENT A HIGH VIEW OF GOD.** Ezekiel did. His view of God is majestic. Only Isaiah comes close to seeing God so exalted and authoritative.
3. **LEADERS SHOULD LEAD WITH CERTAINTY TOWARD GOD'S PURPOSES.** *They will know that I am the Lord* occurs 70+ times in Ezekiel.
4. **LEADERS MUST KNOW THE SOVEREIGNTY OF GOD IN THEIR MINISTRIES.** God of hosts (NIV Sovereign God) occurs 210+ times in Ezekiel.
5. **LEADERS SHOULD MAINTAIN A BALANCED VIEW BETWEEN *WHAT IS* AND *WHAT OUGHT TO BE* IN THEIR MINISTRY.** Chapters 1-33:21 is corrective and is focusing on *what is*. But all ministry can't be correcting the problems in followership. Chapters 33:22-48 focuses on *what ought to be* and gives hope. But all ministry can't be creating expectations for a future which never arrives. Both aspects are needed--creating hope for the future by creating

EZEKIEL continued

expectations for what can be and giving correction that will move toward
that future.
6. **EZEKIEL EMPHASIZES THE NOTION OF GOD CHANNELING
   HIS WORK THROUGH HUMAN REPRESENTATIVES.** The term
   son of man occurs at least 90+ times in Ezekiel.
7. **LEADERS ARE ACCOUNTABLE TO GOD FOR THEIR
   MINISTRY.** While this is taught more directly in other places in
   Scripture, the *Watchman passage* (and others) certainly puts forth the
   notion of the leader being responsible for influencing the people toward
   God's purposes.
8. **OBEDIENCE IS ESSENTIAL TO LEADERSHIP.** Throughout
   Ezekiel is almost extreme in his unconditional obedience to God. Only
   Caleb is comparable in the Old Testament. See especially 24:15-27, the
   death of Ezekiel's wife.
9. **DON'T STEREOTYPE LEADERS AROUND YOU.** Ezekiel was a
   priest. Most in the Old Testament were formal and concerned at best
   with ritual. They were often inflexible and lacked life. Yet Ezekiel
   shows that formal leaders can be powerful leaders and exert tremendous
   leadership. There is evidence of a priestly perspective and influence
   throughout his writings.

For Further Leadership Study
1. Ezekiel's personal processing: Sense of Destiny experiences --several (ch 1,
   ch 2, etc.); Leadership committal (2:1-3:27); numerous obedience checks (ch
   4, ch 5); numerous conflict incidents; crisis--Ezekiel's wife dies (ch 24), fall
   of Jerusalem (ch 33); destiny revelation--the Watchman passage (ch 33).
2. Direct leadership passages: leaders secretly worshipping other gods (ch
   8); Judgment on leadership (ch 11), Pelatiah dies; False prophets
   condemned (ch 13); Lament for Israel's princes (ch 19); elders inquiring
   of Lord (ch 20); shepherds of Israel (ch 34);

Special Comments
A deep book requiring repeated study. The prophetical passages in Part II,
especially, need much further comparative work with other prophecies in
Old and New Testaments. These might be being fulfilled before our very
eyes today. The temple section is disputed territory. Some hold literal
fulfillment. I tend toward a symbolic fulfillment. Ezekiel is an imposing
strong leader and one who is rather intimidating. In tough circumstances he
demonstrated the reality, power, and presence of a glorious God in his life.
Yet it is God's enabling which does it for we are repeatedly reminded of
Ezekiel's humanness via the idiom, son of man.

BOOK	**DANIEL**	**Author:** Daniel

Characters — Daniel, Shadrach, Meshach, Abednego, Nebuchadnessar, Belshazzar, Queen Mother, Darius, Cyrus

Who To/For — Jewish People in general, Babylonians

Literature Type — Chapters 1-6 are historical narratives of 6 major vignettes; chapters 7, 8, 9, and 10-12 each deal with a major vision and its explanation. (Chapter 2 also contains a major vision which gives the framework for all the other visions)

Story Line — Daniel, of royal blood, was carried away in the first captivity during Jehoakim's reign, thus fulfilling the prophecy to Hezekiah in Isaiah 39:7. These royal hostages were then indoctrinated in the higher knowledge of Babylon. Daniel is seen to be a person of integrity. He and his three special friends Shadrach, Meschach, and Abednego are tops in their class. They are given good positions in Nebuchadnezzar's administrative court. Five important crisis events selected from the many possible over a long period of time are given: The so-called forgotten dream, the fiery furnace, tree dream, handwriting on the wall, and the lion's den. In each of these crises the key point being made is that God is ruling behind the scenes and overruling these rulers when He wants to in accomplishing His purposes. The first crisis experience, the so-called forgotten dream has a vision of the future which gives the framework for God's Plan for the Ages. Chapters 6-12 then elaborate on this plan giving more details of specific portions of it. The book closes with Daniel being honored by God for his long and faithful service.

Structure —
I.   (ch 1)   God's Sovereign Preparation of Daniel
II. (ch 2-6) God's Sovereign Rule Over the Nations
III. (ch 7-12) God's Sovereign Rule over History

Theme — **THE MOST HIGH** (sovereign God) **RULES**
- in the affairs of individuals,
- nations, and
- history.

DANIEL continued

Key Words   names for God--Daniel uses many of which *The Most
        High is his favorite, king and kingdoms are important

Key Events   See story line

Purposes
- to show that God is ruling and moving toward His purposes, even though outwardly it appears that disaster has overtaken God's people and plans,
- to show how God shapes a leader He uses,
- to present a framework of God's plan for the Ages,
- to introduce the notion of the Kingdom of God--an eternal kingdom,
- to give insights into power encounters and cosmic level spiritual warfare,
- to encourage God's people to a godly walk in troublesome times, expecting God's ultimate triumph.

Why Important Perspective is a major difference among those who
        follow God and those who don't. Perspective on what
        God is doing in the world allows His followers to identify
        with His work, respond to it, and live with an expectant
        hope of the glory of God. This book shows us that in the
        times in which we live, God is ruling the circumstances
        of our individual lives and of the events of history in
        order to move toward His purposes. He is setting up and
        casting down rulers. On the one hand, He is allowing
        evil to move to its full development and its ultimate
        destruction. On the other, He is preserving good and
        moving toward its full development and final victory.
        God is presented as all wise, all powerful and eternally
        enthroned over all the passing governments. This book is
        also important for it demonstrates that a person of God
        can have a powerful leadership influence in an oppressive
        society and even when there are no religious structures to
        work through. A single life can have deep impact.
        Daniel did.

Where It Fits Daniel lived during the exile phase of era IV Post-
        Kingdom Leadership. This is the interim period awaiting
        coming of Messiah in the Redemptive Drama. In this
        black moment in history when it appears that God's plans
        have been upset, what is needed is a positive view of who

DANIEL continued

> God is. Daniel is just such a person to give this positive view. He saw God not only as sovereign in his own life amid bleak circumstances but also among the rulers for whom he worked and in history in general. The time was ripe for Daniel. And God shaped Daniel for the time. He was a leader born and made.

Leadership Lessons

1. **BIOGRAPHIC GENRE.** The book of Daniel has a good bit of information that is biographic in nature. In fact, a mini-biographic study can be made of Daniel's life. Carefully selected incidents highlight at least six pivotal points in Daniel's life. Of special import is the crisis processing. Crisis processing was the dominant item that shaped Daniel. Many lessons concerning this processing are given in the biographical sketch of Daniel and the in-depth booklet on his life. Daniel's leadership is dominantly by example. He had no organized followers (like a synagogue or temple group). He had no structures through which to lead. His ministry was modeling. And that it was effective can be seen by Ezekiel's (a contemporary) testimony to it (14:14, 14:20, 28:3). Ezekiel classifies Daniel as to righteousness up there with Job and Noah. He also speaks highly of his wisdom.

2. **SUPERNATURAL EMPHASIS.** Daniel's intentional selection of critical events focuses on the supernatural aspects of leadership. God works behind the scenes controlling, revealing, setting up, taking down, giving hope for the future. Each of the events sets up the scene so that an impossible or incredibly difficult situation arises. It is clear that if Daniel or his friends are to escape the situation that only God can deliver. And so when it happens it is clear that God did it. God receives the credit. And Daniel and friends are expanded in their own potential, status, and roles which will affect future ministry. The major incidents include: chapter 1, the food incident; chapter 2, the *so-called* forgotten dream; chapter 3, the fiery furnace; chapter 4, the tree dream; chapter 5, the handwriting on the wall; chapter 6, the lions den. The Daniel 10 incident (warfare in heavenlies) also reveals the supernatural dimension involved in Daniel's leadership.

3. **INTEGRITY.** In chapter 1, Daniel's integrity is tested with the food incident. He passes the test and learns that God can indeed deliver him if he will stand on his convictions. This test is a springboard which launches him into his ministry. He will later face tougher tests for his integrity but they are all rooted back in this test. Throughout the book he is a leader of integrity. His character is impeccable.

DANIEL continued

4. **GIFTEDNESS.** Daniel operated with gifted power. Several times he faced risky situations which would test whether or not God would reveal truth to him. He took those risks. God met him. He operated in gifted power.

5. **SPIRITUAL AUTHORITY.** Daniel (5:11,12 and others) demonstrated spiritual authority. Spiritual authority is the right to influence conferred upon a leader because followers sense in the leader a spirituality they discern is from God. This comes usually in three ways: deep experiences with God, knowledge of God, His ways, and His desires and gifted power. Daniel demonstrates all three of these sources of spiritual authority. Daniel also had positional authority and charismatic authority.

6. **NO BARRIERS.** Six barriers have been previously discussed as being detrimental to those who would finish well. Daniel was faced with four of the six (pride, abuse of power, financial integrity, plateauing) in his long ministry experience yet he never succumbed. He maintained a vital relationship with God and disciplined himself for the long haul.

7. **ENHANCING FACTORS.** 5 items have been previously identified as enhancing the prospect of a good finish. Daniel illustrates all of them in his life:

   a. *Perspective:* Daniel, with his analytical abilities and his supernatural anointing of wisdom and knowledge, had a very high aptitude for getting perspective. His dreams and visions stimulated him in this direction. He sought answers and explanations to them. He had a prophetic curiosity which drove him to get answers.

   b. *Repeated Renewal Experiences:* Over his lifetime Daniel experienced several renewals--that is, deep experiences with God in which God met him afresh. Most leaders will need repeated renewal experiences with God. Some of these will be self-initiated. Others will simply be God breaking in. But however they come, they are needed.

   c. *Disciplines*: Daniel maintained several spiritual disciplines throughout his lifetime including: habitual intake of the word and prayer, extended times of solitude, silence, fasting and prayer. These disciplines served him well. On two of his extended times God met him with renewal experiences and vital revelatory information as well as affirmation.

   d. *Mentors:* Daniel had peer mentors who encouraged and supported him as well as several upward mentors who sponsored him. These were important at critical times in his life and ministry.

DANIEL continued

    e. *Learning Posture:* Daniel exhibits one of the finest learning postures in scripture. It is seen in how he learns in life all around him. It is seen in his continual grasping with and attempting to analyze the various prophetic visions given him. It is seen (Daniel 9) in his study of scripture (Jeremiah 25, 29) and his applicational faith response to it.

8. **SENSE OF DESTINY.** Sense of destiny refers to an awareness that God's hand is on a life uniquely to accomplish special things through it. This is seen in destiny preparation incidents that condition a person to begin to see God initiating that sense of destiny. It is seen in incidents which then clarify and reveal further what the destiny entails. And finally it is seen in fulfillment of that destiny. The prophecy given to Hezekiah long before Daniel's birth came true for Daniel. His unusual revelatory experiences with God continually reminded him that he was special to God and was being used specially to manifest a witness to the living God in the influential center of the worlds strongest empire. The rapid promotions after each major crisis showed God's hand was upon him and guiding him to a top level position in the empire. The revelations about how the empires would unfold in history were a natural extension to his own experiences in the government of three of those empires. Daniel, is a positive example of the observation that has been repeatedly confirmed: All effective leaders in the Bible had a strong sense of destiny. No leader accomplished anything worthwhile without a sense of destiny. The generalization which has been derived from these observations: EFFECTIVE LEADERS HAVE A GROWING AWARENESS OF THEIR SENSE OF DESTINY.

9. **FINISH WELL.** Daniel is the classic example in the Old Testament of a leader who finished well. He demonstrated all of the six characteristics. He had a <u>vibrant relationship</u> with God (note the heavenly affirmation of this--O greatly beloved, highly esteemed). He maintained a <u>learning posture</u> all his life as previously described. His <u>character</u> reflected godliness. He had <u>convictions</u> from God which he stood on (several integrity checks were over just these sort of convictions). He thus demonstrated that God was real via the truth of these convictions. His <u>ultimate contribution</u> set included that of saint, stylistic practitioner, stabilizer, and writer. He fulfilled his <u>sense of destiny</u> (witnessing to God in the empire, revealing God's plans for the empires to come, preserving a sense of a sovereign God in the midst of apparently overwhelming defeat for God's people, leaving a written record of God's interventions and intents).

DANIEL continued

10. **ULTIMATE CONTRIBUTION.** As indicated in the previous point Daniel contributed in at least the following ways: saint (model righteous life), stylistic practitioner (demonstrating a ministry role in an oppressive government) , stabilizer (successful administrator), and writer (recording of his testimony and visions).

For Further Leadership Study
1. Trace out the positive testing patterns for details in chapter 2, chapter 4, chapter 5, and chapter 6. Remember the positive testing pattern has three stages: the test, the positive response to the test, and God's expansion after the successful completion of the test. Daniel is the classic case in the Old Testament of the positive testing pattern.
2. Study Daniel's finish, that is, the vision of the kings of the north and south (chapters 10-12). Ransack it for those indicators of a good finish.
3. Daniel like many effective leaders is a risk taker. How is this seen in the book?
4. Why was Daniel able to *focus* so strongly on his ministry?

Special Comments
This book has special application to us today since we are living in the times it describes. We like these exiles are living in the *times of the Gentiles*. And we like them should live separated lives which attract others to see God as He is. We should worship God in spite of difficulties. We should await His ultimate victory.

BOOK	**HAGGAI** **Author:** Haggai
Characters	Haggai, a prophet; Zerubbabel, a governor of Judah; Joshua, high priest;
Who To/For	the actual prophecies were given to Zerubbabel and Joshua, but the written record was for those Jewish exiles who returned to the land to rebuild
Literature Type	narrative record of important revelations from the Lord to Joshua and Zerubbabel and description of responses
Story Line	Zerubbabel had led a group of Jewish people back to Jerusalem upon the issuing of the decree by Cyrus (536 B.C.). They began to settled down and build the temple but had stopped for various reasons: discouragement, resources, opposition. The time of these prophecies is 16 to 18 years after they had returned. Haggai, a prophet, gets revelation from God which is used to motivate them to get started on the temple again. The revelation answers all the reasons why the work had been delayed.

Structure

I. (1:1-15) The Task Delayed
II. (ch 2:1-9) Discouragement In the Task
III. (ch 2:10-19) Patience in the Task
IV. (ch 2:20-23) Power for the Task

Theme

HAGGAI'S TASK ORIENTED INSPIRATIONAL LEADERSHIP, concerning the building of the temple,

- began with an authoritative word from God which explains the situation as God sees it,
- recognized that along the way toward completing the task discouragement will come and must be counteracted by seeing God's future blessing, and
- counted on God's strength in an overwhelming situation.

Key Words   Lord Almighty (13); On the ...day (time markers, 5), house (8), consider (5)

Key Events   none

HAGGAI continued

Purposes
- to spur the people on to build the temple, the center of hope and inspiration for the returned remnant,
- to give insights on inspirational leadership,
- to show the timeliness and appropriateness of God's revelation to a situation,
- to inspire people of all time to press on in times of discouragement and smallness of the work of God.

Why Important   This book gives valuable insights on inspirational leadership. Stages of reaction by followers to this kind of leadership are illustrated (false satisfaction, false dissatisfaction, false expectation, false fear). Each of these stages is addressed by a timely word from God. Haggai shows the importance of influencing leaders in order to influence the work of God. It also shows how a leader needs to trust God for timely words of intervention. God is continuing to ready Jerusalem for the "fullness of time" and the coming of Messiah. He has not lost sight of that goal even though the people falter.

Where It Fits   Haggai occurs in the Post Exilic phase of era IV. Post-Kingdom Leadership. He is way back at the earliest beginnings of the pre-Messianic period of the Redemptive Drama. It is a time of waiting until the fullness of time was come. It is a time of seeking to rebuild the foundations in the promised land from which Messiah would come.

HAGGAI continued

Leadership Lessons
1. **TASK ORIENTED LEADERSHIP.** Modern leadership theory has identified three major umbrella like leadership functions: a. Leaders must move followers to accomplish achievements, that is, there must be an orientation toward task. b. Leaders must provide an environment (community) conducive to accomplishing task. c. Leaders must inspire followers to want to be a part of the endeavor and to accomplish. Normally a given leader is either dominantly a task type leader or a relationship type leader. Rarely is a leader both of these. Either a task leader or a relational leader can inspire. Haggai, a prophetical leader,[24] was a task oriented leader. His constant thrust was the completion of the task--building of the temple. The book itself is a case study in task oriented leadership.
2. **INSPIRATIONAL LEADERSHIP.** Haggai, a prophetical leader, was also an inspirational leader. He met each stage of the task, with its discouraging feature, with a positive solution which inspired his followers to rejoin the effort.
3. **TEAMWORK.** Not being a relational leader, Haggai needed a team. God brought together Zerubbabel, a political leader and Joshua, a Priest
3. **INFLUENCE MEANS.** Haggai did not have positional political authority, like Zerubbabel, or religious priestly authority, like Joshua. His major means of influence was charismatic (dent of strong personality) and spiritual authority. He dominantly acted with gifted power--getting an authoritative word and then applying it to the situation. In his first leadership act (1:2-11) he overcame the excuses that were given about building the temple (there had been a delay of almost 16 years). His authoritative word gave a divine perspective on what was happening to them economically and why. It was a word with spiritual authority (1:12 ...people obeyed the voice of the Lord their God and the message of the prophet Haggai, because the Lord their God had sent him. And the people feared the Lord). This same pattern of influence means prevails throughout all the stages. Haggai is able by a word from God to head off the excuses at each stage and to inspire both the people and the team leaders.
4. **4 STAGES.** This particular task, rebuilding the temple, had four stages to it as the work unfolded: (1) The Task Delayed--Getting the Task initiated; timing is critical. Haggai overcame the inertial lag with a strong authoritative word from God. It will often take gifted power to break

---

[24]Prophetical leaders, like Haggai, because of their strong corrective bent frequently are task oriented leaders and need real help in relational leading.

HAGGAI continued

through and get the task oriented. (2) Discouragement--after initial momentum, enthusiasm usually wanes, some excuses for pulling back occur. The leader must then re-fire up the people. In this case, the work seemed so small and puny (especially compared to the temple that had once been there). Haggai's answer from God is simple. God reaffirms that it is not the size of a work of God that makes it important but the presence of the living God in it. And He strongly promises that His presence will be there and will accomplish the great things He wants through it. The people again responded. (3) Patience in the Task--having been promised that God would be in this the people immediately look for His blessing. They do not see it and hence could easily become discouraged. Haggai gets a word from God which says blessings will come but are basically conditioned on obedient response. The people again respond. (4) Power for the Task--finally the real issue arises, the need for God's power and protection. Haggai again gets a word from God and convinces the followers of God's provision of power and protection. Frequently, tasks will pattern themselves like this. The major lesson to see is that gifted power is needed to answer objections. Objections will come at each stage. Spiritual authority is needed to convince and overcome. Complementary functions (in this case relational leading) are often needed. It is probably significant that Haggai headed off each of the objections before they were full bloom. He in fact identified the objection for the people (similar to word of knowledge used today in some charismatic circles).

5. **WORK OF GOD.** No work of God, if initiated by Him is small (2:1-9). And any work of God will require His power and presence in it. And the promise of His presence is enough. We can not judge the significance of our efforts whether small or big. God will work through it and bless it according to His purposes. It is enough for us to know that God has called us and He will empower us and will use the work for His purposes.

For Further Leadership Study
1. Study each of the two contexts as leadership acts: a. 1:2-15, b. 2:10-19. Particularly note leadership styles involved in the influence.
2. What is the significance of the two words coming so close together on the same day (2:10; 2:20)?

Special Comments
The following time-line is helpful in catching the flow of the timely revelations. Notice the whole book takes place in about four months.

HAGGAI continued

Haggai Time-Line for Task of Rebuilding The Temple

Time Reference--------------4 months --->

2nd Year 6th month 1st day	2nd Year 6th month 24th day	2nd year 7th month 21st day	2nd year 9th month 24th day	2nd year 9th month 24th day
1st Word challenge to move	Response Began work	2nd word Countering Discouragement	3rd word Countering reward motivation	4th word Encouraging trust in God for power
stage 1 false satisfaction		stage 2 false dissatisfaction	stage 3 false expectation	stage 4 false fear

BOOK ZECHARIAH   **Author:** Zechariah

Characters	Zechariah, a prophet (maybe of priestly line); Joshua (high priest); Zerubbabel (governor).
Who To/For	returned exiles to Jerusalem, Joshua, Zerubbabel
Literature Type	mostly narrative description of visions and application of them; occasional extended Hebrew Poetry passages; numerous prophetic visions (apocalyptic)
Story Line	Zechariah is a contemporary of Haggai. His ten visions in chapters 1-6 come about two months after Haggai's last word. Zechariah seeks to encourage the returned exiles to get on with the work of God. He has a series of visions which are meant to encourage Joshua and Zerubbabel. He then goes on to talk about the future telescopically. Some things have happened. Others partially. Some are yet to be fulfilled.

Structure   I. (ch 1-6)   Visions of Encouragement to Leadership
             II. (ch 7,8)   True Religious Action and God's Promised Blessing
             III. (ch 9-14) Expectation of the Lord's Future Workings

Theme   **THE WORKING OF THE LORD ALMIGHTY**
- involves encouragement in the present to leaders,
- brings correction and hope to sincere followers, and
- reveals His future plans so as to cause anticipation and encouragement.

Key Words   Lord Almighty (NIV)= Jehovah of Hosts (45+)

Key Events   the night of the ten visions

Purposes
- to encourage the exiles who had returned to get on with the work of God--rebuilding of the temple,
- to give long term prophetic messages including the two advents of Christ, (3:8; 9:9; 14:4),
- to unveil truth, authenticating God, His future purposes, plans, and power to carry out His plans,
- to call God's people back to God.

ZECHARIAH continued

Why Important   Zechariah is an unveiler. He sees things that others do
not see. The secret of his strength lies in what he saw--
his visions. And the proof of his vision lies in what he
did--in the midst of a discouraging hour, he saw God, His
persistent purposes and activity, His pervasive presence
and it affected how he lived and those to whom he
ministered. Taken with Joel, and Daniel, and John's
revelation we begin to have a framework of God's intents
and can fall in line with them and respond to them. Even
if details are not always clear--the intent and final
consummation is.

Where It Fits   Zechariah along with Haggai occurs in the Post Exilic
phase of era IV. Post-Kingdom Leadership and hence is
back at the earliest beginnings of the pre-Messianic
period of the Redemptive Drama. It is a time of waiting
until the fullness of time was come. It is a time of
seeking to rebuild the foundations in the promised land
from which Messiah would come. Zechariah sees even
beyond the period of waiting.

Leadership Lessons
1. **GENRE.** Zechariah contains little or no biographical information and
   much that is prophetical. The first section of the book is prophetical and
   seeks to encourage the present situation faced by the team of Haggai,
   Zerubbabel, and Joshua. The middle section of the book seeks to
   encourage the situation directly. And the final section is apocalyptic and
   dealing with the future. As such the book is a difficult source to draw out
   leadership implications.
2. **NAME OF GOD.** The book itself repeatedly uses the name, Lord
   Almighty (NIV) more than 45 times. It is a name for God that has been
   growing in prominence toward the latter part of the destruction of the
   Nation and finds itself prevalent in the post-exilic period. This name for
   God suggests a God who can break into history and intervene. It is this
   God who is encouraging the rebuilding of the temple by Joshua and
   Zerubbabel. The very familiar verse, 4:6, catches the strength of this. It
   is not by might nor by power but by the Spirit of the Lord. All leadership
   will go through moments of searching for power and God will in one
   way or another repeat this same answer. It is the God who can break into
   history who will do it.

ZECHARIAH continued

3. **FUTURE HOPE**. Much of the book points forward to a time yet to be. In the midst of discouragement we are reminded that God will again break into history. Leaders must constantly, especially in the midst of difficult times, encourage their people by pointing forward to God's intervening in history.
4. **PEER ENCOURAGEMENT**. Haggai who is ministering also at the same time as Zechariah received visions from God which were very, very practical and dealt directly with knowledge about the rebuilding of the temple. To have some strong encouragement from a peer whose mystical visions came from God would be very affirming to Haggai. Leaders need affirmation from peers who are very different from themselves as well as affirmation from those like them. The category of lateral external peer fits the kind of function that Zechariah was performing for Haggai.

For Further Leadership Study
1. Different cultures perceive different genre of literature differently. How would visionary literature like the 10 visions in chapters 1-6 strike its original hearers?
2. There is possibly a direct leadership passage, though given in the prophetic future, The Two Shepherds (11:4-17) which could be studied for leadership principles once the context is determined.

Special Comments
A book to be studied for overall intent. This is a difficult book to draw leadership principles from except in the most general sense.

BOOK	**ESTHER** **Author:** uncertain
Characters	Xerxes (King), Queen Vashti, Esther (heroine), Mordecai (hero), Haman (villain), Jews in exile
Who To/For	The Jews in the Persian empire
Literature Type	historical narrative of selected vignettes
Story Line	Xerxes had a six month long celebration for all the major leaders of his empire-military, political, etc. At one of the events (when everyone was drunk), Xerxes commanded his wife, Vashti, to come and dance before the men (probably naked). She refused. This was a bad example that could not be tolerated in this male dominated society. So the King deposed her and announced a beauty contest for his empire. The most beautiful woman would take her place as Queen. Esther, of Jewish descent and the niece of Mordecai, an administrative official, won the contest. Her Jewish background was not known. Mordecai overhears a conspiratorial conversation and sends word via Esther which allowed the King nip the plot in the bud. Haman, an overly ambitious politician, grew in favor with Xerxes. Mordecai refused to toady to him. This angered Haman who secretly plotted to exterminate the whole Jewish remnant in Persia. Mordecai got wind of the plot and fasted. Esther heard of his fast and went to him. Mordecai told her of the problem and asked her to intercede with the king. Esther courageously gains a hearing with the king and requests that he and Haman come to a dinner she will host. The night before the dinner the king can not sleep and while reviewing some historical notes finds out Mordecai has not been rewarded for saving the kingdom. At the dinner he asks Haman what should be done to honor a person in the kingdom. Haman, thinking of himself, specified a public display. The king follows his advice-but it is for Mordecai. Esther does not ask the king about the Jews but instead invites the King and Haman to a second dinner. In the meantime with Mordecai being honored (and a Jew) the handwriting is on the wall. At the dinner Esther accuses Haman of the plot to rid the kingdom of the Jews.

ESTHER continued

Xerxes is astounded. Haman begs with Esther for his life and offends the king by his behavior. He is sentenced to hang. Esther and Mordecai intercede for the Jews and save them. This deliverance becomes the occasion for a feast, the feast of Purim, now held annually by the Jews.

Structure

I. (ch 1,2) Setting the Stage--Providential Background to Esther's Promotion to Queen

II. (ch 3-5) The Crisis and Response--Providential Reason for Esther's Being Queen

III. (ch 6-9) The Intervention and Reversal--Providential Working of God Via His Ready Channels-- Mordecai and Esther

IV. (ch10) The Final result--Reflection on God's Providence in Mordecai's Influence

Theme **THE PROVIDENTIAL WORKING OF GOD**
- involves foresight which includes His use of apparently natural events and responses behind the scenes in *anticipation* of later events,
- will test leadership in the crisis,
- will have timely intervention in unusual yet natural events to protect, and
- will accomplish His purposes in the end.

Key Words The Jews (40+)

Key Events See story line. Pivotal verse: 4:14

Purposes
- to demonstrate God's providential care in the exile,
- to show the historical occasion for the feast of Purim,
- to demonstrate crisis leadership.

Why Important The name of God is not mentioned once in the book and therein lies an important point. A lasting value of the book is to reveal God's acting in providence, God's foresight and activity resulting from foresight so as to accomplish his purposes. We learn that God is hidden but active. His providence is inclusive of individuals and

ESTHER continued

> events. His timing is superb. He has perfect knowledge. He allows man's free will. Yet He controls. Human freedom contributes to Divine purpose. God's providence inspires great confidence and courage. Those, like Haman, who oppose it and do not recognize it are in panic and are punished. God progresses toward His ultimate goal.

Where It Fits   There are about 60 years from the time Zerubbabel and Joshua's ministry to Ezra's ministry. The book of Esther takes place about mid-way during this period. It is therefore in the post-exilic phase of the Post-Kingdom Leadership era.

Leadership Lessons

1. **CELEBRATION**. The book itself commemorates Jewish deliverance in a dark time. It highlights the principle of honoring God for past work in order to keep a present generation motivated toward God. This is a repeated principle seen in the lives of Moses, Joshua, David and others. All leaders should have moments in which God has worked mightily in their ministry for which they celebrate. Note also the court procedure of chronicling history. It was the reading of the past history that prompted Xerxes to honor Mordecai. Historical records can enhance leadership influence.

2. **POWER OF MODELING**. King Xerxes removed Vashti from being queen because of her behavior which would set a bad example for females in the land. People in high places of leadership or prominence can use modeling as a powerful means of influencing others. Xerxes certainly was aware of this. What is needed is leaders who will proactively use this means of influence. It does carry with it dangers.

3. **NETWORKING POWER**. In a critical moment in the history of the Jewish people Mordecai is able to use his connection into the palace via Esther to change the course of history. This is a classical example of networking power.

4. **SENSE OF DESTINY**. Esther 4:14 dramatically highlights the sense of destiny that Mordecai saw and Esther felt. The following events and final deliverance are a classic example of a destiny fulfilled in a leader's life. Both Mordecai, the mentor sponsor/counselor and Esther are part of this destiny.

ESTHER continued

5. **PROCESSES**. This book illustrates several of the process items defined in leadership emergence theory including: destiny processing, power encounter and/or spiritual warfare (seen from the humanistic side), crisis, networking power, sovereign guidance.
6. **POLITICAL PROCESSES**. Within organizations and/or large structures there will always be political manipulation such as Haman was involved in. This is so even in Christian organizations. Leaders should expect this sort of behind the scenes manipulative behavior. It is not ideal. Leaders of integrity should not use such manipulative means to promote their own careers. But it does happen. Experts like Mintzberg[25] should be studied for how power operates in an organization. It is clear that Mordecai was aware of the inherent power structures and clearly used them to save the Jews. Haman and his family were aware of them (note 6:12-14 where the handwriting is on the wall). Top leaders may be unaware of some of the political intrigue going on around them.

For Further Leadership Study
1. Identify and study the individual process items in the book of Esther.
2. Timing is critical in this book. This was a destiny moment. Leaders, like Mordecai, need to be aware of sovereign guidance in their past and recognize critical destiny moments. What if Mordecai had not been sensitive?
3. Why is God not mentioned in the book?

Special Comments
The providence of God is a strong argument for the existence of God. God not only is but He acts. We must respond by trusting and cooperating with this providential God who permeates our every activity. One reading this book apart from the Redemptive Drama may not see God at all. But one reading this book in terms of the movement in the Redemptive Drama have no problem in seeing God in the book and the reason for its inclusion in the canon.

---

[25]See Henry Mintzberg's **Power In and Around Organizations**.

BOOK	**EZRA**	**Author:** Ezra

Characters   Ezra, a priest and scribe highly trained in the Scriptures; King Artaxerxes, Haggai (prophet), Zechariah (prophet), Zerrubabel (political leader), Jeshua (priest), King Darius, Tattenai (governor of Trans-Euphrates),

Who To/For   scattered Jewish people

Literature Type   Historical narrative of selected vignettes from a period of time of about 80 years.

Story Line   Zerrubabel and Joshua had gone back into the land during Cyrus' reign with a remnant to rebuild the temple. They and started and stopped over a period of about 80 years. The temple is finally completed during the time of Darius of Persia (Ezra 6:15). Ezra came in and brought reform. His teaching of the Word was powerful. Conviction, confession and restitution followed his exposing the law of Moses to the people.

Structure   I. (ch 1-6) Incomplete Work Prior to Ezra's Leadership
                 II. (ch 7-10) Ezra's Word Oriented Leadership

Theme   **EFFECTIVE LEADERSHIP IN JERUSALEM UNDER EZRA**
- built on a foundation of that done by Haggai, Zechariah, Zerrubabel, and Joshua,
- involved a call back to Biblical standards for the people in Jerusalem.

Key Words   Jerusalem (40+)

Key Events   under Ezra: second remnant returns under Ezra's leadership; Artaxerxes letter endorsing return to worship; conviction of intermarriage violations, confession of sin, restitution.

EZRA   continued

Purposes
- to give a selected history of the remnants which returned back to the land,
- to show some of the problems that derailed the original remnants work back in the land,
- to demonstrate the importance of the centrality of God's word in a ministry,
- to highlight the on-going sovereignty of God in accomplishing His work in spite of obstacles,
- to highlight the left hand of God's providence, that is, the working through Cyrus, Artaxerxes, and Darius as well as His work through His leaders from His own people.

Why Important   Ezra shows the continuing work of God despite delays, obstacles, and His own peoples' unfaithfulness. It points out the need for continual renewal if God's work is to be kept alive. This same need for renewal will be seen in Nehemiah's and Malachi's works which follow. One of the foci of leadership is to recognize the on-going need for renewal and to inspire so as to accomplish it. What little biographical information we have on Ezra shows him to be a very focused leader. Effective leaders over a life time evince a narrowing trend which focuses them in on their lifetime or ultimate contributions.

Where It Fits   Ezra occurs in the post exilic phase of the Post-Kingdom Leadership Era. Its events take place back in the land and concern the remnant who have returned to rebuild Jerusalem and the temple.

Leadership Lessons
1. **ESSENTIAL INGREDIENT.** From chapter 7 on Ezra appears on the scene. It is clear that he is the strongest leader in the book of Ezra. (its named after him). He has impeccable credentials in the priestly line (7:1-5). He was well educated and well trained (7:6). He could motivate people indicated by a group of people who came with him (7:7). He had networking power and available resources (7:6, 13-26). All of these are important background and pieces of information that explain Ezra's effectiveness. But most important was the fact that God's *powerful presence* was upon the man and his ministry. The phrase the *hand of the*

EZRA   continued

Lord was upon him or its equivalent occurs 6 times (see 7:6, 9, 28; 8:18, 22, 31). In it lies the secret of his destiny and leadership. He is a classic Old Testament illustration of the essential ingredient of leadership. The powerful presence of the Lord in a leader's life and ministry is the necessary and sufficient condition of leadership--that is, the essential ingredient of leadership, first seen in Moses and then traced to Joshua and many others.

2. **FOCUS.** Leadership studies have identified the concept of formation in a leader's life.[26] The strategic formation, that shaping process, that leads a leader on to contribute toward God's on-going program of redemption in his/her unique way leads to a personal ministry philosophy which is described by three umbrella-like concepts: blend (the discovery of values which underlie ministry), focus (the narrowing in on what is to be accomplished) and articulation (the organizing of these values and direction into a coherent explicit conceptual framework). Even with the minimum amount of material available on Ezra it is clear that he had unusual focus in his life and ministry. Note he was well trained (7:6) and well disciplined toward his focus (7:10). He was a teacher of the Bible. He not only knew the material well but he also modeled its use in his own life. And because he had this disciplined bent and focus in life he was able to have a very powerful ministry (see Nehemiah chapters 8-10). Paul advocates this same word oriented focus for Timothy (II Timothy 2:15, 3:16 and others).

3. **DESTINY.** The telltale phrase, *the hand of His God was upon him* says it all. Ezra was a person of destiny. It was clear to others that God was using him for special purposes.

4. **PERSON OF PRAYER.** (8:21, 23; 9:6-15, 10:1 Ezra not only was a disciplined student of the word but he was also a person of prayer as indicated several times in Ezra and Nehemiah. Particularly it is noted that he used the technique of vicarious confession ((:1-15) to help release God's power in the situation he was praying for.

5. **LEADERSHIP SELECTION.** Throughout it is clear that Ezra influence other leaders to work with him. The job was big. He needed help. He recruited some (7:7,28 ch 8, see especially 8:16,17 ,18) and convinced others already there of his views.

---

[26]There are actually three formations that can be studied analytically even though in life they are woven together. God shapes a leader over a lifetime via critical incidents, events, people, life's situations so as to develop leadership character (called spiritual formation), leadership skills (called ministerial formation), and leadership values or ministry philosophy (called strategic formation)

EZRA   continued

6. **RENEWAL/CORRECTION.** Ezra knew the law and its guiding
    principles. There was a preciseness about his application of the word.[27]
    Everything was orderly and by the book. When he found situations
    which did not agree with what he knew was taught in the word, he
    corrected them. Correction--getting back to God's guidelines is usually
    at the heart of renewal.

7. **MINISTRY STRUCTURE INSIGHTS.** Ezra found ways to deliver
    his ministry effectively which is the essence of ministry structure
    insights one of the defined process items of leadership emergence
    theory. Note his use of strategic retreats (8:21ff) and large public
    teaching with appropriate small group interaction with trained group
    leaders (Nehemiah 8) and large group revival meetings (Nehemiah 9).

8. **THE BARRIERS/ENHANCEMENTS.** While there are not indications
    of how Ezra faced the major barriers or pitfalls to leadership there is
    certainly evidence that he had good financial integrity (8:24-36). And
    we see him using power effectively, not abusing it. There are no
    indications of wrongful pride--he is constantly giving God the credit for
    his powerful ministry. We know nothing of his family situation nor of
    any improper conduct sexually. Our picture of him is one who is
    orderly and certainly obeys the law himself. He was a student of the
    word and one who applied it to life's situations. This learning posture
    carried him past the plateau. All in all he (at least in the span of time of
    his life that is available to us) certainly avoided the pitfalls that trip up
    many leaders. In terms of the five factors that enhance a good finish we
    note at least minimum indications of all five: learning posture, renewal
    experiences, perspective, mentoring (at least sponsoring and
    downward), and disciplines.

9. **LEFT HAND OF GOD.** Glasser[28] points out how God uses peoples
    and individuals who are not in the mainstream (His people and his
    direct redemptive program) to accomplish His purposes with or without
    their knowledge. It is just this sort of thing that enabled Ezra's
    networking power.

---

[27]In fact, to me he seems overly legalistic. He applies the truth. But does he apply the truth in love. See
especially the family situations and the registering of lineage.

[28]Dr. Arthur Glasser, long time teacher of a Theology of Mission in the Old and New Testaments in the
School of World Mission of Fuller Theological Seminary, introduces the phrase, *the left hand of God*, to
indicate God's use of instruments not of His own people in order to accomplish his purposes (Pharaoh,
Nebuchadnezzar, Darius, Cyrus, the Assyrians, the Babylonians, etc.) We expect God to move strongly
through His own people, the right hand of God, but we often do not see his indirect work, the left hand of
God.

EZRA   continued

For Further Leadership Study
1. Search through the book of Ezra (7-10) for symptomatic indications of barriers and enhancements to leadership. Jot down any observations you see about leadership that come from this reflection.
2. Explore the concept of speaking the truth in love as seen through Ezra's ministry. Does he come down too hard on the truth side? How is the love side seen?
3. As an encourgement study the entire book for indications of the *left hand of God.*

Special Comments
Ezra knew the word of God. That emphasis, is needed in leader's today. While other leader's of this same era demonstrate other qualities (Nehemiah--prayer, organizational skills, motivational skills; Haggai--timely interventions, revelation from God) and all are important, Ezra shows the power inherent in God's word. The word of God, when central in a ministry, will bring convicting power to bear so as to bring about renewal and reform. What is needed are leaders who are willing to focus on learning, using, and promulgating the word of God.

BOOK	**NEHEMIAH**	**Author:** Nehemiah

Characters   Nehemiah, court official, King Artaxerxes, numerous Jewish people who went back to Jerusalem with Nehemiah, Sanballat (opponent), Tobiah (opponent), Geshem (Arab opponent), Ezra (the godly priest who knew the Word),

Who To/For   For Jewish people

Literature Type   Historical narrative of selected vignettes.

Story Line   The time is about 12 years after the book of Ezra's events. Nehemiah, who serves in the court of Artaxerxes hears of the need of the remnant which has returned to Jerusalem to rebuild the temple. He asks permission of the king to return and provide some organizational oversight to the situation there. He organizes the people to build the wall. There is opposition to this by people who have vested interests in the land. Nehemiah overcomes every obstacle and builds the wall in a short time. He then goes on to bring about reform as the city itself is being rebuilt.

Structure   I. (ch 1-7:3)   Organizing to Rebuild the Wall
II. (ch 7:4-10:39)   Organizing for Reform
III. (ch 11-13)   Organizing for Continuation

Theme   **NEHEMIAH'S ORGANIZATIONAL LEADERSHIP**
- made itself felt in the face of obstacles to rebuild the wall,
- was inspirational in bringing about reform and a covenant in Jerusalem, and
- included drastic steps of separation in order to insure an on-going meaningful religious atmosphere.

Key Words   Remember (6), wall(s) (30+), build (30+), Nehemiah's spontaneous prayers (9+)

Key Events   Nehemiah's petition to Artaxerxes, the trip to Jerusalem, examining the site of the wall, organizing to build, opposition to building, financial integrity of Nehemiah, Repeated opposition against the wall, Completion of the wall, Ezra reads the law, Corporate Confession, Covenant, Centralizing leadership in Jerusalem, Wall Publicly Dedicated, Final Reforms in Response to reading of the law.

NEHEMIAH   continued

Purposes
- to tell of the rebuilding of the walls around Jerusalem,
- to show the importance of networking power,
- to introduce a new kind of leader,
- to describe task oriented inspirational leadership which has organizational issues central,
- to illustrate motivational techniques,
- to show the importance of prayer in leadership,
- to show the importance of the Word in leadership,
- to illustrate perseverance in leadership the midst of opposition and obstacles,
- to show dynamic balance between dependence upon God and activity for God

Why Important   A new order of leadership is seen in this book. Prophet, priest and king have come and gone and still God's work needs accomplishing. God raises up a lay person who is willing to walk by faith in the midst of darkness and opposition. Nehemiah illustrates the basic message of Habakkuk 2:4, My righteous one shall live by faith. His attitude of persevering faith, his continued activity on the wall, and his completing the task illustrate what leadership that mixes faith with obedience can do. Nehemiah lived out the advice of the old Bible teacher who told his students, "Pray as though everything depended on God, and act as though everything depended on you."

Where It Fits   Nehemiah occurs in era IV. Post-Kingdom Leadership, the post exilic subphase. It is a time when the work and plans of God seem minor. The people of God are few--their spirits low. They need inspirational leadership. Nehemiah provides task oriented leadership which inspires the people.

Leadership Lessons

1. **MOTIVATIONAL LESSONS**. Motivational techniques for getting follower ownership includes:
   a. working with them,
   b. sacrificing financially,
   c. taking courageous stands against opposition,
   d. crisis praying,
   e. sensitivity to God in providential ways,

NEHEMIAH continued

    f. working for justice--reforms
    g. competitiveness, pride: each family doing portion near them.
2. **PRAYERFUL SPIRIT.** A spirit of prayer must pervade leadership task situations in the midst of crisis.
3. **OWNERSHIP.** Follower ownership is imperative for accomplishing overwhelming tasks.
4. **COSTLY CONVICTIONS.** Nehemiah was a leader with no compromise on religious convictions even though it be costly.
5. **CONFLICT IN LEADERSHIP.** In major boundary times expect great conflict and opposition from secular people--where threatening change is happening.
6. **OPPOSITION LESSONS.** In dealing with opposition expect:
    a. Ridicule. How did Nehemiah handle it: (1) did not argue--first thing commit to the Lord, (2) he saw the problem in light of God.
    b. Consolidation of opposing force--2 enemies become 4/ Sanballat, Tobiah, Arabs, Ammonites. Nehemiah altered the plans for building and provided a military answers in the midst of the working.
7. **BALANCE BETWEEN ACTION AND PRAYER**. Maintain balance-- pray/work (Nehemiah lived out the advice of the modern teacher who told his students: "Pray as though everything depended on God, and act as though everything depended on you."
8. **PROCESSING.** The book of Nehemiah should be studied in light of leadership emergence theory, that is, processing in Nehemiah's life. Particularly the book shows the importance of conflict processing.

For Further Leadership Study
1. There are numerous leadership acts in chapters 1-6. Each can be analyzed using the basic principles detailed in one of the other handbooks.
2. Nehemiah goes through a major boundary[29] in his life in chapter 1. This is worth analyzing in detail.

Special Comments
Notice in particular the notion of closure (4:6, 6:15,16, 12:27). Nehemiah finished what he started out to do. He built the wall, organized the people, brought about reform and sought to make it a habitual thing.

---

[29]Analysis over a lifetime of a leader identifies major periods of time called development phases. Movement from one development phase to another represents a critical transition and is called a boundary which usually has three stages: entry, evaluation, expansion. See position paper, Boundary Processing available through Barnabas Publishing.

BOOK	**MALACHI**	**Author:** Malachi

Characters   Malachi, a prophet

Who To/For   returned exiles

Literature Type   narrative discussion based on a cyclical pattern of rhetorical question and answer

Story Line   Malachi's ministry to the exiles occurs after Nehemiah's, perhaps as many as 35 years. Nominalism has set in even though Nehemiah's efforts were to build in a continual reforming mindset. Malachi admonishes and calls the people back to God through a series of dialogic questions God asks and answers concerning these returned exiles.

Structure   The structure of Malachi revolves around a series of rhetorical questions which prompt a nominality condition needing correction: Q1 (1:1) How have you loved us? Q2 (1:6) How have we shown contempt for your name? Q3 (1:7) How have we defiled you? Q4 (2:10) Have we not all one Father? Q5 (2:17) How have we wearied him? Q6 (3:7) How are we to return? Q7 (3:8) How do we rob you? Q8 (3:13) What have we said against you?

Theme   **NOMINALITY**, religious form without power and meaning,
- reflects a lack of understanding of God's love,
- is manifested by half-hearted obedience which hinders God's purposes,
- is perpetuated by nominal leadership, and
- ultimately will be corrected by God.

Key Words   Lord Almighty (24),

Key Events   none

Purposes
- to expose nominality--its roots and manifestations,
- to warn that God is going to correct them,
- to show that nominal leaders cause nominality.

MALACHI continued

Why Important   Nominality is much more subtle than outward rebellion. There is an apparent outward following of God. Prophets have spoken directly to the sins of the outwardly rebellious. Malachi shows us that to get to the bottom of nominality we must go to the root causes--the primary one, a lack of sensitivity to God's love for us. If we really understand God's love for us we will not...(here you can fill in proper answers to each of the rhetorical questions).

Where It Fits   Malachi is the last of the post exilic prophets. The context for his ministry therefore occurs in post-kingdom leadership. After Malachi we have no more recorded revelation until messiah comes. This placement assumes Malachi wrote last; others do not agree on this.

Leadership Lessons
1. **GENRE**. We have little or no biographical information on Malachi. What we have is a series of back and forth narratives which bring out problems that Malachi wants to address. They are not pure leadership acts but do contain ideas about influence means. There are two passages, 1:6-14 AND 2:1-9, which are almost direct contexts dealing with leadership. All the rest are indirect information from which some leadership ideas may be cautiously drawn.
2. **IMPROPER MODELING**. Malachi points out that people do not follow hard after God if the leaders (Levites) themselves are nominal. When leadership corrupts the forms of religion so that they have no meaning (1:6-15) then the people will not have vitality in their relationship with God. The leaders were setting a bad example for the people.
3. **SPIRITUALITY AUTHORITY**. The admonition to the priests (2:1-9) indicates that they were failing to follow after God in their own lives. In the corrective statements, Malachi gives one of the major foci of spiritual authority. *For the lips of a priest ought to preserve knowledge, and from his mouth men should see instruction because he is the messenger of the Lord Almighty* (2:7). Leaders with spiritual authority are those who know God and His ways and model His characteristics in their lives. They are in effect representative models of God to those they minister to. Followers must be able to look to leaders and see God's authoritative imprint upon their lives.

MALACHI continued

4. **EBB AND FLOW OF VITALITY.**[30] Throughout the Old Testament history there is a repeated cycle God's renewal efforts with His people, their response, and then degeneration begins again. That is, a leader can always expect nominality to creep into a work over a period of time and must see the need for a-periodic times of renewal. These times of renewal can not be programmed in or they in turn degenerate into forms without function. Malachi reminds us of the need for renewal. Ezra had a good renewal ministry. But some years later there is again need. One can not perpetuate the renewals too often for there is actual need for time to work out implications of renewal in a steady state situation.
5. **SOCIAL BASE PROCESSING.** One of the barriers to finishing well in leadership involves the family. Malachi hits directly on this in his accusation to the unfaithful husbands (2:13-16). A marriage relationship between husband and wife is vital to ministry (see also 1 Peter 3:7 on this).
6. **MAJOR RENEWAL PRINCIPLE.** At the heart of all renewal lies the basic message of 3:7. *Return to me and I will return to you.* Leaders with a renewal thrust must operate out of this principle.

For Further Leadership Study
1. Study the basic questions that structure the book. These probably indicate renewal need in any work of God.
2. Study how the book of Malachi closes. There is need for powerful generational leadership that can see true religious reality passed on in families. Leaders need to take this hint/warning seriously. How are those vertical relationships in the family between parents and children? Renewal begins in the family.

Special Comments
This is the final book closing out the Old Testament. In the intervening years (some 400 or so) there will rise a Pharasaical following of God. In it will be the seeds of nominality. This final message was intended to counteract that tendency and to counteract such tendencies in our present works for God. A major idea in Malachi is that the true motivation for religious activity flows out of love responding to love. This emphasis on right relationships among God's leaders, and the reality of the community manifesting true religion seems to indicate that Malachi, unlike Nehemiah and Ezra, is a relationship leader rather than a task leader.

---

[30]Clinton has tried to capture this ebb and flow idea in his paper, *Structural Time*, which traces sodalities (parachurch organizations) and modalities (church organizations) through time in order to note times of recrudescence (renewal) and times of stability or degeneration.

BOOK	**MATTHEW** **Author:** Matthew

Characters   Mary and Joseph--Jesus' parents, Jesus, John the Baptist--
a prophet who announces Jesus' coming, the twelve
disciples--first followers of Jesus: Simon Peter, Andrew,
James the Son of Zebedee, John, Philip, Bartholomew,
Thomas, Matthew, James the son of Alphaeus,
Thaddaeus, Simon the Zealot, Judas Iscariot; there are
many other people mentioned.

Who To/For   especially for the Jews (those familiar with the Old
Testament), shows many fulfilled prophecies

Literature Type   Historical narrative of selected vignettes with an
emphasis on the 3 years Jesus Christ's ministry and his
crucifixion

Story Line   Matthew writing from a Jewish perspective traces Jesus
genealogy to Abraham the father of the Jewish nation.
He shows his miraculous divine birth, then skips to his
entrance into ministry which begins with Jesus' baptism
by John the Baptist who announces him to be the
Messiah. There follows the temptation of Jesus by Satan
and then Jesus ministry begins. His major teaching is
given. Then are given incidents of his ministry which
authenticate his claims as Messiah. He calls his
disciples--the first 12 major followers. He gives a series
of kingdom parables--each a story with an important
punch line. The death of John the Baptist marks a turning
point in Jesus' ministry. He withdraws and gives special
teaching to his followers. He is basically rejected by the
Pharisees, the major Jewish religious group of his day.
He gives some prophecies concerning his return
following his death and the future of the kingdom. The
book ends with the final week of Christ's life which
includes his death, resurrection, final instructions to his
disciples, called the great commission, and Ascension to
heaven.

Structure   Following the introduction the book is structured around
6 major discourses (given in italics). Each is preceded by
a section of selected narrative vignettes which lead up to
the discourse, all of the narratives emphasize that Jesus is

MATTHEW continued

the King who has come to fulfill the Old Testament predictions.

I. (ch 1,2)	Introduction to the King
II. (ch 3-7)	The Presentation and Proclamation of the King (*Sermon on the Mount*)
III. (ch 8-10)	The Credentials and Messengers of the King (*Charge to the Twelve*)
IV. (ch 11-13)	The Claims of the King About the Kingdom (*Parables of the Kingdom*)
V. (ch 14-18)	The Withdrawal and Identification of the King and His Followers (*The Teaching on Greatness and Forgiveness*)
VI. (ch 19-23)	The Rejection of the King (*Denunciation of the Pharisees*)
VII. (ch 24,25)	The Prophecies of the King's Return (*The Olivet Discourse and Parables of the 2nd Coming*)
VIII. (ch 26-28)	The Trial, Death, and Resurrection of the King (*Exaltation, Enthronement, Great Proclamation*)

Theme   **JESUS, THE MESSIAH KING,**
- is presented with authentication,
- inaugurates and teaches on his kingdom,
- is rejected and crucified,
- is resurrected, ascends to heaven and will return someday to reclaim His Kingdom.

Key Words   fulfill(ed) (17), kingdom (30+),

Key Events   See story line for some. Many more are given.

Purposes
- to present Jesus of Nazareth as the promised Messiah of the Old Testament,
- to show that the kingdom of God (Jewish sensitive synonym uses kingdom of heaven) has come,
- to introduce the nature of the kingdom and its demands on its followers,

MATTHEW continued

- to clarify the telescopic Old Testament prophecies--now see two advents--before they saw both as one,
- to give the proclamation which will establish the movement begun by Jesus into a worldwide channel for redemption,
- to create an expectation for the return of Christ and a conviction about living properly so as to be ready for it.

Why Important   Matthew has more than 60 Old Testament references. It is clear that this opening gospel is intended to connect Jesus story to the Old Testament which went before it. Jesus is the fulfillment of the Old Testament. It was written about him and the events of it, sovereignly superintended by God have led to this moment in history. The central teaching is the arrival of the kingdom of God. Its fundamental conception is the kingship of God. What has been illustrated throughout the Old Testament is now stated conceptually. God is sovereignly reigning and moving toward his purposes. The King, Jesus, interprets this kingship by showing its principles are founded in righteousness. It is a peaceful kingdom. He tells what it means to be a follower in this kingdom. He authenticates his message with miracles and authoritative teaching. The kingdom is now in the presence of the king and all who will submit to His rule in their lives. But it is also yet to come in its fullness.

Where It Fits   Matthew occurs in the Redemptive Drama in Chapter 3, Messiah. Along with the other synoptic(viewing Jesus in the same way--historical tracing) Gospels of Mark and Luke they present us with the story of Jesus, the Messiah King and savior of the world, whose movement in Palestine among a few disciples comprises the N.T. Pre-Church Leadership era. The foundations for the N.T. Church era which is to come are given in these Gospels. By the end of these Gospels we have a good understanding of what led up to the Cross, the central event in the Redemptive Drama. And we begin to realize that Part I of the Redemptive Drama has closed and its great message is done--Salvation has been provided. We are on the verge of Part II, Salvation proclaimed. The

MATTHEW continued

> Gospels with their N.T. Pre-Church Leadership emphasis
> has given us foundational leadership which will launch
> the N.T. Church Leadership Era after the Resurrection
> and Empowerment of the Holy Spirit--the unique
> characteristic of N.T. Church leadership--a decided
> difference from O.T. leadership.

Leadership Lessons

1. **GENRE.** Matthew contains numerous leadership acts and much
   biographical information for which process analysis can be done. This
   biographical information deals both with the disciples and with Jesus
   himself. It contains a few direct leadership contextual units (such as the
   important one, Matthew 20:20-28 which outlines the basics of servant
   leadership). It also has much indirect information which gives teaching
   of Christ which affects character and behavior and can also be applied to
   leaders. Many of these sources could be studied with great profit. I will
   leave most of these detailed studies for Handbook II or for your own self-
   study. I will here give some overall important lessons drawn from
   Matthew.
2. **LEADERSHIP SELECTION.** The Matthew 4:19 passage points out
   the deliberate proactive stance Jesus took regarding leadership selection.
   Effective leaders view leadership selection and development as a priority
   function. Jesus is going to start a movement which will eventuate in an
   institution that will spread around the world. Leadership selection is
   important. Note he recruited from the fringes, in terms of leaders who
   could be shaped, and not from the current religious leadership which had
   very fixed paradigms. Jesus used a basic screening process (see 13:1-23,
   especially 11,12). He taught radical concepts. He clouded many of his
   teachings in parables. He challenged. He demonstrated power that
   would back up his radical ideas. Many could not understand his teaching.
   But those who wanted to understand came for further help. Jesus never
   refused those who came for further help. He explained and clarified. He
   gave them further truth. He tested them on what they heard by giving
   tasks. Those who did them and came back for more became part of his
   following and the potential for leadership. See parabolic teaching for
   screening techniques. See also vignette of Canaanite Woman (15:21-
   28). Of particular import is Jesus emphasis on leadership selection
   praying (see 9:36-38).

MATTHEW continued

3. **RADICAL PERSPECTIVES**. To us, the sermon on the Mount sounds so familiar that we do not recognize just how radical its teachings were to those who heard it for the first time. Leaders who are going to implement change must recruit by promoting challenging, different ideas to potential followers. People were often required to go through paradigm shifts to understand Jesus teaching. That is, they had to throw off old interpretations and accept his new teaching.

4. **SPIRITUAL AUTHORITY.**[1] Matthew clearly traces Jesus' authority. Jesus taught authoritatively (7:29). He backed his teaching with power ministry. Note Matthew's placement of power ministry behind every new narrative presentation. Jesus knew God. He related his knowledge of God and His ways in convincing ways. It is clear from Matthew's ordered treatment that he presents Jesus as one coming with the authority of God. People recognized his authority (8:8, 9). The basic principle of leadership involved is that *Effective Leaders view spiritual authority as a primary power base*. Jesus had no organizational power base through which to work hence spiritual authority was the dominant power base.

5. **LEADERSHIP TRAINING.** Jesus uses screening in selecting and on-the-job training . He uses mentoring techniques: discipling, spiritual guide, coaching, counseling, teaching, sponsoring and modeling. It is in the stream of life that truth is learned and validated. See especially Matthew 10 as part of his training. Emerging leaders must be increasingly released into ministry until they can go it on their own. Matthew 10 is part of that process. Note also the concept of intimacy levels in his mentoring relationships. There was John. There were the three, Peter, James, and John. There was Mary, Martha, and Lazarus. There were the disciples. There were the women financial backers. There were the five hundred. And there were the masses. Leaders will relate to followers at different levels of intimacy and hence empower relationally with different effect.

6. **CONFRONTATION.** Jesus received much opposition from the religious leaders who opposed his new teaching and his authority to give it. Jesus models for his own followers how to approach conflict. He

---

[1]Wrong has helped us see natural power bases for individuals in organizations (force, manipulation, authority, persuasion --where authority breaks down into sub-categories of coercive, inducive, legitimate, competent, personal). Spiritual authority is a hybrid form made up of components: persuasion, legitimate, competent, personal. Spiritual authority is defined as the right to influence conferred upon a leader by followers because of their perceived spirituality of the leader. This perception comes through three major avenues: Godly characteristics in the life, deep experiences with God and knowledge of God and His ways, gifted power. All of these were present in Jesus' ministry. Note the followers have the choice of following or not where spiritual authority is concerned. Many recognized Jesus' spiritual authority and responded. Many chose not.

MATTHEW continued

confronted. He taught. He answered some objections. He challenged
other objections by questioning the underlying ideas behind the
objections.
7. **POWER MINISTRY.** Wimber has popularized the power ministry
concept in recent years.[2] In the breaking open of a new work or new
movement the charismatic leader will assert truth and then must
demonstrate power in order to authenticate it. Jesus authenticated his
authoritative teaching with powerful credentials. See Matthew 8,9 which
follow his great teaching in 5-7. As the movement becomes the church
and the Spirit is given the power authenticator is done by those in the
body who demonstrate power gifts. Apostolic church plants and other
endeavors must be able to demonstrate these gifts if they are to get a
following.[3] The concept of a *power reservoir* (source of available power)
arises when once considers Jesus use of power and his attention to
disciplines (solitude, silence, prayer, fasting). See Luke 5:17. See also
Christ's final comments after coming down from the Mount of
Transfiguration. Note *touched him* Matthew 14:36 and Luke 8:46.
Apparently there is some connection between power and solitude
intimacy with God in prayer.
8. **FOCUS VARIABLE.** Jesus' ministry more than any other leader in the
Bible demonstrates the concept of focus in ministry. He had a long term
perspective and a life purpose that guided him. See especially Matthew
16 (especially verse 21) and Luke 9:51.[4]
9. **AFFIRMATION.** All leaders have a need for affirmation from God
both personally and for ministry. This is not a sign of weakness but of
utter dependence upon God. In its root essence, it is external recognition
from God of the Pauline value of *our sufficiency is of God..* Three times
during Jesus' ministry divine affirmation was given (3:17, 17:5, John
11:42).

---

[2]See John Wimber, **Power Evangelism**, and others.
[3]For purposes of corporate testimony, the gift profile of a local church can be broken up into three major
clusters: power gifts--which authenticate the power and presence of an unseen God, word gifts--which
tell about this God, His demands and His purposes and love gifts--which demonstrate to others the care
and reality of the love of God. There are overlaps in these clusters. Power gifts include: prophecy,
miracles, word of knowledge, word of wisdom, word of faith, healings, discernings of spirits, tongues,
interpretation of tongues. Word gifts include: apostleship, prophecy, teaching, evangelism, exhortation,
pastoral, faith (sometimes). Love gifts include: helps, mercy, pastoral, governments, healings.
[4]The focal variable of a ministry philosophy describes the movement of God to narrow a leader into a
ministry which accomplishes God's purposes through the leader. The focal variable contains such factors
as personality, character, giftedness, ministry structure insights, giftedness and convergence intimations.
A focused life is defined as a life dedicated to narrowly carrying out God's purposes through it by
identifying the major role, life purpose, or ultimate contribution of it, and increasingly prioritizing life's
activities around the focal issues. Ezra in the Old Testament and Paul (besides Jesus) in the New
Testament are the classic representations of a focused life.

MATTHEW continued

10. **FINAL FAITH ACT.** Jesus (like Joseph who also challenged with a final faith act that inspired for long generations) after his resurrection and post-resurrection ministry with the disciples and other followers issues what has become known as the Great Commission (Matthew 28:19,20, Mark 16:15, Luke 24:46-49, John 20:21). This is a prototype of a final faith act. This final culmination of Jesus' ministry is worthy of note leadership wise. One, it contains the promise of the essential ingredient of leadership (the presence of God). Two, it gives a basic focus for all ministries in the N.T. Church Leadership Era to come. Three, it models how closure should be done to a leader's ministry. All that has been done in the leader's life and ministry should form an authoritative backdrop to the closure. Then for the closure there should be blessing (Patriarchal leadership function), there should be a future focus that empowers with hope (inspirational focus), there should be a mandate to act upon (task focus and relational focus in view).

11. **FOUNDATIONAL PRINCIPLE.** The book as a whole illustrates an important leadership principle. Leaders should build upon the past wherever they can. Matthew presents Jesus as the promised Messiah, the culmination of God's Old Testament work. His intentional selection contains many quotes from the Old Testament to show that Jesus is the fulfillment of that revelation. History is important in leadership. Frequently, leaders will give historical perspective in order to validate their present actions.

For Further Leadership Study

Because Matthew is so long and contains so much information on leadership I have just barely touched upon leadership issues in the above 11 major points. Many more could have been selected. I suggest some serious study as given below to fully take advantage of Matthew with regard to leadership lessons.

1. Matthew has a considerable number of parables that need to be studied for leadership lessons. The stewardship parables especially are relevant to leadership.
2. Three major New Testament philosophical models for leadership are introduced in seed form in Matthew--the Harvest Model and the Shepherd Model (9:36-38). The Servant Leader Model is given in Matthew 20:20-28.
3. There are numerous incidents of leadership acts that can be analyzed very profitably for leadership lessons.
4. The leadership style of Jesus should be analyzed by comparative study of the leadership acts.

MATTHEW continued

5. There is much biographical information which yields lessons when analyzed for processing.
6. What place does prayer have in a leader's life and ministry? for intimacy? for power? for vision?
7. What indications, if any, do we have of the 6 barriers and 5 enhancements to leadership in Matthew?
8. What place does speaking a word of faith (e.g. 8:26) have in authenticating a ministry or future perfect thinking?
9. What do we learn about coaching mentoring from Matthew account of sending the twelve (10:1ff)?

Special Comments
The essence of Christianity is given in Matthew. His emphasis in his form of the great commission is on teaching disciples to observe what Christ taught. The essence of Christian practice is seen in Christ's example of life and ministry and in his teaching as given by Matthew. A new world leader has burst upon the scene. His leadership ministry sets the pace. Matthew contains much that will allow us to look into that leadership.

BOOK	**MARK**	**Author:** traditionally, John Mark

Characters — John the Baptist, the prophet who announces Jesus; Jesus, the twelve disciples, a number of individuals in connection with miraculous ministry

Who To/For — Primarily for non-Jewish people (most likely Romans in mind), short, action oriented, accentuates authority and power and noble service, does not begin with connection to Old Testament, does not reference or require understanding of Old Testament to see the good news about Jesus.

Literature Type — Very intentional (shortest of gospels) selection of vignettes during three years of Christ's ministry given in historical narrative

Story Line — Mark begins his story with John's baptism of Jesus. Then there is the temptation followed by the call of Simon, Andrew, James and John. Each of these incidents and the ones to follow are super brief compared to the account of the same incident in Matthew or Luke. The action is swift and brief to the point. Jesus Galilean ministry-many vignettes in quick accounts follows up through chapter 9. Chapter 10 gives the Judean and Perean ministry and chapters 11-16 give the ministry near Jerusalem including the last several days--the crucifixion and resurrection. The incidents chosen show power, action, and service. There are a number of supernatural miraculous type of incident backing up Jesus claims as Son of God.

Structure   I.   (ch 1:1-13)   The Spiritual Nature of Christ Amazing Service.
           II. (ch 1:14-13:37) The Characteristics of Christ's Amazing Service
           III. (ch 14,15)   The Central Fact of Christ's Amazing Service
           IV. (ch 16)   The Continuation of Christ's Amazing Service

MARK continued

Theme   **JESUS, THE SON OF GOD,**
- became the mighty (authoritative) wonder working servant of God and,
- died for all, the supreme act of service.

Key Words   Multitudes (17); Action words indicating no nonsense, getting right with it translating the Greek word eutheos (40+): in KJV words such as straightway, anon, as soon as, forthwith, immediately, shortly. In NIV at once, without delay, began to, then, immediately, as soon as. Key verses include Mark 1:14,15 which gives the central appeal of the book and 10:45 which shows Jesus role in that appeal.

Key Events   Many in common with Matthew and Luke but some unique to Mark only include: Parable of Lamp on Lamp Stand (ch 4), Parable of the Growing Seed (ch 4), Healing of Blind Man at Bethsaida (ch 8).

Purposes
- to present Jesus as a divine servant of God,
- to highlight Jesus divinity from an empirical viewpoint,
- to focus on the supernatural perspective of Jesus' ministry.

Why Important   After clearly stating that Jesus is God this book goes on to say that He is a servant of God. The natural response you would expect is that if someone were God you would expect people to serve him/her. Yet the heart of the Gospel is just this. Jesus came to serve us not the other way around. (10:45) The wonder working God became the servant of God in order to provide the supreme service to humanity--the basis for their reconciliation to God. And so this book goes on to defines issues of what being a servant of God means in terms of its nature, its values, and its results. It shows the sense in which Jesus, the Son of God is a servant of God. Though Equal in nature with God there is one sense in

MARK continued

which Jesus became the servant of God. He became the servant of God in order to create the good news of salvation for human beings. The Servant of God is the savior of humanity. What governed his service? Empathy, suffering, and sacrifice are the values Mark highlights of Jesus servant ministry. He was identified with those he came to save. The results of his service was a finished work of salvation whereby sinful men and women could come to God and be reconciled. And it is this result that is at the heart of the continuation of the movement begun and traced in this book--Go into all the world and get man and women to believe and follow. The model of service has been set--God himself became a servant to bring others to God--we can do no less than follow the model.

Where It Fits Mark occurs in the Redemptive Drama in Chapter 3, Messiah. Along with the other synoptic(viewing Jesus in the same way--historical tracing) Gospels it presents us with the story of Jesus, the Messiah King and savior of the world, whose movement in Palestine among a few disciples comprises the N.T. Pre-Church Leadership era. The foundations for the N.T. Church era which is to come are given in these Gospels. Mark, like each of the synoptic Gospels has its own unique slant on Jesus. It is a book full of leadership source material and its intentional selection warrants close scrutiny and comparative study with the other two Gospels.

Leadership Lessons
1. **GENRE**. Mark, though much briefer than Matthew, does in fact carry the same basic source material for leadership lessons. Since most of the vignettes of Mark are repeated in a somewhat modified form in either Matthew or Luke I will not repeat the lessons mentioned in them. But I will simply give some overall leadership lessons suggested by Mark, as a whole.
2. **MOVEMENT THEORY**. Mark is the briefest of the Gospels. As such it is the easiest to read at one sitting and get a fairly quick overview of the highlights of Jesus' three years of ministry. In retrospect it is easy to see that he was intent on propagating a movement that would last beyond his

MARK continued

earthly ministry. Four out of five of the Gerlach and Hine factors[5] for establishing a movement are seen in Jesus' Ministry. Face-to-face recruitment of new members, personal commitment, an effective ideology, and opposition to the movement from within the old order are all seen. The fifth, a small group structure that can fit into the society and its tied together by personal and ideological ties, was founded in seed form and blossomed in the opening chapters of the Acts.

3. **SERVANT LEADERSHIP.** Marks central theme is Jesus as the authoritative wonder working servant of God. The New Testament servant leadership model introduced in Matthew is expanded conceptually by Jesus ministry in Mark. The thrust of servanthood is vertical and horizontal. Jesus is a servant of God and the nature of his service is to help people. He does this with great power yet caring for those he serves. The image of a servant is not that of a poor and helpless person but one who has power but who uses that power to serve others.

4. **PROPHET WITHOUT HONOR SYNDROME.** Emerging leaders are often not recognized in their own locale (6:1-6). Former paradigms or perceptions are hard to overcome.

5. **VALUES ESSENTIALLY DETERMINE ACTION.** (7:20) Ministry essentially flows out of being.

6. **PARADIGMS.** Mark seems to focus on the concept of paradigms blocking reception of new ideas. (2:21,22; 6:1-6; 9:19, 12:35,37)

For Further Leadership Study
1. Many leadership acts and biographical information sources can be studied for detailed leadership lessons.
2. The parable of the sower (Mark 4:1-9, and explanation) is a paradigm which helps one unlock all the parables.
3. Credible leaders keep their word? What leadership lessons about promises are seen in the narrative about King Herod in Mark 6:14-29?

Special Comments
This book illustrates in depth the great servant passage in Philippians 2:5-11.

---

[5]Gerlach, L.P. and and Hine, V.H., **People, Power, Change: Movements of Social Transformation. New York**: Bobbs-Mderrill Co. (1970). The personal face-to-face recruitment of new members by committed individuals in the movement use their own pre-existing significant social relationships. This similar to McGavran's notion of people movements except that the ties are social rather than ethnic. The commitment is characterized by separating the convert in some significant way from the established order (or his/her place in it), identified with a new set of values, committed to changed patterns of behavior. The ideology must codify values and goals, provide a conceptual framework by which all experiences or events relative to these goal may be interpreted. It must motivate and provide rationale for envisioned changes. It must define the opposition. It must form the basis for unifying the widespread structure.

BOOK	**LUKE**	**Author:** Luke

Characters   Jesus, Zechariah, Elizabeth, parents of John the Baptist, Mary, Jesus' mother, Joseph, his human father, John the Baptist, the twelve disciples, and many in connection with ministry vignettes. Luke includes a number of women, and also gentiles.

Who To/For   Addressed to Theophilus, most likely a Greek nobleman; from the focus of the book and things selected, it appears to be written especially for the Greeks, a cultured people who loved beauty, balance, consistency, symmetry, courage, and ability in a person.

Literature Type   Historical narrative of selected vignettes with an emphasis on the early events leading up to Jesus' birth, one event from his childhood, and many events of the 3 years Jesus Christ's ministry and his crucifixion. There is an unusual number of parables (35) with 19 of them unique to Luke.

Story Line   Luke writing from a Gentile, medical and a missionary perspective and having seen the impact of this Gospel among Gentiles writes to present a logical overview of Jesus' life and ministry so as to attract Gentiles to see him not only as a Jewish Messiah but as a Gentile Savior. Luke is interested in the human race and gives all kind of details that show this interest. It is clear that Luke is showing Jesus as the ideal representative of the human race, one who identifies with it and is interested in all facets of it. The story fills in much more detail than either Matthew or Mark including expanded coverage of the birth events, an early childhood experience, and many incidents and parabolic teaching. The story follows Jesus geographically as well as time wise in his ministry. It gives the Galilean ministry and also the Perean ministry, a mainly Gentile province. It moves on to cover the Jerusalem ministry, the final days.

Structure
I. (ch 1:1-4:13)   Introduction to the Son of Man
II. (ch 4:14-9:50   The Galilean Ministry of the Son of Man
III. (ch 9:51-19:28) The Perean Ministry of the Son of Man
IV. (ch 19:29-24)   The Climax of the Son of Man's Earthly Life

LUKE continued

Theme **JESUS, THE SON OF MAN** (ideal representative of all humankind)
- identified with all humankind, Jewish and Gentiles, men and women and
- became the savior of all humankind in order to lift human beings to their fullest potential (a relationship with God and a meaningful life).

Key Words Son of Man (26), all (seven different Greek words are translated by English all)(150+), sinner (16),

Key Events Many, but nearly 1/2 of Luke is unique and not seen in Matthew or Mark including the sending of the 70 (in a Gentile region), miracles which especially emphasize those of healing and mercy, revealing the sympathetic, human side of Christ

Purposes
- to present Jesus as the ideal human being who fully identified with the human race in becoming its Savior,
- to give a historical record of Jesus' life which is especially contextualized for Gentiles,
- to give the positive side of Jesus' ministry, glad acceptance of His person and work (contrast with Matthew's which gives a sad rejection).

Why Important Luke presents Christ as the perfect human being, the great teacher, the intellectual who understands human nature, and the purest of religious persons. The Jew was characterized by deep religious feeling (Matthew appeals to them). The Roman by strength of will for action (Mark appeals to them), and the Greek by great intellectual power. To the Greek people are Homer, and Plato and Aristotle--great thinkers. The Greeks were the representatives of universal humanity, and the great ideal toward which they worked was the perfect person. But by making their gods in their own image, they made imperfect gods who had vices as well as virtues. So their religion was unspiritual and debasing. Their hearts were not satisfied--restless and despairing. The presentation of Christ in Luke's gospel has in view these characteristics and needs. Jesus is seen as a person of wisdom, courage, ability, balanced character. He identified himself with all

LUKE continued

humans--the fallen and despised, the bereaved, the despondent, the diseased. He was a sociable man. We see Jesus in all kind of social situations. He is a person of cosmopolitan interest. The whole human race is in view, Jews and Gentiles, women and children. The human perfection the Greeks sought is thus seen to be fulfilled in Jesus. The human perfection which they sought is here manifested, their intellectual hunger could be satisfied, and their religious aspirations may now be purified and realized.

Where It Fits   Luke occurs in the Redemptive Drama in Chapter 3, Messiah. Along with the other synoptic(viewing Jesus in the same way--historical tracing) Gospels it presents us with the story of Jesus, the Messiah King and savior of the world, whose movement in Palestine among a few disciples comprises the N.T. Pre-Church Leadership era. The foundations for the N.T. Church era which is to come are given in these Gospels. Luke, like each of the synoptic Gospels has its own unique slant on Jesus. It is a book full of leadership source material and its intentional selection warrants close scrutiny and comparative study with the other two Gospels.

Leadership Lessons
1. **SUPERNATURAL POWER**. Jesus is presented in the Gospel of Luke as the ideal representative of humankind. He was fully human. As such, Jesus will need God's power in his ministry just as we did. Luke, the only Gentile writer who has gone through major paradigm shifts concerning the Holy Spirit (see Acts presentations of the Holy Spirit ministry) writes post-reflectivel viewing Jesus' ministry and uses terminology fitting the Apostolic age given in the Acts. He focuses on supernatural power, using terminology like filled with the Spirit, in the power of the Spirit, the power of the Lord was present for healing, because power was coming from Him for healing, power has gone out from me, the finger of God, Jesus' prayer ministry and extended times of solitude (notice the unusual mention of times of solitude--power reservoir concept). The basic lessons for leaders are at least two: a. Ministry which is effective can not be done without the power of the Holy Spirit. b. Solitude times are times of renewal and infilling of God's presence and power.

LUKE continued

2. **COMMINICATION.** Luke presents Jesus as the master communicator. Luke has some of the most powerful parables and he shows how Jesus uses them to communicate with impact.
3. **INCARNATIONAL MODEL.** Jesus is presented in Luke as the ideal reprersentative who identified with all humanity--Jews, Gentiles, men, women, rich, poor, people of high status and of low. Leaders who want to be effective must incarnate their ministries (contextualize them as well) with the people they are seeking to reach.
4. **FOUNDATION CRITERION FOR A MINISTRY.** In a unique passage, Luke 10:17-20, Jesus gives a fundamental principle that should undergird all leaders. More important than success in ministry is the relationship of the leader to God. Ministry essentially flows out of being not doing.
5. **PRAYER MINISTRY.** More than any of the other Gospel writers Luke emphasizes the importance of Jesus' prayer life to his ministry. Luke demonstrates the *Ministry Prayer Principle* (If God has called you to a ministry then He has called you to pray for it) and the *Prayer Encouragement Principle* (Get your prayers from God and tell your people your are specifically praying for them (22:31-34).

For Further Leadership Study
1. Luke's parables should be studied for communication principles.
2. Luke has a number of leadership acts not occurring in Mark or Matthew. These should be studied for leadership lessons.
3. Luke gives biographical information which should be studied for processing.

Special Comments
Luke must be studied because in depth because of its large amount of unique material. The concept of Jesus as the ideal representative of the human race highlighs Luke. It carries to the highest form the teaching of Psalm 8 on the son of man and of the kinsman redeemer of Ruth.

BOOK	**JOHN**	**Author:** John

Characters   Jesus, John the Baptist, Andrew, Simon Peter, Philip, Nathanael, Jesus' mother, Nicodemus, Samaritan Woman, Lame man at Bethesda Pool, Woman caught in adultery, the Pharisees, Man born blind, Lazarus, Mary, Martha

Who To/For   For all who might follow Jesus

Literature Type   Historical narrative of selected vignettes

Story Line   After nearly a lifetime of following Jesus, John reflects back and assembles what are to him important events and details from Jesus life. The selection is with a specific purpose--John 20:30,31 *of the many things that Jesus did I have selected some crucial ones that you might come to see that Jesus is indeed God and that you might trust in him for the eternal life that he gives.* John introduces his story of Jesus with a philosophical explanation. Jesus is the incarnate God who was recognized by John the Baptist. Following this recognition disciples are called. Then John begins to select incidents that will answer three questions: **Who is Jesus? What is faith? What is life?** Generally the incidents are organized time wise. The incidents are sometimes miracles. Sometimes they are dialogues with individuals or groups. Many of the incidents reveal Jesus in intimate conversations with people. But all do something to answer the three questions. There is a long section which relates his intimate time with his disciples just before Jesus is to be crucified. There is a post resurrection story about restoring Peter.

Structure   The book is not so much structured analytically, that is, in sections relating to one another, as it is in terms of intentional selection to carry out the purpose of the book. The narratives do flow in terms of chronological time.

    I. (ch 1)   Jesus, the Eternal God, Manifest in the Flesh
   II. (ch 2-12) Jesus, the Eternal God, Manifest To Others
 III. (ch 13-17) Jesus, the Eternal God, Manifest To His Own
 IV. (ch 18-21) Jesus, the Eternal God, Final Manifestations

JOHN continued

Theme   **JESUS, THE ETERNAL GOD,**
  * became a human being,,
  * revealed the Father and His love, and
  * offered eternal life (salvation) to whoever trust Him.

Key Words   Father (121), love (57), world (78), Son (40+), believe
(98), life (52)

Key Events   many (everything is intentionally selected)

Purposes
  * to present Jesus as the eternal God, who became human in order to relate people to the Father,
  * to appeal to people to trust in Jesus as their Savior,
  * to emphasize the motivating force of love in the Gospel story,
  * to bring to completeness the unveiling of Jesus as God that is suggested in the synoptic Gospels.

Why Important   This book unveils God to us. In it we see that no one, but Jesus, has intimacy with God so as to reveal God as He did. We see the nature of God (a loving being seeking His own) and the laws that govern His activity (grace and truth) fleshed out in a human being who relates to people. We have illustration after illustration showing these divine principles in action. We see that we can be related to this God. We see how--by believing and committing ourselves to Him. We see the touch of eternal life that is generated when this happens--how new life comes, a purpose and meaning in living. We have evidence that convinces us of the unveiling being given in the book. There is certainly information given, information that moves the heart and is wrapped up in human experience. But the final appeal is to the will. Human beings can choose or reject this evidence and this person.

Where It Fits   John is grouped in this manual with the synoptic Gospels for ease of comparative study but it, though covering events and analysis of Pre-Church Leadership, is written long after the fact of that transition time. John, unlike the other Gospels, was written not to trace the

JOHN continued

historic emergence of Jesus but to philosophically teach who he was, what he came to do, and how people can respond. It was written at the close of the first century in light of where the church was at that time and its need to interpret the basic facts of the Gospels which gave Jesus history. It is a post-event reflection back by one of the participants. Its intentional selection shows careful thought.

Leadership Lessons

1. **PARADIGMS**. This is a book about paradigms.[6] There is difficulty in paradigm shifts because of entrenched old paradigms. Leadership frequently has vested interest in old paradigms and therefore oppose new paradigms and their implications. John intentionally selects materials that will show the new paradigm being introduced about who Jesus was and what Jesus did. He shows that it will take a supernatural breakthrough to see the new paradigm. The conflict passages show how the entrenched paradigms with vested interest oppose the new. A negative response to a paradigm will drive one deeper into the old paradigm (12:37-41). The contrast is also given with many who go through the paradigm shift and see Jesus for who he is. Need is the key driving force for accepting a new paradigm and is the main lesson for leaders in this book. Leaders must create or utilize need in followers in order to get new paradigms accepted.

2. **INTIMACY WITH GOD**. John makes it clear that intimacy with God is the secret to Jesus' leadership. He knows the Father. He sees the Father work and He works. He is one with the Father. John presents union life (John 14, 15, John 17) in metaphor which certain people will sense quickly (Paul uses conceptual teaching which others will grasp).

3. **FINISHING WELL**. Jesus gives the essence of finishing well, the underlying focus of the six characteristics we have identified previously. The essence is indicated in Jesus intimate prayer with the Father in John 17. See whole context but notice the phrase, *I have brought you glory on earth by completing the work you gave me to do.*

---

[6]See the position paper, **The Paradigm Shift** (God's Breakthrough Processing That Opens New Leadership Vistas), available via Barnabus Publishers. A paradigm is a controlling perspective which allows one to perceive and understand REALITY. .A paradigm shift is the change of a controlling perspective so that one perceives and understands REALITY in a different way.

JOHN continued

For Further Leadership Study
1. John intentionally traces the conflict with the *Jews*. Extended passages show Jesus in confrontation with them. Study the passages to see what principles can be derived for leadership in conflict situations.
2. Numerous leadership acts are included in John and should be studied for leadership lessons.
3. Biographical information also is plentiful and should be studied for processing.

Special Comments
John was written long after the actual time of the events and details it describes. Reflective thoughts long after an event usually will highlight the essential and most important things that remain influential in one's mind. Such is the case with John's Gospel. We come face to face with the essential issues on who Jesus is and how we are to respond to him. Each item included in this book has been chosen with special care. We should study each asking the three questions, Who is Jesus? What is life? What is faith? The book is meant to move us emotionally and volitionally even more so than just to inform us. Philosophically this is one of the most challenging books in the New Testament. While it has so much that appears simple and easy to understand on first reading it also contains much that is profound.

BOOK	JAMES	Author: James, brother of Jesus

Characters   none

Who To/For   To Jewish Christians who were scattered abroad

Literature Type   exhortive teaching emphasizing practical application of Christian teaching to everyday life

Story Line   None

Structure

I.	(ch 1)	True Faith Tested By Temptation
II.	(ch 2)	True Faith Manifested in Wise Living
III.	(ch 3)	True Faith Manifested in Wise Words
IV.	(ch 4-5:6)	True Faith Manifested in Underlying Motivations
V.	(ch 5:6-20)	True Faith Endures and Prays

Theme   **CHRISTIAN FAITH** which has the ring of authenticity,
- is tested and strengthened by temptation,
- is manifested in life style,
- is illustrated by control of one's words,
- is rooted in character with proper underlying motivations, and
- waits for the Lord's coming with expectant prayer answering faith.

Key Words   faith (16), works (15)

Key Events   none

Purposes
- to show that the Christian faith that is real manifests itself in a life of outward godliness and good works,
- to illustrate both negatively and positively what faith isn't and what it is,
- to show how Jesus' teachings were applied in church settings.

Why Important   Shows how the teaching of Christ was applied. This very practical book is the seedbed for Christian ethics. It illustrates how teaching affects lifestyle. This book shows that faith is not real if it does not work out in life. As Morgan implies (see Handbook page 272), true

JAMES continued

Christian faith produces life that corresponds to God's will; while life contrary to God's will denies true faith.

Where It Fits This is one of the earliest of books of the New Testament Church leadership Era. It is in Chapter 4 of the Redemptive Drama, The Church.

Leadership Lessons

1. **GENRE.** The book of James contains only indirect material with the one exception of 3:1,2 which deals with leadership responsibility and possibly 3:13-18. which deals with wisdom a frequently seen gift, or natural ability, or acquired skill of a leader. It is therefore dealing largely with Christian character, much of which applies to Christian leaders as well. I will not detail any of these lessons since any standard exegetical/practical commentary will list many of these lessons and values for Christian character.

2. **BALANCE.** Whereas transition times, apostolic breakthroughs, and new works often need a strong emphasis on supernatural power (see Gospels, Acts) James points out a balance. On-going testimony requires a large dose of love gifts. It is the practical application of Christianity to life's situations which demonstrates the reality of faith in an unseen God. Established works will need love gifts. *Leaders need to realize that love gifts carry great power and impact just as the more spectacular supernatural power gifts do.*

3. **PARADIGMS.** James perspective on the historical story when compared with Paul's use of the same historical context show how paradigms control what is seen of reality. James is writing from a very practical application of Christianity. Paul is explaining a theoretical understanding of salvation. *Different paradigms can serve equally well for users of them.*

4. **STATUS/PRESTIGE.** A major leadership stumbling block is that of giving special status/privilege to those having power. James warns against this. Frequently, people are put into church leadership because of their money or secular standing and not because they meet spiritual requirements. *Leaders need to be wary of dangers involved in leadership selection for wrong reasons.*

5. **COMMUNICATION.** James confirms the emphasis in Proverbs of the importance of controlling one's words. *Leaders because of their visibility and ascribed power impact others by what they say even in private conversations and hence they should be especially careful.*

JAMES continued

6. **SPIRITUAL WARFARE.** James gives some information about personal spiritual warfare. Resistance of Satanic influence is coupled with submission to God. Both must be done deliberately.
7. **PRAYER OF FAITH.** Elijah, one of the great Old Testament leaders, is used as an example of effective prayer. Leaders need effective praying in their ministries.
8. **ELDERS/ HEALING PRAYER.** The 5:13-18 passages points out the importance of corporate leadership in healing prayer and necessitates some basic prerequisites to this effective praying.
9. The 5:19,20 highlights the basic mentoring accountability function among lateral mentors.

For Further Leadership Study
1. Study the Old Testament passages on Elijah for lessons on prayer.
2. Study the 1:12-15 passage to learn about the importance of testing and the stages involved in temptation.
3. One of the barriers to leaders finishing well relates to money. James has several passages warning about money. These should be studied as warnings by leaders who don't want to be trapped by that barrier.

Special Comments
The structure is difficult in James. There is subtle weaving of positive and negative illustrations which are symptomatic of larger issues. The thrust is not so much on analytical learning but on emotional, volitional, and affective learning. James seeks to move the hearer to feel, respond, and act.

BOOK	ACTS	**Author:** Luke

Characters   Jesus, Peter, John, the Sanhedrin, Barnabas, Ananias and Sapphira, Stephen, Phillip, the Ethiopian Eunuch, Saul (Paul), Ananias, Aeneas, Dorcas, Cornelius, James the brother of John, Herod, James, John Mark, Silas, Lydia, Timothy, Priscilla, Aquila, Apollos, Eutychus, Felix, Festus, Agrippa, Bernice

Who To/For   addressed to Theophilis, a high gentile official; but for all who are interested in the beginning of the church

Literature Type   Historical narrative generally flowing chronologically but tracing the expansion of the church beyond the Jews

Story Line   About half of the book tells of the formation of the church in Jerusalem and its early expansion to Jews, Samaritans, and finally to Gentiles. The latter half of the book traces the breakout of the Gospel to Gentiles in Asia and Europe. Acts begins with Jesus' post resurrection ministry to the disciples and his Ascension to heaven. Then the disciples are gathered at Jerusalem praying when the Pentecost event, the giving of the Holy Spirit to the church happens and Peter gives a great public sermon. Early church life is described. Peter and John imbued with power heal a lame man at the temple gate and are put in prison. They are threatened and released. An incident with Ananias and Sapphira shows the power and presence of the Holy Spirit. Stephen an early church servant has a strong witness and is martyred for it. General persecution on the church breaks out. The believers are scattered and preached the gospel where ever they go. Phillip, another early church servant leads an Ethiopian palace administrator to Christ and has ministry in Samaria. Saul, the persecutor of Christians, is saved on the road to Damascus. Peter demonstrates Godly power in several miraculous events. Peter is divinely chosen to preach the Gospel to a Gentile, Cornelius. Herod kills James and imprisons Peter. Peter is miraculously delivered. The story line now switches to follow the missionary efforts of Barnabas and Paul (formerly Saul) to Cyprus and Asian minor. It then goes on to follow Paul's efforts which go further into Asia

ACTS continued

minor and Greece. Paul makes a return visit to Jerusalem where he is accused by the Jewish opposition in Jerusalem. Eventually after several delays and hearings he is ordered to Rome. The book ends with the exciting journey to Rome, including a shipwreck.

Structure

There are seven divisions in Acts each concluding with a summary verse.[7] The summary verses: 2:47b, 6:7, 9:31, 12:24, 16:5, 19:20, 28:30,31

I.	(ch 1-2:47)	The Birth of the Church in Jerusalem
II.	(ch 3-6:7)	The Infancy of the Church in Jerusalem
III.	(ch 6:8-9:31)	The Spread of the Church into Judea, Galilee, Samaria
IV.	(ch 9:32-12:24)	The Church Doors Open to the Gentiles
V.	(ch 13-16:5)	The Church Spreads to Asia Minor
VI.	(ch 16:6-19:20)	The Church Gains a Foothold in Europe
VII.	(Ch 19:21-28)	The Travels of the Church's First Missionary To Rome (The Church on Trial in its Representative Paul)

Theme

THE GROWTH OF THE CHURCH

- which spreads from Jerusalem to Judea to Samaria and the uttermost parts of the earth,
- is seen to be of God,
- takes place as Spirit directed people present a salvation centered in Jesus Christ, and
- occurs among all peoples, Jews and Gentiles.

Key Words

Holy Spirit (Ghost) (54); name (referring to Jesus Christ) (30+); Peter (50+), Paul or Saul (140+)

Key Events

Jesus' Ascension, Pentecost, Cornelius' conversion, Paul's conversion, 1st Missionaries out of Antioch, churches established in Asia minor, Jerusalem council, churches

---

[7]In linguistic theory, these are called discourse markers. A discourse marker signals the end of large structure of linguistic material larger than paragraphs. In English we do not have good names for units larger than paragraphs. We use sections, divisions, parts etc. to describe large units. The identification of a discourse marker helps to authenticate the breakdown of a large book into meaningful divisions.

ACTS continued

> established in Greece and Europe, Paul tried before Felix, Festus, and Agrippa

Purposes
- to show the legitimacy and the process whereby Christianity spread beyond Judea all the way to Rome and made salvation available to all people everywhere,
- to show the continuity of authority and power from Jesus through Peter and the Apostles to Paul,
- to demonstrate the good character and innocence of the central figure (Jesus) and the leaders of the Christian movement,
- to show the fact that Christianity was not hostile to true Judaism but rather was an outgrowth of its central features under the direction and activity of the God of the Jews through their Messiah by the Holy Spirit,
- to examine the nature, the cause of the hostility, and the process by which there came to be a gulf between the Jewish leadership and the Christians.

Why Important   This book in one sense is apologetic. In fulfilling its purposes it establishes that the leading characters of the movement were basically law abiding citizens. Christianity's bad reputation (founder crucified as a Roman criminal, early leaders jailed, riots where ever it goes) comes from those who were jealous of the movement or were threatened by it economically. It answers such questions as: Can a person who is a law-abiding Roman citizen consider Christianity to be true and legitimate? How does Christianity relate to Judaism? Why don't Jews and Christians continue to worship together in the temple and the synagogue since they both claim to worship the same God? How did the separation between Jews and Christians come about? The book also traces the movement begun by Jesus among Jews as it expands to the Gentiles and shows that incorporation of Gentiles into Christianity was of God's doing. Paul and Peter are both authenticated as apostolic. This is the pivotal book in the Drama of Redemption. From Genesis on God has been moving to reconcile all humanity to Himself. The Jews as a channel in the Old Testament failed to accomplish these purposes. But God now forms

ACTS continued

a channel, the church, which will be a blessing to all the nations. In fact, its major purpose is to do just that. This book tells how that happened and connects the church to all of God's preparatory work in bringing the Messiah.

Where It Fits   Though written much later the book of Acts covers the earliest history of Chapter 4, The Church, in the Redemptive Drama. It deals with the N.T. Church leadership era including its spill over into the Gentile world.

Leadership Lessons
1. **GENRE.** The book of Acts contains numerous biographical vignettes which yield excellent sources of process analysis. There are numerous leadership acts. Acts 20:13-38 is a direct leadership passage. I will leave analysis of these to individual detailed studies. Overall lessons seen in the book as a whole or special contributions of specific lessons will be given here.
2. **TRANSITION LESSONS.** When moving from one leadership era to another there are usually numerous lessons associated with the turmoil, new structures being discovered, functions of leadership, paradigms being changed, etc. Acts is such a transition book. Acts is introducing the New Testament Leadership Era which is very different in leadership issues from the N.T. Pre-Church Leadership Era. Some of these topics which will yield specific lessons are indicated below:
   a. Going from a movement to an institution (structures) that will carry it beyond just a Jewish application.
   b. Face-to-face to Large Recruitment
   c. Commitment levels--Barnabas contrasted with Ananias and Sapphira Incident (issue of truth and integrity involved in commitment)
   d. Continual Structural changes (Jewish, modified Jewish--add service leadership, contextualized Gentile, contextualized mission structure, contextualized local church structures)
   e. Persecution--Opposition is real; solidifies movement; martyrs seal importance of commitment; sovereignly spreads movement
   e. New Paradigms (Acts 10 Gospel for all; Acts 13 Proactive Sending Structure; Acts 15 Contextualized Theology all right; 2nd Missionary Journey--local church structures and leadership)
   f. Wide spread decentralized loosely connected local churches geographically spread throughout Palestine, Asia Minor, Greece, Rome: ideology the major tie.

ACTS continued

In transition times, *leaders will face added complexity in their leadership.* The rate of change can be increased. Change dynamics[8] are affected drastically by the complexity of transition times.

2. **CENTRALITY OF WORD BASED MINISTRY.** Luke makes it clear that the Word of God (Old Testament, revelatory, and New Testament in the Making) is central for the spread of the church movement. He continually points out in sermons or testimonies how well the leaders knew and used the word of God. The church meetings concentrate on studying the word. See Peter's sermons; Acts 2:42; 6:7 Notice the metonymy which emphasizes the spread of Christianity and the central place of the Word in it (same for 12:24, 19:20); See Stephen's speech; See Phillip's witness (especially 8:35ff); Paul's public teaching (e.g. 13:16ff); Acts 17:11; Acts 18:25; Acts 19:8-12; Acts 20:32. Leaders today must have this value--*God's word is central to my ministry.*

3. **SUPERNATURAL POWER**. Luke emphasizes the ministry of the Holy Spirit in power. See Acts 1:8 promise of power from on high; Acts 2, coming of Holy Spirit; Acts 3, Peter and John healing the cripple, Acts 4:8, 31; 5:12-16; 5:32; 6:5, 8, 19:11 and many others. In a transition time, messages must be backed by supernatural power in order to gain a hearing. Particularly is this true of societies which are used to power being a natural outcome of religion. In the earliest stages of Apostolic work the power cluster of gifts dominates followed by word gifts and love gifts. As the Gospel gains a foothold the word cluster dominates with love second and power occasionally. As the work matures love gifts will move toward an equal level with word gifts and power gifts will be used for critical breakthroughs. *Leaders need to be aware of gift cluster profiles and how they change over time. Leaders will need to be able to see power demonstrated in their ministry.*

4. **APOSTOLIC MINISTRY.** Ephesians 2:20 indicates the foundational ministry that apostles and prophets have. Acts illustrates the basic kinds of functions or characteristics of Apostolic ministry. Some of the Apostolic functions include: a. demonstration of power in order to authenticate God's work, b. evaluation of new works for genuineness, c. appointing of leadership, d. impartation of gifts, e. evaluation and preservation of orthodoxy and orthopraxy. *Apostles (and prophets) carry special leadership authority and responsibility.*

5. **PROCESSING.** The Acts illustrates a number of classic processing examples. a. Double Confirmation (see Paul and Ananias, ch 9),

---

[8]See **Bridging Strategies--Leadership Perspectives for Introducing Change** published by Barnabas Publishers. This manual introduces change dynamics principles.

ACTS continued

    b. Destiny Revelation (see Paul, Acts 9, 22, 26) see also 16:8), c.
Obedience /Integrity Check (positive and negative patterns, see Barnabas
and Ananias/Sapphira--Acts 4), c. ministry challenge (see Paul/Barnabas
in Acts 13 and Paul in Acts 16), d. spiritual warfare (see Paul 16:16ff),
e. ministry affirmation (see Paul Acts 18:9-11). There are others but this
will suffice to indicate the importance of Acts for illustrating major
process items. *Leaders should be aware of processes God uses to shape
leaders and the patterns through which God takes leaders.*
6. **MENTORING.** Acts illustrates a number of important mentor
relationships.[9] Barnabas sponsors Paul and links him into the center of
Jewish Christianity. He also links him into the major Gentile Christian
center. There are numerous downward examples of mentoring seen in
Paul's ministry. Paul particularly models the whole concept of ministry
being personal. *Effective leaders recognize the importance of relational
empowerment.*
7. **PARADIGMS/ PARADIGM SHIFTS.** Like the book of John, Acts is a
major source of study for understanding how paradigm shifts occur. Acts
2 (empowerment) , 7 (resistance to new paradigms because of vested
interests in old paradigms, softening of Saul preparing for paradigm shift
to come), 9 (experiential breakthrough), 10 (gospel for all) , 11 (how to
communicate a paradigm shift to others who haven't experience it), 13
(power encounter), and 15 (contextualization) all contain very important
paradigm shift material. Kinds of paradigm shifts include cognitive,
experiential, and volitional. Causes instigating paradigm shifts seen in
Acts include: experiencing supernatural power, receiving visions, power
encounter, dialogic give and take with those having experienced
paradigms shifts with those not.

For Further Leadership Study
1. Study each of the discourse markers (2:47b, 6:7, 9:321, 12:24, 16:5,
    19:20, 28:30,31)for distinct contribution to understanding the spread of
    Christianity.
2. Study Acts to identify specifically Apostleship and Prophetical functions.
3. Study the paradigm passages for lessons about paradigm shifts. Acts 10
    is particularly instructive in identifying stages.
4. Study the supernatural passages to understand when and how experienced
    and to establish absolutes, guidelines, and suggestions concerning power
    and the Holy Spirit. Be sure to study these historical passages along with

---

[9]See **The Mentor Handbook** published by Barnabas Publishers which details nine basic types of mentors:
discipler, spiritual guide, coach, counselor, teacher, sponsor, contemporary models, historical models,
and divine contacts. Almost all of these are seen in brief form in Acts.

ACTS continued

comparative teaching in epistles and particularly from Paul's viewpoint in
his later life as he instructs Timothy. Paul has experienced great power in
his life and ministry (supernatural visions, deliverance power, power
encounters, healings including raising from the dead, etc.). Yet notice
what he says to Timothy about leadership. What place do all these things
have in his mentoring of Timothy?

5. Study Acts 7 to see intentional selection of Stephen as he reviews Old
Testament history in a nutshell. What is important? What does he
include? What does he not include? What implications for leadership are
involved in this intentional selection? Study especially the summary
statements of the various Old Testament leaders particularly noting his
Ultimate Testimony for them.

6. Study Acts for illustrations of spiritual gifts. This is helpful when
teaching on spiritual gifts to emerging leaders.

7. Study the direct contextual source of leadership, Paul's Farewell Address
to the Ephesian Elders (Acts 20:13-38) for its very important specific
leadership lessons.

8. Acts 15 is a particularly important leadership act with various leaders
involved in the influence process. It should be studied carefully to
identify lessons.

9. There are many communication lessons available from the numerous
public messages and private conversations included in Acts. There are
also important cross-cultural communication lessons involved in some of
these passages.

10. What is the importance of the Kingdom of God in the spread of the
Church? When is it mentioned? Why?

Special Comments

In addition to its own purposes the book of Acts gives background
information that is helpful in understanding the Pauline letters. Acts was not
listed in the 20 most important books to be studied for leadership. It should
have been. It is a must for it ushers in the New Testament Church
Leadership Era of which we are a part.

BOOK	**1 THESSALONIANS** **Author:** Paul

Characters   People involved: Paul, Silas, Timothy

Who To/For   To the young church at Thessalonica, Greece

Literature Type   a letter containing teaching and exhortation

Story Line   none

Structure   Each chapter follows a cyclical structure of an explanation or teaching with exhortation followed by a reminder of Christ's return. See return passages: 1:10, 2:19; 3:13; 4:13-18; 5:1-11, 23

     I.   (ch 1)   The Thessalonican Church: Symptoms of Genuine Apostolic Work; Waiting for Christ's Return

     II.   (ch 2)   The Thessalonican Church: Paul's Foundational Ministry; Reward At Christ's Return

     III.   (ch 3)   The Thessalonican Church: Timothy's Report of Their State; Blameless and Holy At the Lord's Return

     IV.   (ch 4)   The Thessalonican Church: Exhortations As to Moral Life Style; Expanded Teaching on 2nd Coming--The Rapture

     V.   (ch 5)   The Thessalonican Church: Aware and Ready and Corporately Alert; Kept by God's power for the Return

Theme   **THE SECOND COMING OF THE LORD,**
- was a value founded in the Thessalonican church,
- is a true motivation for apostolic work,
- provides a goal toward which to endure,
- will result in a present concern for pure living, and
- will fill you with a joyful expectation.

Key Words   coming of the Lord, return of the Lord, day of the Lord (altogether 6 times); comfort or encouragement (6);

Key Events   A future event is describe via exhortation and teaching about it: the day of the Lord (introduced in Joel and

1 THESSALONIANS continued

elaborated on in Zephaniah) is seen here to involve Christ's return, be a day of judgment where motivations will be searched out, and Christ's own will be united with him for ever.

Purposes
- to clarify teaching on the second coming,
- to encourage those whose believer relatives had died before Christ returned,
- to emphasize the return of Christ as an ever present motivating factor for the Church,
- to introduce the notion of the day of the Lord as synonymous with Christ's coming and a day of judgment and reward,
- to vindicate Paul's apostolic ministry and motivations while at Thessalonica,
- to affirm the Thessalonica church while at the same time exhorting them on to continued progress.

Why Important   This book connects the second coming of the Lord with the day of the Lord given in prophecies of Joel and Zephaniah. It helps focus the church with expectancy to the future when Christ will return. This book is meant to encourage. There is coming a new age in which human history will be perfected. This book says that new age will be ushered in by Christ's personal return. It connects an expectant view of this great triumphal return with present Christian experience. Human nature is built so as to need a future hope. Without it there is but pessimism and despair. This book gives us an ultimate hope, a motivation to live, love, and labor always with a view to the return of Christ.

Where It Fits   This is the earliest of the Pauline epistles and occurs in Phase B, Gentile, of the New Testament Church Leadership Era. This of course is in Chapter 4, The Church, in the Redemptive Drama.

1 THESSALONIANS continued

Leadership Lessons
1. **GENRE.** 1 Thessalonians contains mainly indirect source information for leadership lessons. It does however contains many illustrations of leadership values and ideas seen in other bible books. One passage does deal with spiritual gifts which is an important leadership concept and one passage deals directly with followership, an important leadership idea.
2. **PERSPECTIVE.** The book as a whole teaches the importance of having perspective. Paul is giving a future perfect long term perspective yet one which reaches back (beforemath) with powerful implications for present living. Here the day of the Lord (a strong Old Testament teaching dealing with God's justice and vindication concerning accountability) is identified with the second coming of Christ. Leaders constantly need a broader perspective. *A leader's view of the return of Christ should play an important motivational undergirding for ministry.* It should bring hope as well as influence present conduct.
3. **INFLUENCE MEANS.** Leadership style[10] refers to the way a leader uses his/her authority as a leader to influence followers. Three Pauline styles are identified in this epistle. One of them, the *Father-Guardian style* (2:10-12), is a directive style which refers to a leadership style similar to a parent-child relationship and has as its major concern protection and encouragement for followers. The other two, are non-directive styles including imitation modeling (1:6,10) which refers to the conscious act of modeling as a means for influencing followers. The *nurse style* (2:7-9) is a behavior style characterized by gentleness and sacrificial service and loving care which indicates that a leader has given up rights in order not to impede the nurture of those following him/her. Early on in Paul's ministry we are introduced to the notion that he will be a multi-style leader and will adjust style to fit the needs and maturity level of the followers. The major power base used by Paul is spiritual authority and persuasion.

---

[10]In most of the Pauline epistles I will refer to influence means and talk about leadership style as well as power bases used in influencing followers. Leadership style refers to the individual expression a leader utilizes to function in his/her leadership role. This individual expression includes his/her methodology for handling crises, problem solving, and decision making as well as relationships to peers and followers and influence techniques (especially persuasion methods). Leadership style embraces such categories as how the leader: motivates followers, relates to followers, is perceived in his/her role by followers, solves group problems, attempts to bring about obedience among followers, resolves differences. Ten Pauline leadership styles include: Highly directive--apostolic, confrontation, father-initiator; directive--obligation persuasion, father-guardian, maturity appeal; non directive--nurse, imitator; and highly non-directive--consensus, indirect. See **Coming to Conclusions on Leadership** Styles available through Barnabas Publishers. Helen Doohan has done an outstanding study on Pauline leadership including the evaluation of leadership style. See Doohan's **Leadership in Paul.**

1 THESSALONIANS continued

4. **BALANCED CHURCH MODEL.** The Pauline affirmation formula (1:3) contains the results of a corporate ministry. The results faith, love, and hope are loosely tied to the functions of the three gift-clusters: power, love, word. The Thessalonian church was a balanced church. Paul mentions all three results in giving testimony to their corporate effect on themselves and others. Notice in other epistles he does not necessarily give all three affirmation labels; sometimes 2 or 1 or maybe none (Galatian).

5. **MENTORING.** Contemporary models (1:6) always play an important role in the early stages of young Christians. Young Christians are challenged by Christian models. And they see that Christianity can be real.

6. **TRANSPARENCY.** (2:3-6). Paul here models a characteristic that is important for those who use relational empowerment and have very personal ministries. See also 2 Timothy 3:10ff. A major leadership lessons observed in comparative study of leaders is: EFFECTIVE LEADERS RECOGNIZE THE IMPORTANCE OF RELATIONAL EMPOWERMENT IN THEIR MINISTRIES. Transparency is vital to this principle.

7. **WORD CENTERED MINISTRY.** It is clear that Paul exercised a strong word centered ministry. See (2:13) for an example of gifted power involving word gifts.

8. **REALITY OF SPIRITUAL WARFARE** (2:18; 3:5) Paul does not major on hunting out demonic activity in every issue but he does reckon with its power as being real.

9. **PRAYER MINISTRY** (1:2,3; 2:13, 3:10-13, 5:17) It is clear that along with a strong word centered ministry, Paul had a strong prayer ministry undergirding his ministry. He illustrates in this epistle the basic ministry prayer principle: *If God has called you to a ministry then He has called you to pray for that ministry.*

10. **FOLLOWERSHIP.** 1 Thessalonians 5:12,13 gives a followership exhortation. Followers are to hold their leaders in high regard. They are to know them. They are to respect them. The Greek word, proistamenous, is also translated as ruling over you. This could be a leadership gift.

11. **SPIRITUAL GIFTS PASSAGE.** 1 Thessalonians 5:19-22 is one of the numerous minor passages touching on spiritual gifts. Indicated in the passage are two gifts: prophecy, and discerning of spirits (by implication).

1 THESSALONIANS continued

For Further Leadership Study
1. The list of exhortations in 1 Thessalonians 5:12-20, are particularly instructive as they are a leader seeking to directly influence behavior of followers.
2. Who wrote this book? What are the leadership implications of Paul's gesture of sharing the credit for writing this book?

Special Comments
This is the first of the Pauline letters. It is written to a place where he was resident for a very short time. It is interesting to see how much he had accomplished and taught in that short time. Note how much he refers to as having introduced it before. Note also the first of the New Testament passages referring to spiritual gifts (prophecy and by implication discerning of spirits) in chapter 5.

BOOK	**2 THESSALONIANS** **Author:** Paul
Characters	People involved: Paul, Silas, Timothy
Who To/For	To the young church at Thessalonica, Greece
Literature Type	a letter containing teaching and exhortation
Story Line	none
Structure	Each chapter follows a cyclical Structure corrective explanation on the day of the Lord followed by a benediction/prayer for the Thessalonicans. See benediction/prayer passages: 1:11,12; 2:16,17; 3:16-18

   I. (ch 1) The Thessalonican Church--Suffering as It Awaits the day of the Lord; 1st Prayer: Worthy of Calling

  II. (ch 2) The Thessalonican Church--Correcting False views about the day of the Lord; 2nd Prayer: Encouragement

 III. (ch 3) The Thessalonican Church--Praying and Working as it Waits; 3rd Prayer: Peace

Theme **THE DAY OF THE LORD**
- is yet future and will be realized by a powerful personal catastrophic return of Jesus,
- has not yet happened and will be preceded by a Satanic display of power through a lawless leader finally defeated by Jesus, and
- necessitates a faithful prayerful perseverance and an industrious life style.

Key Words day, day of Lord (3)

Key Events As in 1 Thessalonians a future event, the day of the Lord, is described with more details as to events that will precede it.

Purposes
- to correct a misunderstanding about the day of the Lord already having happened,

2 THESSALONIANS continued

- to give encouragement during a time of severe persecution,
- to give exhortation as to what expectancy entails--a prayerful anticipation but an industrious and fruitful life style.

Why Important   This book clarifies the day of the Lord by giving two aspects of it: a gathering together (as in 1 Thessalonians 4:16,17) and the revealing of catastrophic judgment (2 Thessalonians 1:7). It further corrects attitudes and conduct while we wait for that return. There is a powerful restraining force, the presence of the Holy Spirit, which holds back utter sinfulness and lawlessness.

Where It Fits   This is one of the earlier of the Pauline epistles and occurs in Phase B, Gentile, of the New Testament Church Leadership Era. This of course is in Chapter 4, The Church, in the Redemptive Drama. The letter is a follow-up letter trying to clear up some misconceptions, probably arising from the first letter.

Leadership Lessons
This small book contains some of the same leadership lessons that are given for the first epistle to the Thessalonians. The following are the distinctly different ones that occur.
1. **MENTORING.** (1:3, 4, 11, 12) Paul illustrates an important social dynamic principle which is especially important in relational empowerment. Goodwin's expectation principle states that followers tend to live up to the genuine expectation of leaders they admire or respect.
2. **PERSPECTIVE/ ULTIMATE JUSTICE.** (1:6,7) Knowing that there will be an ultimate accounting and justice served gives the philosophical underpinnings for living in a society that has numerous situations manifesting injustice. That this ultimate justice will be involved with the day of the Lord gives us a strong reason for hoping for the return of Christ.
3. **MODELING.** One of the strongest means of teaching truth with impact involves modeling it and explaining it (3:6-13).
4. **DISCIPLINE.** (3:14,15) One ultimate aim of discipline is to warn a brother or sister in order that they might return to the Lord. This important leadership function is frequently avoided in today's church world. Two things are to be noted. Those under discipline are to be treated with respect as brothers or sisters in the Lord. Yet if the discipline

2 THESSALONIANS continued

is to have teeth they must in effect be cut off from inclusion in the church--its activities, its goals, its ministries, etc.

For Further Leadership Study
1. What is the import of Paul's mentioning the Kingdom of God in this letter to a church?
2. What does 2:9 tells us about power gifts?

Special Comments
Utter lawlessness is yet to be revealed.

BOOK	**1 CORINTHIANS**	**Author:** Paul

Characters   People mentioned or involved: Paul, Sosthenes, Crispus, Gaius, Chloe, Cephas (Peter), Stephanas, Apollos, Fortunaus, Achaicus

Who To/For   The young church at Corinth

Literature Type   a letter containing teaching and exhortation

Story Line   Paul got wind that the church at Corinth was having many problems including improper view of wisdom, divisions, immorality, lawsuits, disputes over marriage and its dissolution, disputes over certain practices, impropriety in worship, misunderstanding and improper stress of certain spiritual gifts, an incorrect doctrinal view of the resurrection. He wrote to correct perspective on these various issues.

Structure

I.	(ch 1,2)	Problem About Wisdom
II.	(ch 3,4)	Problem About Divisions
III.	(ch 5)	Problem on Toleration of Immorality
IV.	(ch 6)	Problem of Lawsuits Among Believers
V.	(ch 7)	Problems About Marriage
VI.	(ch 8-10)	Problem on Doubtful Practices
VII.	(ch 11)	Problem on Worship Practices
VIII.	(ch 12-14)	Problem About Spiritual Gifts
IX.	(ch 15,16)	Problem About Resurrection

Theme   **CHURCH PROBLEMS, INDIVIDUAL AND/ OR CORPORATE**
- can be solved,
- by submission to God concerning His truth for them.

Key Words   grace (10); emphasis carried by repeated diverse problems not so much by actual repeated words though there is repeated words within treatment of a problem

Key Events   none

1 CORINTHIANS continued

Purposes
- to answer the questions posed about the many problems arising in the Corinthian church,
- to defend Paul's apostolic conduct,
- to demonstrate how leadership confronts and resolves problems in the church,
- to show that belief and conduct are both important in the life of the church,
- to stress the interaction between a church and its culture and thus highlight the need for the church to impact its surrounding environment or else be impacted by it.

Why Important   This is an urban book full of great warnings for our modern church today. Churches which fail to impact their surrounding areas are usually impacted by them. And because this is so, such churches will be problematic churches. And most of the leadership effort will be spent on correcting the church rather than carrying out the task of the church to those around. The Corinthian church illustrates this and is a warning to others. Many of the problems in the Corinthian church were problems in the society: religious license, moral laxity, social disorder. Morgan (see Handbook page 210) points out two central truths of this letter. A church which fails to fulfill her task in the city will be invaded by the spirit of the city. Such a thing happens when a church is not what it ought to be, that is, is untrue to her essential nature of being and developing toward the potential God intended. The secret of an effective church lies in its progress toward realization of its life in Christ. It is an interdependent body, united in one Spirit and under the organizing influence of that Spirit. That same Spirit gives gifts individually to members of that church that the church as a whole may fulfill its task of bringing glory to God.

The book also points out one of the major functions of leadership--problem solving. It also gives teaching on each of the problems--some of which we would not get anywhere else in the Scriptures. But apart from this direct teaching there is this indirect and

1 CORINTHIANS continued

powerful overtone of the book which is essentially then one of the major lessons of the Corinthian letter--the church is responsible for the religious life of the city, for the moral standards of the city, and for the social life of the city.

Where It Fits   This is one of the earlier of Paul's epistles, written probably on his Third Missionary Journey--perhaps in the spring of 57A.D. It occurs in Chapter 4, The Church, in the Redemptive ERA. It is one of the most helpful books in dealing with important lessons for N.T. Church leadership.

Leadership Lessons
1. **GENRE.** 1 Corinthians is a series of leadership acts in which Paul the outside leader who founded the church and moved on now seeks to do concerning range of major problems that have arisen. There is biographical information, leadership acts, and even some direct individual verses directed at those who are influencing in the church. This book is filled with leadership lessons because it is an example of a leader confronting typical leadership issues that do arise in local churches.
2. **COMPLEXITY OF LEADERSHIP.** Leadership is complex. Paul deals with a whole range of problems including moral issues, philosophical issues, practical everyday issues, theological issues, conceptual issues, methodological issues. Problems in a situation are a main reason for the existence of leaders. Leaders must see problems not as hindrances to leadership but as the warp and woof of leadership responsibility. Problems actually can become challenges to those who can carry a positive attitude. It is in the midst of problem solving that much creative thinking emerges.
3. **GIFTEDNESS.** Leadership has much to do with giftedness. Both personally and corporately giftedness is important. This book shows that leaders need to know the doctrine of giftedness and especially the sub-set of spiritual gifts thoroughly. Ministry problems will arise because of misperceptions on giftedness. Leaders must deal with these problems with balance. This book should be studied in depth for its contribution to teaching on giftedness. There are references to giftedness throughout the book, not just chapters 12-14. The topic of giftedness is much broader than 1 Corinthians. There are some 15 or so lists in the Scripture referring to gifts. Perspective on gifts only comes when all the passages

1 CORINTHIANS continued

are brought together and looked at from a leadership perspective.
Detailed specific lessons on giftedness is left for comparative treatment.[11]
This topic is particularly important when a leader begins to think of
deliberate development in his/her own life or in the life of emerging
leaders. The Corinthians passage (12-14) first list of gifts emphasizes
come and go gifts. The second list and others which follow also
emphasize permanent gifts.[12] It shows that when the body gathers the
Holy Spirit impart gifts as are needed.

3. **STEWARDSHIP MODEL.** (4:1-5) One of the important New
   Testament Philosophical leadership models is the stewardship model.
   The model is given in the Gospels, particularly in the stewardship
   parables. Paul amplifies that model here and affirms it here. Leaders
   who operate with a stewardship model must see themselves as Servants
   of Christ, and as those entrusted with God-given resources.
4. **LEADERSHIP STYLES.** When dealing with problems leaders often
   have to come down with directive or highly directive leadership styles.
   Paul does so here using a Father-Initiator style (4:14,15) . This style is
   related to the Apostolic leadership style. This style uses the fact that the
   leader founded the work as a lever for getting acceptance of influence by
   the leader. Paul also uses the Apostolic style (9:1,2) which is described
   as a method of influence in which the leader assumes the role of
   delegated authority over followers, receives revelation from God
   concerning decisions, and commands obedience based on this delegated
   role and revealed truth. One of the most important leadership styles
   illustrated in this book is the confrontation style--another highly directive
   leadership style. The confrontation style is an approach to problem
   solving which brings the problem out in the open with all parties
   concerned, which analyzes the problem in light of revelation, and which
   brings force to bear upon the parties to accept recommended solutions.
   Since this book is filled with problems there are many instances of this
   leadership style. Note that all three of the highly directive leadership

---

[11]I teach an entire leadership course dealing with giftedness. My book, **Spiritual Gifts**, deals with the
narrow focus of spiritual gifts. Many specific lessons about spiritual gifts and leadership are given there.
But giftedness goes beyond and includes the whole giftedness set made up of natural abilities, acquired
skills, and spiritual gifts. Usually one of these components dominates for a given individual (we call that
dominant component the focal element). A self-study manual, **Developing Leadership Gifts,** is on the
drawing board and already has rough draft material for many of the chapters. That booklet, will treat in
detail the lessons referred to above.

[12]In leadership emergence theory these descriptions of gifts are termed vested and non-vested. Other
passages focus on one or the other. The Romans gifts passage, 12:3-8, focuses on vested gifts. The
Ephesians passage, 4:7-16 also focuses on vested. 1 Corinthians with its several lists focuses on both.

1 CORINTHIANS continued

styles are used. This is often the case when a leader is faced with many problems or crises in a church and the followership is not very mature.

5. **SERVANT LEADERSHIP.** Another of the New Testament Philosophical Leadership models is the servant leadership model. Christ introduced this in the Gospels and carefully announced that it contained one of the distinguishing leadership qualities between Christian leadership and secular leadership. *Leaders lead by serving and leaders serve by leading.* One of the strong testimonies to this dynamic balance and tension is given by Paul in the 1 Corinthians 9. Here Paul shows that he gives up his rights as a strong leader in order to serve those being led.

6. **DISCIPLINE.** (9:24-27) Paul advocates discipline in a leader's life in order that a leader may finish well. Few leaders finish well. One enhancement to finishing well incudes spiritual disciplines and other disciplines. Paul here shows that these will be needed throughout one's leadership. He, himself, is here about 50+ years of age. Disciple is still needed. One of the disciplines needed is that of Bible study. In the very next chapter, Paul gives one of the more important reasons for Bible study of the Old Testament. It is to derive lessons and values which will enable us to be better leaders. Paul advocates discipline in the body as a whole in order to purify it (ch 5). Discipline is only effective if the church as a whole enforces it.

7. **STRUCTURE.** Paul, in his explanation of giftedness in the local church, helps leader's understand the structure of the local church. It is an interrelated group of people with diverse gifts which serve to complement each other. Further, Paul shows that orderliness is compatible with the ministry of the Holy Spirit through this structure.

For Further Leadership Study

1. This a major book contributing to giftedness theory and must be studied in depth and comparatively with other gifts passages for major lessons.
2. Each of the problems should be studied in depth to understand the confrontation leadership style.

Special Comments

This book highlights an important doctrine. The resurrection of the Lord. That truth is essential to the whole Christian message. In it lies the affirmation of God of all that Christ was and did. In it lies power that will enable. In it lies the future hope of things being made right.

BOOK	**2 CORINTHIANS**	**Author:** Paul

Characters   People mentioned or involved: Paul, Timothy, Titus

Who To/For   The young church at Corinth and other churches in Achaia (Greece)

Literature Type   a letter containing teaching and exhortation

Story Line   Paul had heard back from the church in response to his first letter. They had basically responded positively to his exhortations. It was clear, however, that at least some of them had personally misunderstood Paul, his ministry, and motivations behind his actions. Understandably then one can see why this letter is so personal and emotional. Paul's character and ministry are on the line. He writes to explain himself and does so in the first section of the book. The writing of the letter is compounded by the fact that he has a delicate task--asking the Corinthians for money to help out in a sister church situation. He does this in the middle portion of the letter and thus we are given teaching on giving that nowhere else occurs in the Scriptures. Paul then goes on in the final section of the book to defend his apostolic authority.

Structure
    I. (ch 1-7)   Paul's Apostolic Ministry and Motives
    I I. (ch 8,9)   Paul's Appeal to the Corinthians
    III. (ch 10-12) Paul's Defense of His Authority

Theme   **PAUL'S APOSTOLIC DEFENSE,**
- involved an explanation of his personal conduct, motives, and view of the ministry,
- was in harmony with his plea for the Jerusalem gift, and
- concluded with an overwhelming refutation of arguments opposing his Apostolic authority.

Key Words   ministry and related words (18); personal references to Paul himself (many); apostle(s) (6); grace (25)

Key Events   none

Purposes
- to correct the overcorrection the Corinthians had made in regards to the immorality problem mentioned in the 1st letter,

2 CORINTHIANS continued

- to explain his motives and ministry among the Corinthians so as to correct misrepresentations being circulated about him,
- to establish his spiritual authority among them,
- to give further instruction about the offering,
- to bring to light ministry values that ought to undergird a leader.

Why Important   No other book in the Scriptures so exposes the inner life of a leader in terms of leadership values. A leadership value is an underlying assumption which affects how a leader behaves in or perceives leadership situations. It is a mindset which gives meaning to ourselves and explains why we do things or think things. It can relate to a belief, personal ethical conduct, personal feelings desired about situations, and ideas of what brings success or failure in ministry. Our values might be rooted in personality, is certainly related to our heritage and our experiences in leadership which have shaped us. About 19 major Pauline leadership values (and many lesser related ones) are exposed in 2 Corinthians. These can be very instructive for today's leaders. The book also exposes the notion of spiritual authority and its ultimate aims. While other power bases are necessary in the ministry it is this power base, spiritual authority, which should be a priority of an effective leader for God.

Where It Fits   This is a book about leadership in the church era--the age in which we live today. 2 Corinthians was most likely written on Paul's third missionary journey. He had been a Christian for about 21 years. So we are getting some mature leadership advice. Because Paul had been misunderstood by some in his first letter to the Corinthians he goes into personal details about his reasons, motivations, and ministry philosophy--leadership values. This letter then unfolds for us insights into apostolic leadership, spiritual authority, and leadership values of the most prominent church leader to the Gentiles. Many of these values, though uniquely and personally Paul's, will fit many church leaders today.

2 CORINTHIANS continued

Leadership Lessons

1. **MINISTRY PHILOSOPHY AND VALUES.** Ministry philosophy is key to a leader's overall influence and ultimate achievement. 2 Corinthians exposes us to Pauline leadership values and thus helps us begin to see the underpinnings of Paul's ministry philosophy. A ministry philosophy is a strategically organized set of values which guides a leader in his/her application of personal giftedness, calling, and influence to the leadership situations he/she faces so as to achieve God-given purposes and leave behind an ultimate contribution for a life-work. It is made up of values learned via experience and flowing from one's beingness. Below are given 19 Pauline values identified in 2 Corinthians which help explain Paul's motivations and actions in his dealing with the Corinthians. I have generalized from specific statements applying uniquely to Paul to possible application statements that may fit other leaders.

   (1) Divine Appointment. *LEADERS OUGHT TO BE SURE THAT GOD APPOINTED THEM TO MINISTRY SITUATIONS.*
   (2) Training Methodology. *LEADERS MUST BE CONCERNED ABOUT LEADERSHIP SELECTION AND DEVELOPMENT.*
   (3) Personal Ministry. *LEADERS SHOULD VIEW PERSONAL RELATIONSHIPS AS AN IMPORTANT PART OF MINISTRY.*
   (4) Sovereign Mindset. *LEADERS OUGHT TO SEE GOD'S HAND IN THEIR CIRCUMSTANCES AS PART OF HIS PLAN FOR DEVELOPING THEM AS LEADERS.*
   (5) Integrity and Openness. *LEADERS SHOULD NOT BE DECEPTIVE IN THEIR DEALINGS WITH FOLLOWERS BUT SHOULD INSTEAD BE OPEN, HONEST, FORTHRIGHT, AND FRANK WITH THEM.*
   (6) Ultimate accountability. *LEADERS ACTIONS MUST BE RESTRAINED BY THE FACT THAT THEY WILL ULTIMATELY GIVE AN ACCOUNT TO GOD FOR THEIR LEADERSHIP ACTIONS.*
   (7) Spiritual Authority--Its ends. *SPIRITUAL AUTHORITY OUGHT TO BE USED TO MATURE FOLLOWERS.*
   (8) Loyalty Testing. *LEADERS MUST KNOW THE LEVEL OF FOLLOWERSHIP LOYALTY IN ORDER TO WISELY EXERCISE LEADERSHIP INFLUENCE.*

2 CORINTHIANS continued

(9) True Credentials (competency and results). *A LEADER SHOULD BE ABLE TO POINT TO RESULTS FROM MINISTRY AS A RECOMMENDATION OF GOD'S AUTHORITY IN HIM/HER.*

(10) True Competence (its ultimate source). *A LEADER'S ULTIMATE CONFIDENCE FOR MINISTRY MUST NOT REST IN HIS/HER COMPETENCE BUT IN GOD THE AUTHOR OF THAT COMPETENCE.*

(11) Transforming Ministry. *FOLLOWERS WHO ARE INCREASINGLY BEING SET FREE BY THE HOLY SPIRIT AND WHO ARE INCREASINGLY BEING TRANSFORMED INTO CHRIST'S IMAGE OUGHT TO BE THE HOPE AND EXPECTATION OF A CHRISTIAN LEADER.*

(12) Prominence of Christ in Ministry. *A LEADER MUST NOT SEEK TO BRING ATTENTION TO HIMSELF/HERSELF THROUGH MINISTRY BUT MUST SEEK TO EXALT CHRIST AS LORD.*

(13) Servant Leadership. *A LEADER OUGHT TO SEE LEADERSHIP AS FOCUSED ON SERVING FOLLOWERS IN JESUS' BEHALF.*

(14) Death/Life Paradox. *THE FIRSTFRUITS OF JESUS RESURRECTION LIFE OUGHT TO BE EXPERIENCED IN THE DEATH PRODUCING CIRCUMSTANCES OF LIFE AND OUGHT TO SERVE AS A HALLMARK OF SPIRITUAL LIFE FOR FOLLOWERS.*

(15) Motivational Force. *LEADERS SHOULD USE OBLIGATION TO CHRIST (in light of his death for believers) TO MOTIVATE BELIEVERS TO SERVICE FOR CHRIST.*

(16) True Judgment Criterion. *LEADERS SHOULD VALUE PEOPLE IN TERMS OF THEIR RELATIONSHIP TO GOD IN CHRIST AND NOT ACCORDING TO THEIR OUTWARD SUCCESS IN THE WORLD (even in the religious world).*

(17) Unequally Yoked. *CHRISTIAN LEADERSHIP MUST NOT BE DOMINATED BY RELATIONSHIPS WITH UNBELIEVERS SO THAT NON-CHRISTIAN VALUES HOLD SWAY.*

(18) Financial Equality Principle. *CHRISTIAN LEADERSHIP MUST TEACH THAT CHRISTIAN GIVING IS A RECIPROCAL BALANCING BETWEEN NEEDS AND SURPLUS.*

(19) Financial Integrity. *A CHRISTIAN LEADER MUST HANDLE FINANCES WITH ABSOLUTE INTEGRITY.*

These certainly do not exhaust the values implied in 2 Corinthians but do reflect a number of important contexts explaining Paul's views on ministry and motivating factors for his own leadership actions.

2 CORINTHIANS continued

2. **FINANCIAL SAFEGUARD.** Leaders must be open and honest with followers concerning giving and finances. Churches and parachurch organizations have financial needs just like any other organization in society. These needs must be met. How leaders influence followers with respect to meeting these needs is important. Paul demonstrates this delicate matter in 2 Corinthians. Some observations concerning his handling of financial matters include:
   a. Motivational techniques include relating giving to the issue of absolute surrender. True freedom to give flows from a life given to God.
   b. Motivational techniques involve competitive comparisons with others who are poorer and yet give beyond expectations.
   c. Willingness to give, not the amount given, is the criterion for giving.
   d. Resources in the wider body of Christ will include surplus and great need. Where there is surplus giving should shift resources to needs.
   e. Integrity in the handling of money is essential.
3. **SPIRITUAL AUTHORITY INSIGHTS.** Paul demonstrates the essentials of spiritual authority in his defence of his apostolic authority. Spiritual authority is the right to influence conferred upon a leader by followers who willing follow that leader because of their perception of spirituality in the leader as demonstrated by a godly life (character), gifted power, and deep experience with God. Paul's entire letter emphasizes these elements: character, gifted power (both in revelation, and in application to the situation including spiritual warfare, and in deep experiences with God in which he has seen the sufficiency of Christ put to the test and sufficient.
4. **AUTHORITY/POWER.** An apostolic leader must demonstrate God-given power, in order to validate his/her authority, in correcting major problematic/crises situations in a church. While Paul would prefer their willing response to his appeals he is prepared to enforce his analysis and solutions with God-given power. See 2 Corinthians 13.
5. **PERSONAL EXPERIENCE /SPIRITUAL AUTHORITY.** The essence of God's processing of a leader, that is, shaping that leader by sovereign experiences, is demonstrated in 2 Corinthians in Paul's sharing of his personal experiences with God. 2 Corinthians 1:3,4 give the basic underlying accomplishment of any processing. The book itself is filled with *deep processing*--that is, process incidents dealing with maturity of character. Spiritual authority is a by-product of deep processing.

2 CORINTHIANS continued

For Further Leadership Study

1. Some fifty process items have been codified in leadership emergence theory[13]. Identify the kinds of process items that Paul indicates in his various relating of incidents.
2. Study the notions of influence, power, and authority to understand the basic power bases a leader has to undergird his/her leadership influence[14]. Which kinds of power forms does Paul use in 2 Corinthians?
3. Paul's view of giving is not tithing, something many present day leaders advocate. His view is proportionality. We give freely, not in obligation. We give liberally as we can. We give recognizing that God enables us to give. We give recognizing that we are stewards. Everything we have (not just a tenth) belongs to God. We are simply using it for His purposes in our lives. Compare these ideas with the Old Testament view of the tithe.
4. Study other Pauline books with a focus on leadership values to add to the identified Pauline leadership values. It is generally accepted that Paul wrote 1,2 Thessalonians before 1 and 2 Corinthians and over the next nine years wrote the rest of his epistles with 2 Timothy being the last and occurring about ten years after 2 Corinthians? Did any of these values identified in 2 Corinthians change over the rest of his lifetime? What new values do we see added as we study each of the later epistles? What leadership values are stressed in his three last books, the pastoral epistles? These especially should be informative as he is dealing specifically with leadership issues.

Special Comments
This book can be studied with great profit for leadership processing information in the life of Paul. Many process items can be identified and helpful lessons from them.

---

[13]See my manual **Leadership Emergence Theory**. Page 31 gives the complete list. These are defined throughout the book.
[14]See my manual **Leadership Emergence Theory** which defines power bases. Pages 192-194 gives these definitions which include: force, manipulation, persuasion, and authority forms (coercive, induced, legitimate, competent, personal, and spiritual authority).

BOOK	**GALATIANS**	**Author:** Paul

Characters   People mentioned or involved: Paul, the Apostle, James, the Lord's brother, Peter, Titus, Barnabas

Who To/For   the churches of Galatia (a Roman province in Asia Minor), the people were migrants, Gauls, from western Europe

Literature Type   a letter containing teaching and exhortation

Story Line   Paul was concerned with some of his churches in the Asia minor region. Judaizers (apparently Jewish believers who felt that it was necessary to become circumcised and keep Jewish traditional law in order to become real Christians) had come in after Paul. They were leading these new converts to Christianity astray in Paul's thinking. What they were teaching contradicted Paul's view that our essential relationship to God depends on Christ's work on the Cross and nothing else. In an almost scathing letter Paul writes to the churches in Galatia denouncing this fundamental error.

Structure
    I. (ch 1,2)   Paul's Gospel--Divinely Revealed
    II. (ch 3,4)   Paul's Gospel--Distinct From the Law
    III. (ch 5,6)   Paul's Gospel--Demanding Freedom

Theme   **PAUL'S GOSPEL** (of salvation by faith alone)
- rests upon divine revelation,
- stands apart from the law, and
- frees believers from any salvation regulation.

Key Words   faith (21), law (32), gospel (12); grace (7)

Key Events   Paul refers to some past Events visit of Paul to Jerusalem after three years as a convert, visit of Paul to Jerusalem fourteen years later, Peter's visit to Antioch

Purposes
- to counter the teaching of the Judaizers who added works to faith as an additional condition of salvation,

GALATIANS   continued

- to clarify and defend the Gospel as revealed to Paul, that is, that salvation is by faith alone in the finished work of Christ on the cross,
- to show that this Gospel was compatible with Old Testament revelation,
- to show the purpose of the law,
- to show that sanctification (perfecting of the believer) is the work of the Spirit and not something we do to add to our salvation.

Why Important   The essence of the Gospel is highlighted in this book. In the midst of controversy a person usually focuses on the main points of the controversy. So with Paul in this letter. The essence of the Gospel lies in what Christ has done at the cross for the believer. To add anything to that is to deny the efficacy of that work--that is, if salvation can come in any other way then the Cross was not necessary. This is a white hot letter. There are core issues and periphery issues it is clear that this issue is core with Paul. In terms of leadership the book is invaluable because of Paul's defense of spiritual authority. This book (and 2 Corinthians) provide the only exceptions to the general rule that spiritual authority doesn't have to be defended; let God defend it.

Where It Fits   This is a book about leadership in the church era--the age in which we live today. Galatians was most likely written on Paul's third missionary journey just after 2 Corinthians. He had been a Christian for about 21 years. So we are getting some mature leadership advice. This is an example of when a leader must take a strong stand where there are differences with others since this is dealing with a core issue--the meaning of the Gospel. This letter then unfolds for us insights into apostolic leadership, spiritual authority, and leadership values of the most prominent church leader to the Gentiles. It shows a confrontational leadership style.

Leadership Lessons
1. **DIVINE CALLING.** A major value of Paul's includes the following: (1) Divine Appointment. *LEADERS OUGHT TO BE SURE THAT GOD APPOINTED THEM TO MINISTRY SITUATIONS.* Paul repeatedly opens his epistles with phrases to remind his readers that his leadership

GALATIANS   continued

was instigated by God. This value is especially needed when a leader faces conflict and must confront. Both for the leader's personal reassurance and for the power needed with followers. Here Paul is going to confront the Galatians on a doctrinal matter which in his mind is core. It is at the very heart of the Gospel. It concerns the work of Christ. Paul needs divine backing for this task. Hence, he refers to his calling and then gives testimony showing it to be true. Leaders with weak calls or none at all will usually fade in the midst of discouragement or conflict demanding confrontational styles.

2. **INFLUENCE MEANS.** Paul uses several leadership styles in getting at this major problem. Remember leadership style refers to the individual expression a leader utilizes to function in his/her leadership role. This individual expression includes his/her methodology for handling crises and problem solving. Frequently, problem solving and crises, require heavy handed leadership styles, that is, highly directive styles such as apostolic or confrontation. And that is the case here. The apostolic style is a method of influence in which the leader assumes the role of delegated authority over those for whom he/she feels responsible, receives revelation from God concerning decisions, and commands obedience based on this delegated authority and revelation concerning God's will. The confrontation leadership style is an approach to problem solving which brings the problem out in the open with all parties concerned, analyzes the problem in light of revelation and which brings force to bear upon the parties to accept recommended solutions. Though Paul would probably wish to use less demanding leadership style the problem is so serious and the believers so immature in it that he must use highly directive leadership styles. The problem is intense and Paul's reaction is intense. This is the harshest language of any of his epistles. He does not affirm this church at all. In most epistles, in his opening words of greeting or introduction he gives affirmation to the church. From that positive note he builds. But not so in Galatians. It is serious business from the word go.

3. **SPIRITUAL AUTHORITY.** The very nature of spiritual authority requires that followers recognize it and follow it willingly. Therefore, a general rule concerning spirituality is, don't defend it.[15] Let God defend it.

---

[15]My study of spiritual authority has led me to identify 10 basic guidelines. Two of the ten are dealt with in this lesson on spiritual authority. The ten are (two dealt with in boldface): (1) One who learns spiritual authority as the primary power base for ministry must recognize the essential Source of all authority: God. (2) God's delegated authority does not belong to the person exercising it. That person is merely the instrument God uses. (3) The person who is the instrument of delegated authority is

GALATIANS   continued

If followers choose to disregard it they will answer to God. But in two cases in the New Testament, Paul does defend his spiritual authority. The fundamental issue allowing this is that his spiritual authority is tied to the doctrinal issue under fire. If he has no spiritual authority then his revelation of the Gospel has no authoritative backing. So he defends. His method of defense is instructive: a. authenticates his salvation and calling with irrefutable testimony, b. declares that his understanding of the Gospel came not from human sources but from God, c. shows how his understanding of the Gospel has backing of Peter and other Christian stalwarts, d. shows how the Galatian's understanding of the Gospel negates the necessity for Christ's work on the cross, e. uses historic Old Testament teaching to affirm his own view, and then f. simply exhorts based on his completed presentation. He concludes with his personal testimony of suffering and ministering for Jesus. His suffering for his understanding of the meaning of the Gospel (the cross) validates his claim to truth. Note his use of spiritual authority is in accord with his controlling value about it (4:19). Spiritual Authority--Its ends: *SPIRITUAL AUTHORITY OUGHT TO BE USED TO MATURE FOLLOWERS.* Spiritual authority is never used for personal gain but for the benefit of followers (2 Corinthians 10:8).

4. **MODELING.** See 6:1 where Paul exhorts the Galatians to do individually with one another what he himself is doing with them corporately.

For Further Leadership Study
1. Individual verses that should be studied and why:

What	Why
1:15, 16	retrospective understanding of destiny preparation processing, step forward in seeing focus of ministry
1:13	the subtlety of the error (even Barnabas, Paul's mentor)

---

responsible to God for its exercise. (4) A leader is one who recognizes God's authority manifested in real-life situations. (5) Subjection to authority means that a person is subject to God Himself and not to the person through whom it is coming. (6) Rebellion against authority means that a person is not subjecting himself/herself to God, though it may appear that the person is rejecting some impure manifestation of God's authority through the human instrument. (7) People who are under God's authority look for and recognize spiritual authority and willingly place themselves under it. (8) **Spiritual authority is never exercised for one's own benefit, but for those under it.** (9) a person in spiritual authority does not have to insist on obedience--that is the moral responsibility of the follower. (10) **God is responsible to defend spiritual authority.**

GALATIANS   continued

<u>What</u>   <u>Why</u>

3:26-29   what does no differences between these important categories mean in light of the context?

4:1,2   study the word epitropous (guardian) to understand the law's place in maturing believers

4:21ff   Paul's use of allegory

5:16-26   life in the Spirit; note especially 5:22, the standard for godliness in character

6:1,2   reciprocal living commandment, basis for lateral mentoring accountability

Special Comments
Christian liberty is highlighted in this book. Liberty is not license to do anything we want--it is life in the Spirit, controlled by the Spirit. Its results are evident--its lack too is evident. Strong leadership is needed in crisis situations.

BOOK	**ROMANS** **Author:** Paul
Characters	Paul, Abraham, David, Adam, Christ and many personal acquaintances of Paul in the church at Rome (see Romans 16).
Who To/For	to the church at Rome (many of whom were personal friends of Paul)
Literature Type	a carefully thought out letter containing teaching and exhortation concerning the essentials of the Gospel. There is much reasoned out teaching included in this book.
Story Line	The church at Rome was located in a strategic position. Paul hopes to visit it and be sent on from it to missionary service in Spain. This letter is paving the way for that. But there is more. Paul had faced enough opposition from Judaizers (see Acts and Galatians) that he saw the strategic necessity of getting into print a clear exposition of the Gospel and getting it to a predominantly Gentile church where it would be spread to many others. Rome with its strategic position in the empire is ideal. So Paul writes a carefully thought out letter, one that includes many of the arguments he had used previously in his ministry. But now he puts it all together. He explains clearly the needs of humanity, both Jews and Gentiles, before God--their sins have separated them. He shows how God met that need in Christ's perfect work on the Cross. He then shows the basic inner need of a believer-- to live above sin's controlling power. He explains how that too was part of the work of the cross. He goes on to explain how this work of Christ and the Gentile acceptance of it mesh with God's previous work with the Jews. Finally he shows that the Gospel has practical ramifications in everyday life.

Structure I. (ch 1-8) The Gospel and the Individual
                                            A. (1-4) How God delivers from Sins
                                            B. (5-8) How God delivers from Sin
               II. (ch 9-11) The Gospel and Israel
               III. (ch 12-16) The Gospel and Daily Living

ROMANS continued

Theme   **GOD'S GRACIOUS PROVISION OF CHRIST'S
             RIGHTEOUSNESS TO EVERY BELIEVER** (the gospel of God),
- encompasses an individual's total need before God,
- is consistent with redemptive history, and
- applies to all of life's relationships.

Key Words   justify (and related words) (7); faith (37); Christ (39);
                 Holy Spirit or Ghost (26); spirit (7); grace (25)

Key Events   events not in focus, except as abstracted for purposes of
                 teaching

Purposes
- to announce his intended visit to Rome,
- to help stabilize the church at Rome with foundational truth which he
  had been learning over the past several years, including the Gospel, the
  ministry of the Holy Spirit, spiritual gifts, disputed practices, and several
  others,
- to explain the rejection of Christianity by the Jews in terms of God's
  overall plan to reach the world,
- to spur the Roman church on to missionary effort.

Why Important   This letter pulsates with missionary concern. It first
                  shows the need that all fallen humanity has and then
                  shows the perfect salvation God has provided for that
                  need. All people everywhere, Jew and Gentile, have
                  need for it. Those who accept this salvation do so and are
                  declared righteous in the eyes of God. They also begin to
                  see righteousness imparted in their lives. All creation is
                  moving toward a climactic event when all of God's
                  believers will be perfected. Paul's desire is that all people
                  everywhere hear and respond to this message. We have in
                  this book the clearest explanation of the whole
                  redemptive drama in teaching form. Of particular
                  importance to a believer desiring to see righteousness
                  imparted and lived out is the explanatory section in
                  Romans 6-8 which shows the process for victory in a life.

ROMANS continued

Where It Fits   Romans was probably written just a short time after
Galatians, perhaps in 58A.D. Again it is the work of a
mature Christian who has grappled with the meaning of
the Cross both for salvation and for Christian living
(sanctification). It occurs in the N.T. Church Leadership
era and details important insights on leadership.

Leadership Lessons

1. **GENRE.** There is very little biographical information in this book. The
giftedness passage is directly important to leadership. Most of the rest of
the book is indirect. Therefore I will share basically overall implications
for leadership from the book.
2. **PERSONAL MINISTRY VALUE.** Paul believed that ministry should
be personal. He exemplifies the relational empowerment lessons.
EFFECTIVE LEADERS SEE RELATIONAL EMPOWERMENT AS A
PRIMARY MEANS OF LEADERSHIP. The book of Romans, more
than any others of Paul's ministry shows this. In all of Paul's epistles
taken collectively there are 60 names of people with whom he had
personal ministry. There are about 35 personal names included in this
book alone. These were people Paul and ministered to in various places
on the mission field. He had never been to Rome when he wrote this
epistle.
3. **WORD CENTERED MINISTRY.** Paul demonstrates in this book just
how word centered he is. He shows a vast knowledge of and ability to
use the Scriptures.
4. **UNION LIFE.** Paul abstractly teaches the union life message (double
union--joined with Christ in death, metaphor, and in His resurrected life--
victory). Union life is the starting point of the Christian life, and the
source of victory in the life. Whereas John teaches this metaphorically
and in relational language, Paul teaches it conceptually. Romans 8 is the
highpoint of this union life message. Nowhere else in all the Bible is a
future perfect paradigm so emphasized as here, the 8:28-30 passage
shows the certainty of the paradigm. The whole of Romans 8 points out
the beforemath implications. This message provides the central content
of one of Paul's major thrusts of leadership (see Colossians 1:28,29 for
the statement of it). The victory is real and certain (Romans 6). The
battle is real and not automatic (Romans 7). The two fold source of

ROMANS continued

appropriated victory is available , relationship in the family and empowerment by the Holy Spirit for life power (Romans 8).[16]

5. **PERSPECTIVE.** (1-8 on the Christian life, ch 9-11 on God's working). The difference in leaders and followers is perspective. The difference between leaders and effective leaders is better perspective. Here, in Romans, Paul highlights the necessity of perspective. An overall view of the Christian life can aid development. A perspective on how God is working allows one to see present ministry in terms of a wider perspective. The basic lesson affirmed: *Effective leaders perceive present ministry in terms of a lifetime perspective.*

6. **GIFTEDNESS.** The Romans passage on spiritual gifts emphasizes vested gifts and hence the responsibility for leaders to develop to their potential and use those gifts for God.

7. **MENTORING.** Another use of Goodwin's expectation principle is seen in Paul's exhortation to the Romans (15:14-16).

8. **MISSIONARY EMPHASIS.** The book as a whole carries a strong missionary emphasis. Paul is thinking strategically. He is on is way to Spain. He wants the Rome church to become a part of his ministry. His teaching on the Gospel in Rome highlights its universal appeal to Gentiles. Rome is in a strategic location. If this church can catch the missionary vision it will be in a place to mobilize others. Note how many mobile people it has there already (see Romans 16--remember Paul hadn't been there).

For Further Leadership Study

1. Go through Romans and mark in your Bible the indications that Paul is a Word centered leader.
2. Mark the number of times the Holy Spirit occurs by name prior to Romans 8 and after Romans 8. Then mark the number of occurrences of the Spirit in Romans 8. What implications does this have for life power?
3. What great warning is given to leaders in the New Testament Church Leadership Era in Romans 11:20-22?

Special Comments

Leaders who want to develop believers to maturity must know Romans 3-8.

---

[16]Every leader will go through several times in his/her life during a life time in which power will be greatly needed. Two major power gates have been identified: life power, gifted power. Here Paul is emphasizing the need for life power and provides the knowledge for one to enter that Life Power Gate.

| *BOOK* | **EPHESIANS** | **Author:** Paul |

Characters   not in focus

Who To/For   to the church at Ephesus; possibly to all the churches in this region, the Roman province of Asia Minor.

Literature Type   an exhortive letter with teaching and several beautiful prayer passages.

Story Line   Ephesus was an important place in Paul's ministry. There was a good acceptance of the Gospel (see Acts 19). Later he exhorts the elders of that church in a quick stop over on his way to Jerusalem. He writes this epistle to them. Finally, 1 and 2 Timothy are written to Timothy who is ministering at Ephesus. It is to this group of people who had responded so well to Paul's ministry that he most clearly communicates what he has been learning of the essence of the church and its place in God's redemptive program. The first half of the book provides this exalted view of the church seen from above. This ideal picture deserves a response adequate to it--a church which manifests in the world its essence. And that is what Paul writes in the last half of the book--exhortation and teaching which is meant to make the present church move toward the ideal church.

Structure   I. (ch 1-3) The Church and Its Highest Purposes
II. (ch 4-6) The Church and Its Earthly Testimony

Theme   **THE CHURCH AND ITS ULTIMATE PURPOSES**
- were planned in eternity past,
- were founded and revealed in history by the Apostles' witness, and
- demand a unique Christian life style.

Key Words   walk (8); grace (12); unity or one (20)

Key Events   none in focus

Purposes
- to reveal perspective about the church in its highest purposes,

EPHESIANS continued

- to show the importance of unity in the body,
- to show that the high calling of the church places demands on believer's lives,
- to give practical instruction which would help the believers live up to that high calling.

Why Important   The revealed wonder and ultimate purposes of the church demand a unique Christian expression of life style. In short, that is the essence of the message of Ephesians. This book gives us the full and final truth concerning the Church. The plan of the Church existed in God's thoughts from eternity. It will last into eternity. We can count on it and act upon it.

Where It Fits   Probably written about 4 years after the book of Romans, perhaps around 62 A.D. This book lines out the high purposes of the church. It shows how future perfect thinking can affect us today. Again as with Romans, this is the work of a mature church leader and it contains many leadership lessons for the N.T. Church Leadership era.

Leadership Lessons
1. **GENRE.** This book contains no biographical information. There is one direct leadership contextual passage and an important gifts passage. There is an important passage on spiritual warfare which leaders must know since they will be involved in it frequently in their ministries. There are a few verses which indirectly teach some important leadership truths. Other than that, the material is generally an indirect source of leadership lessons.
2. **PERSPECTIVE.** The book of Ephesians is for leaders in the N.T. Church Leadership Era to study. For it gives perspective on the Church, which is seen in light of God's great cosmic purposes. It inspires leaders and give them confidence as they struggle in their local contexts with their local churches. This book gives hope and spurs leaders on to believe what can happen with local churches. They see themselves as part of something much bigger. They must do this also with their followers.
3. **LEADERSHIP, ESSENTIAL PURPOSE.** The Ephesian passage on giftedness and its purpose for the church (4:7-16) could be interpreted to mean that the major gifts indicated by metonymy (Apostles, prophets, evangelist, pastors, teachers) are given to a wider body than just local churches. In any case, whether these are local or regional, their major purpose of leadership is to develop people in the body to do the ministry and to mature them in the things of Christ. These leaders are given to

EPHESIANS continued

work with the body of Christ to enable it to do ministry. Evangelists main
ministry is to equip the body (presumably other emerging evangelists). Each
of the major leadership gifts are basically to do the same thing.
4. **ULTIMATE PURPOSE.** An individual leader usually recognizes little-by-
little over a lifetime of development that *ministry flows out of being*. Part of
that beingness includes knowing who we are. Ephesians 2:10 points out that
each person, including every leader, is unique and God has unique purposes
for them.
5. **ISOLATION PROCESSING.** This is an outstanding book to study in
terms of processing. Paul is in isolation. One of the major lessons to see
in the midst of isolation is that God is sovereignly controlling in it. See
3:1 and 4:1 and 6:20 for indications of this recognition of sovereignty.
6. **SPIRITUAL WARFARE.** Paul gives actual teaching on spiritual warfare.
See Ephesians 6:10-18 for some surprising lessons not usually emphasized
by those involved in deliverance ministries and spiritual warfare.
7. **PRAYER MINISTRY.** That Paul has a prayer centered ministry as well
as a word centered ministry is seen in the great prayers of Ephesians. See
8. **UNITY.** A major leadership goal is to create a corporate value in the
body of unity among the diverse parts.
9. **TECHNIQUE.** The whole structure of the book as a whole yields an
important leadership communication principle. Theory must lead to
practice. Theory properly understood motivates to application. Lack of
application in the life of people as individuals and the church as a whole
indicates that truth has not been communicated in its highest purposes and
with its potential motivational intent.

For Further Leadership Study
1. Why does Paul include Prophets in Ephesians 2:20 as part of the
foundation upon which the church is built? Most could see why Apostles
are there, but why Prophets?
2. Study Ephesians to learn lessons about isolation processing. What one
major result of isolation can you see?
3. Study the spiritual warfare passage (6:10-18) for major lessons on
spiritual warfare? What is emphasized? Power gifts? Skills? Character?
4. Study the great prayers in Ephesians in order to learn how to pray and
how to pray with vision and how to pray with a future perfect attitude.
See 1:15-23; 3;14-21.
5. Ephesians contains the only command from Paul to appropriate the Holy
Spirit's power. For what purposes?

Special Comments
A book using a future perfect paradigm logic.

BOOK	**PHILIPPIANS** **Author:** Paul
Characters	People mentioned or involved: Paul, Timothy, Epaphroditus, Euodia, Syntyche, Clement
Who To/For	To the Church at Philippi in Macedonia
Literature Type	A warm positive letter written from prison involving much testimony, some teaching, and some exhortation.
Story Line	The Philippians had sent a gift which had reached Paul while he was in prison. This letter is the thank you note. But Paul couldn't help but add a few other things, like what was happening to him and how it contained lessons for all. Weaving throughout the whole letter is a desire for unity among the Philippian church which is based on one's attitude toward other believers. It is clear that Paul sees his life as a model for the believer's at Philippi. His selection of material has that end. This book illustrates what it means to be *in Christ* in daily life. There is a note of joy throughout it, a sense of life with a purpose, a sense of destiny in life, and a thankful attitude for life and its problems, opportunities, and experiences.
Structure	The structure does not strictly follow an analytical procedure as Paul's epistles often do. There is testimony, spontaneity of feeling, and illustrative digression. There is teaching drawn from the testimony. And there is application to the Philippian situation.

I.   (ch 1)   Rejoicing in Prison --Spirit of Christ Real And Sufficient
II.   (ch 2)   Rejoicing in Service--The Mind of Christ Real And A Model
III.   (ch 3)   Rejoicing in Purpose--The Power of Christ Available
IV.   (ch 4)   Rejoicing in All Things--Peace of Christ Sufficient

Theme   **PAUL'S MODEL OF THE NORMAL CHRISTIAN LIFE**
- is a life in union with a personal Christ (a Christ-centered life),
- is expressed joyously in all circumstances, and
- is worthy of emulation by others.

PHILIPPIANS continued

Key Words	Joy, rejoicing (18); in Christ, him, the Lord meaning union (10); Jesus, Christ, the Lord (43); words indicating the Christian consciousness: mind, minded (8)
Key Events	Paul imprisonment serves as the backdrop for sharing what his life in union with Christ means

Purposes
- to thank the people for their gift and the love and concern behind it,
- to express what life in Christ can be in spite of circumstances,
- to help patch up the division between Euodia and Syntyche,
- to let them know that Timothy and Epaphroditus will be visiting and that he himself hopes to come soon,
- to motivate all to continue on toward finishing well.

Why Important   Philippians, probably more than any of Paul's letters, presents the positive aspects of union life. It illustrates union life (in Christ, to live is Christ) and its fruit in a real life situation which would normally be depressing. Its keynote of joy in the midst of difficult isolation processing is a model for believers. The song in chapter 2 on the theological aspects of the incarnation (and one of its major teaching--attitude) is another plus in this book as is the vignette on Paul's testimony showing a sense of destiny purpose for his life. The section in chapter 4 on living and learning from circumstances because of inward resources of union life in Christ illustrates the standard for believers concerning God's processing in life.

Where It Fits   Several epistles, all occurring in the N.T. Church Leadership Era were written about the same time. These include Philemon, Colossians, Ephesians and Philippians. All deal with specific lessons for N.T. Church leaders.

Leadership Lessons
1. **ISOLATION PROCESSING.** This book is written toward the end of Paul's ministry. He is in prison. He is set aside from his normal ministry.

PHILIPPIANS continued

It is a time of isolation.[17] Isolation lessons include: recognition of God's sovereignty in it (prisoner of the Lord), getting God's perspective on it (1:12-14), the need for deep relationships and prayer backing (1:3-7), importance of a reciprocal prayer ministry when in isolation (1:9-11, 19), the importance of modeling throughout it (the whole book), reevaluation of life purpose (3:12-14).

2. **MODELING.** Probably more than any other of Paul's writings the book of Philippians deliberately invokes modeling as a major means of influence both by deliberate example and by teaching it plainly (3:15-17, 4:8,9). Modeling is a technique whereby a leader is transparent with followers concerning life and ministry with a view toward influencing them to imitate him/her. In fact, followers do imitate leaders whether they want it or not. It thus behooves leaders to deliberately strive to model in such a way as to demonstrate what Christian living is all about. A contemporary model is a mentor who uses modeling in order to set ministry examples for emerging leaders.

3. **RELATIONAL MINISTRY.** The book of Philippians mentions by name five of the leaders with whom Paul had personal relationships. Paul had a high value on relational empowerment as a means of influence. More than 100 people are mentioned by name in the Pauline epistles. With most of these Paul had a personal touch which changed their lives. With a number of them he had extensive mentoring which empowered them in ministry.

4. **INFLUENCE MEANS.** The entire book is a major leadership act with Paul being the leader, the Philippian church with its leadership and followership being the followers and the seeds of disunity of the church at Philippi being the prompting situation. Leadership styles which Paul uses include maturity appeal and imitation modeling. His power bases include spiritual authority, personal authority, and persuasion. Some of the more important lessons: a. Women are involved in a vital ministry in

---

[17]The isolation process item refers to a setting aside from normal ministry in which the leader learns a deeper dependence upon God. It usually is a very trying time in the life of a leader. Frequently, it includes a brokenness experience. But great lessons flow from this experience with God. Lessons which enhance spiritual authority.

PHILIPPIANS continued

the church. b. Unity in a church is foundational to a joyous testimony.
c. Partnership in the ministry includes emphathetic concern, prayer, and
giving. d. Leadership must be diverse enough to meet the needs of the
church in its situation (overseer and deacons). e. Reciprocal relationships
are critical. f. The basis for reciprocal relationships is looking our for the
interest of others. g. Humility is a major trait for all who serve in
leadership.

5. **LEADERSHIP ACCOUNTABILITY.** Paul, in 2:14-18, exhorts the
Philippian church to a testimony that will stand out among the
unbelievers around them. As a basis of his appeal he reminds them that
as a leader he will give an account of them on the day of Christ and that
he wants to do so with joy. He wants his ministry with them to have
counted eternally.

6. **FOCUSED LIFE.** Isolation processing usually forces evaluation of life
and ministry. Paul, in a strongly worded appeal models for leaders in the
Philippian church the importance of a focused ministry. Note his
testimony of his life before Christ and then the paradigm shift afterwards.
Note that he is pressing on in his life to attain that for which he was
called--the essence of a focused life which is a deliberate focusing on life
purpose and a desire to fulfill that purpose.

7. **VIBRANT TESTIMONY.** Joy is a fruit of the Spirit that distinguishes a
believer from an unbeliever particularly in distressing circumstances.
Paul in isolation processing and trying circumstances not only models joy
but exhorts it for his followers. His own joy in the midst of non-joy
circumstances forms the basis for a strong persuasive appeal. One of the
characteristics of finishing well is a character which exemplifies the fruit
of the Spirit. Paul certainly shows forth that kind of character here.

9. **CENTRALITY.**[18] Union life with Christ is the secret of this vibrant
testimony. The book as a whole is demonstrating the value of union life.
It sets the norm for what union life looks life in everyday living. The
phrase in Christ carries special significance meaning in union with Christ
as is translated several times by the Good News version. This union life
is not a goal for the believer but should be the norm from which life is
lived out.

---

[18]Centrality is one of eight spirituality components identified in **The Mentor Handbook**. Centrality
involves a growing awareness of who Christ is and how the believer can appropriate Union Life (Christ
in the believer as the believer--the victory aspects of Romans 6-8; including the double union in death to
the controlling authority of sin in a life and in victory--joined to a resurrected Christ in victory d). The
awareness moves along a continuum including: Christ as Savior, Christ as Lord, Christ as strength, Christ
as Union Life.

PHILIPPIANS continued

For Further Leadership Study
1. Note the phrase the Spirit of Jesus Christ(1:19). Why is this used? Where else does the phrase or its functional equivalent occur?
2. In what way does the book portray use of Goodwin's expectation principle[19] as a means of persuasion?
3. Note the inclusion of the great passage on Christ in 2:5-11. What does this say about leadership and status and influence means?

Special Comments
A positive testimony such as the book of Philippians, to use Paul's own words, *shines like stars in a universe for a crooked and depraved generation.* It should be the norm for mature believers. The Philippians are mature believers. As such Paul uses leadership styles on the non-directive end of the continuum--meaning that the believers have the freedom to follow or not. But because they are mature they will probably choose to follow willingly his persuasive appeals.

---

[19]Goodwin is a Christian leader who formulated a statement reflecting a social dynamic that is frequently used by mentors with their mentorees. Emerging leaders tend to live up to the genuine expectations of leaders they admire or respect.

BOOK	**COLOSSIANS** **Author:** Paul
Characters	People mentioned or involved: Paul, Timothy, Tychicus (will carry the letter), Onesimus (Philemon's ex-slave), Aristarchus, John Mark, Jesus Justus, Epaphras, Luke, Demas, Nympha, Archippus
Who To/For	The Church at Colosse, a city in Asia minor east of Ephesus.
Literature Type	An exhortive letter keying on a problem and using teaching as the basis for the exhortation
Story Line	There are several churches in the immediate area (Laodicea, Hierapolis). In Rome, Paul has seen an ex-runaway slave, Onesimus, get saved and grow in the Lord. He belonged to a Christian, named Philemon, in this region and wanted to return to make amends. Paul is going to send Tychicus, a respected brother, back with Onesimus. Hence he takes the time to jot off several letters for them to take. Ephesians, Colossians, and Philemon are the result. The Colossians are being bothered by a cultic group who claim to have inside information on religious issues and practices. They are seeking to proselytize the Colosse believers into practicing some of their religious rites. Paul pens one of the most dynamic chapters on who Christ is (see also John 1 and Hebrews 1 for other such chapters). Based on who Christ is and what He has done--Paul strongly exhorts them to avoid these cultic practices. He also puts in shortened form some of the teaching he has just penned to the Ephesians. In this letter it is clear that Christ should have the pre-eminent place in the lives of believers because of who He is and what He has done.
	Whereas Ephesians focuses on the Church whose head is Christ, Colossians focuses on the Christ who is the head of that church.

Structure			
	I.	(ch 1-2:5)	Christ, Preeminent in His Person and Work
	II.	(ch 2-6-23)	Christ, the Source of Christian Knowledge and Life: Warning Against Cultic Practices
	III.	(ch 3)	Position With Christ, the Motivation for Christian Guidelines and Living
	IV.	(ch 4)	Further Christian Guidelines

COLOSSIANS continued

Theme	**A CLEAR UNDERSTANDING OF CHRIST AND HIS WORK AND HIS RELATIONSHIP TO HIS CHURCH,**

- will result in rejection of man-made efforts towards religious fulfillment and
- will form the basis for practical Christian living.

Key Words   known, knowledge, wisdom, understanding (14)

Key Events   none

Purposes
- to show that the most important religious truths center in the person and work of Christ and are available to all followers of Christ,
- to warn against both cultic ritual and cultic knowledge which claims to add to one's spirituality,
- to warn against human wisdom, legalistic practices and the need for angelic worship,
- to show how Christ's work at the cross overcame principalities and powers.

Why Important   Colossians 1 (along with Hebrews 1 and John 1) gives a tremendous passage on the person and work of Christ who is the head of the church. Wisdom and knowledge is wrapped up in Him. A believer is complete in Him and needs to center his/her life in Christ. Religious practices do not add on to our essential salvation in Christ. This book relates the work of the Cross to the problem of cultic special revelation and shows that the essentials are all in place. We just need to see them worked out in our lives.

Where It Fits   Several epistles, all occurring in the N.T. Church Leadership Era were written about the same time. These include Philemon, Colossians, Ephesians and Philippians. All deal with specific lessons for N.T. Church leaders.

Leadership Lessons
1. **GENRE**. This book written at the same time as Ephesians is much like it in genre. It contains no biographical information. There is an important foundational passage on spiritual warfare which leaders must know since they will be involved in it frequently in their ministries. There are a few

COLOSSIANS continued

    verses which indirectly teach some important leadership truths. Other than that, the material is generally an indirect source of leadership lessons.

2. **SPIRITUAL WARFARE.** The 2:13-16 passage gives an important foundational fact about spiritual warfare. The spirit world which would oppress (in the Colossian case, most likely religious spirits that would bind to legalistic religious pursuit and chasing after special religious knowledge) have already been essentially defeated. The victory can be counted on in spiritual warfare in the present. This is a past perfect paradigm with aftermath results that can be appropriated by faith.

3. **MAJOR PAULINE VALUE.** Paul had as a major goal in his ministry the task given in Colossians 1:24-29). He believed that the Gospel given him and the task given him applied to the Gentiles in an effective way. His goal was to see Gentile believers mature in their union with Christ.

4. **PRAYER CENTERED MINISTRY.** Paul's intercessory ministry for this group of Christians whom he had never visited was strategic in scope and the essence of an intercessory ministry. See especially 1:3,4,5, 9, 10,11,12; 1:29-2:5. The last passage, 1:29-2:5 is especially intercessory in its nature.

For Further Leadership Study

1. Study 1:29-2:5 to learn of one essential ingredient of intercessory praying. See 1:29 agonidzomenos (struggling) and 2:1 agona (struggling) correlate with Romans 15:30 to see the context of sunaonisasthai (striving together). The cognate root is used with prayer and describes the struggle involved in prayer. How could Paul who had never seen these followers struggle with such energy for them (only in prayer).

2. Colossians 2:15-17 gives important leadership principles for how the body operates when it is gathered. What do you see there?

Special Comments

Colossians gives another view of the Cross besides the Roman's vicarious aspect. Colossians shows the power unleashed at the Cross in the supernatural realm. Principalities and powers lost a decisive strategic battle at the Cross. We are made aware of spiritual powers in Job and their effect in the physical world but we have no inkling of what to do about them except to live righteous lives and have faith in God's purposes in our situations. In Daniel we see that there are opposing forces in the spiritual realm and that warfare is going on even as we intercede. Prayer catalyzes spiritual warfare. Somehow truth is important-- Daniel was certainly seeking truth. In Ephesians we learn that we can have victory and how righteousness, truth, faith, and prayer combat spiritual forces. But Colossians (2:13-15) gives the basis for victory--both in our personal lives and over spiritual forces.

BOOK	**PHILEMON**	**Author:** Paul

Characters   People mentioned or involved: Paul, Timothy, Philemon, Apphia, Archippus, Onesimus, Epaphras, Mark, Aristarchus, Demas, Luke

Who To/For   Philemon, a fellow worker in the Gospel, probably the head of the church meeting in his home

Literature Type   A very personal letter which makes a special appeal to Philemon.

Story Line   Onesimus, a run away slave from the household of Philemon, somehow made his way to Rome. There he got converted and came into contact with Paul while Paul was under house arrest. He grew in the Lord and became close to Paul. Paul sends him back to his master, Philemon to make amends. He sends along this letter (and the letters to the churches in Colosse and Ephesus). The letter asks Philemon to free Onesimus willingly. It is a strong appeal based on Paul's maturity and previous relationship with Philemon.

Structure   I. (verses 1--7)   Positive Lead In to the Plea
        II. (verses 8-21   The Plea--Using Obligation/ Persuasion In a Powerful Way
        III. (verses 22-25)   Possible Follow-up of the Plea

Theme   **PAUL'S SPECIAL PLEA TO PHILEMON**
- was a request to receive back a former runaway slave, named Onesimus,
- was based on his special relationship to Philemon,
- involved strong persuasion yet left the final decision to Philemon, and
- models the application of Christian principle to a social institution.

Key Words   none

Key Events   the past event--Onesimus running away is in view and a future event--the return of Onesimus and the reading of the letter with the appeal

PHILEMON   continued

Purposes
- to appeal on Onesimus' behalf for Philemon to receive him back, forgive him, free him, and accept him,
- to model tactfulness in dealing with Christians on important issues,
- to highlight the importance of Christian restitution,
- to show the power of the Gospel--life in Christ changes every relationship individuals have,
- to show that our relationship to others tests our relationship to Christ,
- to show how the Gospel impacts social institutions: social evils are to be ended willingly by individuals whose transformed lives can no longer tolerate them.

Why Important   This book shows the power of the Gospel to transform lives and to transform society. It was written in the same time span as the epistle to the Ephesians and the epistle to the Colossians. Those lofty epistles, with great doctrinal truth, were companion letters being carried to churches in the same area. The three taken together serve to emphasize just how important this little epistle was. Its inclusion in the Scripture shows us how important the Gospel is in everyday life. Here is one illustration of three transformed lives, a very complex social problem, and how the Gospel requires love to be applied. We see Paul practicing what he taught others and asking them to do the same.

Where It Fits   This little book was written along with Ephesians, Philippians, and Colossians about two thirds of the way through Paul's ministry. It is vintage Paul and show how a mature leader in the Church era utilizes gentle yet powerful influence means to motivate and bring about change in a specific situation. This is a prison epistle and shows how productive ministry can flow, even in a major isolation period of Paul's life.

Leadership Lessons

1. **INFLUENCE MEANS**. This book demonstrates the importance of spiritual authority and three specific leadership styles as the essence of influence means with a mature follower. Paul is attempting to influence

PHILEMON   continued

Philemon to accept back a runaway slave, Onesimus. He uses three kinds
of leadership styles to bring about that influence. Leadership style refers
to the behavioral patterns that a leader exhibits when attempting to
influence the attitude and actions of followers in a given leadership act.
How a given leader influences others depends upon several factors:
personality bent toward task or relationship, the leadership function being
attempted, the follower maturity, and the leader-follower relationship.[20]
Philemon is a mature believer. Paul has a very special relationship with
him and others in his church. Normally Paul is a task oriented person
(here he is too--the task to link Onesimus back into the situation); but
here he is also very relationship oriented. The function is a delicate one.
Discipline of run away slaves is expected and even demanded. Paul is
trying to circumvent this normal social response with the hope of
redeeming Onesimus for the Gospel's sake. Of the ten Pauline leadership
styles identified in his epistles, three are seen here with one being in
focus: father-initiator, maturity appeal, and obligation persuasion. The
father-initiator leadership style uses the fact of the leader as having
founded the work as a lever for getting acceptance of influence by the
leader. The *maturity appeal* leadership style is a form of leadership
influence which counts upon godly experience, usually gained over a
long period of time, an empathetic identification based on a common
sharing of experience, and a recognition of the force of imitation
modeling in influencing people in order to convince people toward a
favorable acceptance of the leader's ideas. An *obligation persuasion*
leadership style refers to an appeal to followers to follow some
recommended directives which persuades, not commands followers to
heed some advice; leaves the decision to do so in the hands of the
followers, but forces the followers to recognize their obligation to the
leader due to past service by the leader to the follower; strongly implies
that the follower owes the leader some debt and should follow the
recommended advice as part of paying back the obligation; and finally
reflects the leader's strong expectation that the follower will conform to
the persuasive advice. It is this last leadership style that is in focus in the
book. Spiritual authority is a power base from which a leader exerts
influence. Leaders using spiritual authority as the power base for
influence do so by modeling, persuading, and teaching and not by
command or demand. They look for willing response from followers not

---

[20]See my booklet, **Coming to Some Conclusions on Leadership Styles** available through Barnabas
Resources, 2175 N. Holliston, Altadena, Ca 91001. There I discuss more thoroughly these factors
affecting leadership style. I also define more fully the three Pauline styles referred to in the following
discussion.

PHILEMON   continued

a forced response. Followers perceive spirituality in a leader and are thus
open to that leader's influence. This spirituality is seen in a leader
because of demonstration of supernaturally gifted power, deep
experiences with God, and modeling of godly character. Paul here
illustrates how a godly leader with spiritual authority dominant as the
power base influences a mature follower toward an important life
changing decision.

2. **MENTOR SPONSOR.** Mentors frequently co-minister with mentorees in
order to enhance the mentorees status and standing before followers. (See
Philemon 1, 2 Corinthians 1:1, Philippians 1:1, Colossians 1:1, 1
Thessalonians 1:1, 2 Thessalonians 1:1) Mentors sponsor mentorees. One
way is to co-minister with them. Mentorees tend to rise to the level of the
mentor in the eyes of followers in terms of status and authority--though they
must always eventually earn their own way. Co-authoring is a way of
sponsoring and giving prestige and initial credibility to a mentoree.

3. **RELATIONAL VALUE.** Paul believed that leadership selection and
development and training should be done in a personal/ relational
manner. A *leadership value* is an underlying assumption which affects
how a leader behaves in or perceives leadership situations. One
important value seen in Philemon and almost all of the Pauline epistles
concerns personal ministry. *Leaders should view personal relationships
as an important part of ministry.* This dovetails with another Pauline
leadership value: *Leaders must be concerned about leadership selection
and development.* Paul constantly had about him people whom he related
to very personally (mentor relationships) in order to train and release
them into ministry. Notice even in this small very personal epistle to
Philemon how Paul exudes personal relationships and how each are being
trained: Timothy, Philemon, Apphia, Archipus, Onesimus, Epaphras,
Mark, Aristarchus, Demas, Luke.

4. **PRAYER ENCOURAGEMENT PRINCIPLE.** Leaders encourage
their people by praying for them and telling them what they are praying
for them. The prayer encouragement principle seen in Jesus ministry
(Luke 22:31,32) should be part of each leader's repertoire of influence
means for development of followers. Here Paul demonstrates it as he so
often does. This little epistle also illustrates the ministry prayer principle:
*If God has called you to a ministry then He has called you to pray for
that ministry.*[21]

---

[21]This principle first occurs in the final public leadership act of Samuel in 1 Samuel 12. It reoccurs across
the scriptures in many varied leadership situations. It is an absolute in force.

PHILEMON   continued

5. **ISOLATION PROCESSING AND RESULTS.** Productive ministry is often rooted in isolation times. For the most part isolation is a setting aside of a leader from normal ministry in order to develop a deeper relationship with God. But here we see as in the other prison epistles how these times can be productive times in reflection, divine contacts, and production of lasting achievements (Pauline epistles). Productive ministry in the future is often rooted in these isolation times. Contacts, seed thoughts, and evaluation which come in this time may lead to an expanded productivity in the future. Notice how Paul views his isolation situation sovereignly--a prisoner of Christ Jesus.

6. **MENTOR SPONSOR.** Mentor sponsors use influence to link their mentorees to resources, people and situations that will develop them. Paul sponsors Onesimus. This illustrates how mentor sponsors use their influence on behalf of mentorees. It is interesting that church history makes note of a Bishop Onesimus in this region. It is also held by some New Testament scholars that Onesimus and Philemon were the gatherers of the Pauline epistles and thus helped facilitate the New Testament canon.

7. **SOCIAL ISSUE.** Major wrongs in society can be changed by individuals. Paul attacks a major evil social institution, slavery, by hitting at its roots. He stresses the transforming power of the Gospel, both to change a slave and a slave holder and himself. When the essence of the Gospel is understood it will cut at the root of issues like slavery. For the historical case study illustrating just this approach to changing slavery see John Woolman's story of ridding the Quakers of slavery. Notice also Paul's change tactics. See especially his tactfulness and approach to getting a hearing--*just a little bit of sugar makes the medicine go down in the most delightful way* (Philemon 4-7). Notice also his gentle accountability threat (Philemon 22).

For Further Leadership Study
1. Study the Pauline leadership styles: apostolic, confrontation, father-initiator, obligation-persuasion, father-guardian, maturity appeal, nurse, imitator, consensus, and indirect conflict style. Paul exhibits styles all along the leadership style continuum which runs from highly directive to highly non-directive. The obvious implication of this was that Paul used a multi-style approach in his leadership influence depending on many factors including leadership function, relationship involved, and maturing of people being influenced.

PHILEMON   continued

2. Study further the personal names listed in this epistle for any indications of what happened to them.

Special Comments
This is one of the five one chapter books in Scripture. It is small enough to be mastered and yet profound enough to challenge us all.[22]

---

[22]The one chapter books in the Bible ought to be a challenge for Bible students. They are small and hence easy to master. Yet they are important enough to be included in the Bible. And if the intentional selection notion is valid they contribute something special that can't be found elsewhere. The one chapter books include: Obadiah, Philemon, 2 John, 3 John, Jude.

BOOK	**1 PETER** **Author:** Peter

Characters none in focus

Who To/For specifically to Jewish Christians who lived outside of Palestine but also generally to all those who are undergoing suffering

Literature Type A general letter containing little of anything personal. It teaches by reflecting on basic issues of Christianity as they have been experienced by Peter and the implications of these insights for people going through suffering.

Story Line Toward the end of his life, Peter is aware of numerous believers scattered about in Asia who are undergoing persecution. He views these things as part of God's sovereign working in the lives of the believers and seeks to establish them in their faith by revealing how these processes will be used by God to mature them.

Structure

I.   (ch 1:1-12)   Introduction--Suffering, Salvation and God's Purposes

II. (ch 1:13-2:10)   Submission to Present Circumstances-- Special Privileges Spurring Us to Holiness, to Love and Growth

III. (ch 2:11-4:11)   Submission to Demands of Special Relationships: Pilgrims, Citizens, Servants, Family, Innocent Sufferers, Opposition, 2nd Coming

IV. (ch 4:12-ch 5)   Submission in View of Special Trials

Theme **PRESENT PRESSURE CIRCUMSTANCES IN OUR LIVES**,

- are under God's sovereign control,
- are used by Him to perfect us in our character and in our trust of Him,
- will be accompanied with God's grace, and therefore
- demand on our part a submissive spirit to them.

1 PETER continued

Key Words   suffer, sufferings (15); words looking forward to hope
       such as glory, glorify (16); grace (10)

Key Events   none

Purposes
- to encourage those going through difficult times to see those times as God's means for perfecting them,
- to exhort believer's to recognize God's sovereign control over circumstances in their lives,
- to testify to the grace of God in preserving and establishing a believer in the midst of these circumstances,
- to give a model of the power of the Gospel over a lifetime of processing in a life (Peter's),
- to give a model of a leader (Peter) who is finishing well and can testify to these truths in his own life.

Why Important This book coming out of a lifetime of experience testifies to the grace of God to shape and establish a believer through the circumstances and relationships around that believer. The book begins with this message (1:2) and closes with it (5:12) and weaves it in to every portion. Thus it gives probably the most exhaustive treatment in Scriptures of the sufficiency of God's grace for encouraging, enabling, and establishing a believer. Peter has experienced this grace throughout his own lifetime. He speaks from experience. We have to listen to him. This book probably as much as any shows how important the return of Christ is as a motivating factor for having us appropriate the grace of God and purify our conduct in the circumstances around us (when Jesus Christ is revealed, the glories that would follow, when Jesus Christ is revealed, reason for the hope, end of all things near, when his glory is revealed, share in the glory to be revealed).

Where It Fits This book, written near the end of Peter's life occurs, in the N.T. Church age after the church had broken out of its Jewish cocoon and spread to the Gentiles. Again it is

1 PETER continued

> filled with N.T. lessons for Church leaders by one who
> had spent his adult life leading churches. He himself had
> suffered and now gives advice to those who will be
> fellow sufferers for the sake of Christ.

Leadership Lessons
1. **GENRE.** 1 Peter contains source material which deals with giftedness, leadership style, the New Testament Philosophical Model--The Shepherd Model, authority/submission. It has one direct contextual leadership passage--1 Peter 5:1-4.
2. **LEADERSHIP STYLE.** Peter uses a maturity appeal style (see especially 5:1-4, 5-7) in his persuasion attempt to influence his hearers. Maturity appeal is a form of leadership influence which counts upon Godly experience, usually gained over a long period of time, an empathetic identification based on a common sharing of experience, and a recognition of the force of imitation modeling in influencing people, in order to convince people toward a favorable acceptance of the leader's ideas. He uses also imitation modeling as a leadership style--the conscious use of modeling to influence. Both of these are highly indirect styles of leading and depend upon maturity in followers to respond. The situation is one in which the hearers are facing persecution and trying times. A heavy handed highly direct style would be too much of a burden for them under the kind of pressures they are already facing. So Peter emphathetically adjusts his leadership style to fit the situation.
3. **AUTHORITY/SUBMISSION.** Peter's strongest appeal for submission in tough situations is Jesus himself (1 Peter 2:20-25). Peter advocates submission in terms of governmental issues, social issues, marriage relationships, church as a whole. The end result of submission even in unjust situations is testimony to the glory and grace of God. Submission is seen in its essence as to God (5:6,7) and for His purposes.
4. **SPIRITUAL WARFARE.** (5:8-9) Two warnings to head off spiritual warfare include discipline and alert minds. Alertness has to do with expectancy that we will receive warfare. The admonition is to resist Satan, resting on our faith (Christian truth) and taking courage from the fact that others are standing firm too.
5. **SHEPHERD MODEL.** 1 Peter 5:1-4 is a direct leadership context and should be studied in detail. Highlights of this leadership passage include: a leadership style of maturity appeal; the appeal for accepting responsibility of leadership willingly and not from other improper motivations (like money); an appeal for modeling as a basic influence means; an appeal to share in Jesus reward when He returns.

1 PETER continued

6. **GIFTEDNESS.** (4:7-10) is a leadership gifts passage. It contains one role (the hospitality function) and two generic gift categories: use of word gifting, and use of love gifting. The essence of the thrust is that these diverse gifts should be used with gifted power and for results that honor God. In order to see the concept of generic categories, this passage should be correlated with the Hebrews 2:1-4 which uses a generic category as well as a specific spiritual gift and with Romans 12:3-8 which also has the possibility of one generic category. The major importance of this passage is an external confirmation of giftedness in the early church by someone other than Paul (the Hebrews passage does this too).

7. **EMPOWERMENT.** Peter encourages by repeatedly emphasizing that it is the grace of God which will sustain through these hard times. Empowerment at its ultimate always goes back to God. Probably the most important thing Peter does for us is to warn us that suffering (conclusion 4:19) and persecution are normal and that we should expect them.

8. **SOCIAL BASE.** The 1 Peter 3:1-6, and 7 give helpful information of relationships between husbands and wives. Both receive help. The end result of the admonishment is that social base processing is seen to have a direct and vital impact on spiritual issues.

For Further Leadership Study
1. Exegete the 1 Peter 5:1-4 passage and list your major principles of leadership.
2. Study the 1:3-8 to catch the essence of all processing, its purposes in God's sovereignty.

Special Comments
The range of teaching in this epistle is quite broad touching on theological topics of election, inspiration of Scripture, salvation, sanctification, the church, the believer's relationship to political authority and others. It also deals with a broad range of practical applications of Christian truth. Peter's Christianity ramifies throughout all his perspectives and relationships in life.

BOOK   **2 PETER**   **Author:** Peter

Characters   not in focus, Peter and Paul mentioned

Who To/For   to believers in general, perhaps the same as those in 1
                 Peter (3:1)

Literature Type An exhortive general letter full of warning

Story Line   In 1 Peter, Peter was aware of danger from without the
                 church (persecution and heavy suffering) in sidetracking the
                 believer. In this little epistle he points out the dangers from
                 within the church, false teaching, for sidetracking the
                 believer. Again the answer has to do with the grace of God.

Structure   I. (ch 1) Provision for Growth--Inner Life, knowledge of Christ
               II. (ch 2) Deterrent to Growth--False Teaching
               III. (ch 3) Stimulus for Growth--the Day of the Lord

Theme   **YOUR KNOWLEDGE OF FOUNDATIONAL
               CHRISTIAN TRUTH,**
               - **must be life-transforming knowledge,**
               - **will be opposed and denied by false teachers, and**
               - **must reveal itself in positive on-going progress (growth),**
                 the ultimate solution to these negative pressures.

Key Words   *knowledge (6); judgment (4);*

Key Events   none specifically; the mount of transfiguration experience
               that Peter, James, and John had with Jesus is alluded to; a
               future event--the fulfillment of the Day of the Lord--is
               pointed to.

Purposes
- to warn against false teachers who can lead believer's astray,
- to establish believers in a growth mentality,
- to motivate toward growth by making believers aware of the Day of the Lord
- to model a Christian leader finishing well.

Why Important   This book highlights the responsibility for a believer to
                  grow. In 1 Peter the sufficiency of grace to enable a believer
                  to stand fast in the midst of suffering and persecution was
                  asserted. But it is not enough to just stand fast. There must

2 PETER continued

> also be growth. Being in the grace of God carries with it responsibility for growth. The final admonition gives a two fold growth thrust: grace, experiential knowledge of Christ.

Where It Fits   This book, written near the end of Peter's life occurs, in the N.T. Church age after the church had broken out of its Jewish cocoon and spread to the Gentiles. Again it is filled with N.T. lessons for Church leaders by one who had spent his adult life leading churches. His final appeal is for people to grow up in their experiential knowledge of Christ.

Leadership Lessons
1. **GENRE.** 2 Peter contains source material much like that of 1 Peter. Its most important contribution is the portrayal of a leader who is finishing well (1:12-15). Peter has walked with Jesus for a long time and he is finishing well. We need models of those who finish well.
2. **CERTAINTY OF WORD.** One of the important things Peter models at the end of his lifetime is a conviction about the Word of God (1:19-21).
3. **HOPE.** At the end of his life Peter still has conviction that God enables and brings growth in a believer's life (1:3-9). He sees a dynamic tension in the growth process. There is the aspect of God's provision in union life (1:4) but also the responsibly appropriate and grow in the Christian life (1:5-9).
4. **PERSPECTIVE.** Peter adds to the concept of the day of the Lord by describing characteristics of the times near the end. There will be false teachers who will lead people astray. But God will act in judgment (3:10). And there will be new heaven and earth--hope for the believer.
5. **FINAL CHALLENGE.** Peter finishes well. His last exhortation is one to grow in an experiential understanding of Jesus.

For Further Leadership Study
1. Note the stages of growth that Peter describes in 1:5-9. This is Peter's equivalent of Paul's fruit of the Spirit (Galatians 5:22,23).
2. When looking back after a long life one usually remembers key items. What pivotal point does Peter remember about Jesus' processing?
3. Which of the barriers are mentioned in the description of the false teachers?

Special Comments
Peter's death is near (1:14) and he longs to leave behind an ultimate contribution that will help believers continually remember some of the essential insights that have proven true for him (1:15). Thus we have 2 Peter. And every time we read it and study it and use it in our lives we partake of a blessing he imparted to us.

BOOK   **1 TIMOTHY**   **Author: Paul**

Characters   Those mentioned or involved: Paul, Timothy, Hymenaeus, Alexander

Who To/For   To Timothy, a protégé of Paul, who is helping advise church leaders in Ephesus

Literature Type A personal letter with powerful advice backed by years of experience

Story Line   Paul had helped found the church in Ephesus (Acts 19). It became an indigenous church. Later he met with the elders of this church in a stop over on his trip back to Jerusalem (Acts 20). At that time he warned them of problems that would arise in the church. Later he also wrote an epistle to them (along with the ones to Colosse and Philemon). At that time there were no major problems as witnessed by the general nature of the letter. Several years later the problems he warned about have arisen. He sends Timothy to try to minister to the situation and advise the church elders. Timothy runs in to a number of problems which he does not know how to handle. This epistle is written to Timothy to help him in that situation.

Structure   There is a lack of well integrated structural sections in this book. It is written by an older person--who throws in asides (certain of his words and phrases will remind him of important things he has learned in the past--and he will divert to include them). There is a purpose statement which loosely integrates every thing that is said. See 1 Timothy 3;14,15.

    I.   (ch 1,2)   Paul's Advice on Major Problems in the Church
    II.   (ch 3)   Paul's advice on Local Leadership Selection
    III. (ch 4)   Paul's Personal Advice to Timothy on How to Handle Himself
    IV. (ch 5)   Paul's Advice on social Problem on Widows
    V.   (ch 6)   Paul's Miscellaneous Exhortations

1 TIMOTHY   continued

Theme   **LEADING GOD'S PEOPLE, AS MODEL REPRESENTATIVES OF GOD'S TRUTH,**
- requires confrontation against false doctrines and practices,
- involves selection of quality local leadership,
- demands personal development as a leader, and
- outworks itself in meeting social needs for the believers.

Key Words   godliness (8), good (three different Greek words) (23), conscience (4), doctrine (8), teach, teacher (7)

Key Events   none in focus

Purposes   See 1 Timothy 3:14,15 for a stated purpose.

- to give Timothy advice on numerous church problems including: confronting false doctrine and troublesome leaders propagating it, instruction on church prayers, selection criteria for overseers and deacons, spirit practices, Timothy's lack of boldness, how to properly rebuke in the church, handling of support of widows, financial support of church elders, accusations against elders, attitudes of slaves, attitudes toward money, Timothy's personal conduct, giving.
- to encourage Timothy to confront the problems,
- to encourage Timothy to develop personally and warn him against the consequences of failure to develop,
- to model several mentoring styles including: contemporary model, counselor, teacher, spiritual guide,
- to show the complexity of leading a church which has the truth of the Bible as its central controlling guidelines.

Why Important   Church leadership is desperately needed at all times. This book gives advice and warning to church leaders on the necessity for their own personal development and for how to go about problem solving. It shows that the true function of the church is the proclamation of the truth in the world about it. And the leader of the church must have as a true function the exposition, application, and modeling of that truth. The leader(s) is key. He/she must be loyal to truth, consistent in outward life and inner life, and maintaining a learning posture personally.

1 TIMOTHY   continued

Where it Fits   In the redemptive drama Timothy occurs in Part II
Salvation proclaimed and chapter 4, the church.
Throughout this era God is inviting people everywhere
(Acts 15:14) to be reconciled to Himself. His instrument
for this is the church. When churches are started, where
ever they are, there will always be a need for leadership.
There will always be problems both within the personal
life of the leaders and in the congregation. The problems
in the church are part of the reason for existence of
leaders. They must be confronted. Problems in the
church will not be solved without a leader who is
developing. This book, addresses leadership issues at a
specific church in a specific culture. Yet its advice is
broad enough to be multi-culturally acceptable--certainly
in the problem solving methodology if not the actual
solution. This book is also peculiar in that it is
addressing the problem of indigenous leadership which
needs help. How can an outside consultant be accepted
by them, have authority with them and be useful to them
yet without destroying their indigeneity? Such
is the task Paul faces in writing and giving leadership
information to Timothy.

Leadership Lessons

1. **MENTORING.** Experienced leaders need to be mentoring others and all
   leaders need mentoring. All leaders will need various kinds of mentoring
   help throughout their leadership time-line. Paul's ministry to Timothy
   demonstrates four of the nine mentor roles that mentors can take with
   mentorees: contemporary model, spiritual guide, teacher, and counselor.
   These roles of course require a special relationship between mentor and
   mentoree. Paul had that with Timothy.
2. **GIFTEDNESS.** Giftedness needs to be motivated and developed.
   Aspects of a leader's giftedness can be neglected, grow cold, and be
   ineffective. See 1 Timothy 4:14 for Paul's admonition.
3. **BALANCE.** Effective leaders maintain a balance between personal
   development and ministry productivity. Doing and being must be kept in
   balance throughout a leader's life. It is clear that Paul saw both as
   important to Timothy.
4. **DISCIPLINE.** Discipline of leadership must be done carefully and upon
   good evidence. The best antidote to this is proper leadership selection

1 TIMOTHY   continued

and on-going development. Nevertheless this will be an on-going problem and must be done and done properly with a view to redeeming the leader and protecting the church. Leaders need to be disciplined carefully for reputation and character are at stake and can ruin leadership. Discipline must occur after investigation and upon reliable evidence. Leaders who fail need to be rebuked publicly in church in order to warn the church, maintain credibility for high standards of leadership, and as a basis for recovery. Cover-ups hurt everybody both leaders and people.

5. **COMPLEXITY**. Leadership is very complex. A major focus, that is, an on going function that leaders must perform is problem solving: doctrinal--attacks from without and within, which will split the believers and woo some away, problems of integrity (conscience), problems of character, problems of hypocrisy in public worship and in leadership, submission problems from men and women, subtle inroads of culture that weaken the gospel--contextualization balance, leadership selection, loss of heart for ministry, lack of leaders developing themselves, lack of confrontation by leaders of problems, unusual emphases which over balance Christian practice, social problems in the church, finances in the church, wrong views toward stewardship of resources, etc.

6. **LEADERSHIP GUIDELINES**. Patterns or guidelines for local church leadership in this specific church include:

   a. *a knowledge of what it is not and what it is*. Paul shows that local leadership is not--controversial teachers of laws that bind people, results in hypocritical use of ministry as a means of financial gain. He shows that it is a plurality yet a strongly led plurality--Timothy's role was to inspire, correct, and move this leadership and church toward correcting its problems.

   b. *qualifications for leaders which include character and conscience.* Paul's list of qualifications focuses on integrity and deals mainly with character not giftedness. At least three kinds of leaders are seen in this specific local church situation: elders (overseer--two kinds--ruling and word gifted), deacon (service oriented), and roving apostolic function (Timothy--probably regional influence). Notice that a *good or clear conscience* is stressed as fundamentally important in a leader (see 1:5,18-20, 3:9, 4:1,2). Early ministry is where foundational character is solidified. Timothy is urged to solidify his inner life in this regard and warned of the consequence of not doing so. Controversial teaching should be avoided--stick to the fundamentals-- notice the *truth asides* that Paul *inserts*--all are core and central to Christianity (1:15; 2:3,4,5,6; 3:1; 3:16; 4:9, 10; 6:15)

1 TIMOTHY   continued

   c. *Strong local church leadership is not incompatible with plurality.*
     Frequently strong leadership is associated only with authoritative
     structures. And frequently weak task oriented leadership is associated
     with plurality. This does not have to be.
   d. *Emphasis on selection is maturity in character, not riches, position, or*
     ability.
   e. *Testing and time is involved in selection of local leadership.* Too quick a
     selection is warned against as leading to pride and problematic leadership.
   f. *The spirituality factors of exteriority and interiority in the leader's life*
     must be kept in balance. Reputation without is crucial to a leader; a
     leader can sway followers and deceive them--but usually a bad
     character is recognized by non-followers external to the situation.
     Personal inward growth in a leader is a must and should lead to and be
     consistent with outward behavior.
7. **FINANCES**. Finances can be a blessing and a curse. Having or not having
   wealth is not the issue. It is the stewardship of resources that is the major
   issue. What they are used for is what is significant. There are dangers of
   having financial resources--they can subtly turn away trust from God to trust
   in the resources. Paul admonishes to use resources well.
8. **SPIRITUAL WARFARE**. Paul gives several pieces of advice and
   caution concerning spiritual warfare including:
   a. *Spiritual warfare is a natural part of the ministry.* Paul doesn't make a
     big thing over it nor does he avoid it. He simply assumes spiritual
     warfare as part of the cause of the problems that Timothy faces.
   b. *Maintain balance with regard to spiritual warfare.* Paul does not see
     spiritual warfare as the cause of everything. On the other hand, natural
     causes are not the source of everything either. Paul does not even
     advocate some special means of dealing with it other than use of truth
     and righteousness. He does not attack the spirit world directly nor
     does he give any special instructions about it (Perhaps that is because
     he had already done this in his letter to the Ephesian church). His
     inclusion of spiritual warfare is not in focus but is subtly woven into
     the normal discussion. (see 1:18-20, 3:6, 3:7, 4:1)
   c. *Paul has spiritual authority to discipline indirectly.* (See 1:18-20--
     where Paul disciplines indirectly, handing over to Satan)
   d. *Paul identifies areas of Satanic involvement*: doubt and matters of
     conscience, pride, deceptive teaching and lustful indiscipline.

1 TIMOTHY   continued

For Further Leadership Study
1. Study the mentoring roles that Paul works on in his relationship with Timothy as illustrated in this book. What empowering tasks of a spiritual guide, counselor, teacher, or contemporary mentor are illustrated?
2. What to Paul are core doctrines that must be foundational to a local church? See his asides on doctrinal truth and his emphasis to Timothy.
3. Which of the qualifications for leaders are specific to this situation? Which can be generalized and seen in other local church cultural situations in the New Testament? How do you know?
4. 1 Timothy 2:11-13 (entire context is 1-14) should be studied as a cultural problematic issue regarding women and abuse of authority. This is not a general admonition against women in leadership but a specific cultural issue being dealt with--the issue is abuse of authority and influencing the church improperly. Forming a major doctrine on an unclear text dealing with a problem issue is questionable (like excluding women in ministry because of this text).
5. Giftedness development and impartation of gifts suggested in this letter need further comparative study in other Pauline letters.
6. Both the *harvest* and *shepherd models* of philosophy are in view in this letter. However, due to the development of the church the emphasis is more on the shepherd model--internal nurture and problem solving. But see the subtle emphasis in the truth asides toward harvest model thought.
7. Two principles of discipline are highlighted: the *Principle of Validity* (Is it true?), the *Principle of Public Discipline* (the value of warning). Both of these need to be studied for wider confirmation.
8. Issues of conscience must be addressed in leadership. Paul gives here some basics but much more needs to be done with conscience.
9. The model for plurality needs to be traced to other situations for wider confirmation. Is this one of several configurations or the ideal? Is it culturally suggested? What other models are allowable?
10. Can a leader's personality be changed? Timothy does not seem to be very confrontational (Titus does seem to be so). In this situation Paul knows that confrontation is a must. Paul seems to think that Timothy can become confrontational, and more authoritative. Do these kind of assumptions hold for other leaders in Scripture? Can bold authoritative leaders become gentle? Can gentle leaders become bold?

Special Comments
This major book contributing to leadership is a must for personal study and application and for teaching for the church. It should fundamentally form a leader's ministry foundations in the Church leadership era.

BOOK	TITUS	**AUTHOR: PAUL**

Characters People mentioned or involved: Paul, Titus, Artemas, Tychicus, Zenas, Apollos

Who To/For To Titus, a protégé of Paul, who is confronting church problems on the island of Crete

Literature Type an authoritative personal letter to Titus containing strong advice, teaching, and exhortation.

Story Line Titus is a gentile and is one of Paul's protégés who has traveled with him and learned ministry via on -the-job training. Frequently he is sent on ministry assignments which involve confrontation. Such is the case in the church at Crete. Leadership is lacking. Daily life is basically unaffected by Christian teaching. There is little difference between a Christian and any other Cretian as to daily life. Paul sees the problem as one of leadership. Titus is sent to select, develop and establish leadership that can turn the church around. He needs authority to do that--authority that a person like Paul has. Paul seeks to give that authority vicariously through this letter which would be read by the believers in Crete.

Structure

I. (ch 1:15-16) Leadership--An Essential Basis for a Well Ordered Church

II. (ch 2:1-14) Application of Practical Teaching--An Essential Function of a well ordered Church

III. (ch 3:1-11) Godly Living--An Essential Outward Sign To Society of A Well Ordered Church

Theme **SETTING THE CHURCH IN ORDER**
- involves the appointing of qualified leaders,
- requires leaders who are sound in teaching and who model a Christian life style, and
- necessitates leaders who exhort others to practical Christian living.

Key Words sound (5), good works (6), good (11)

TITUS continued

Key Events   none in focus

Purposes
- to give Titus authoritative backing in the eyes of the Cretian church,
- to give Titus perspective on leadership selection,
- to give Titus perspective on how leadership can best influence the situation--teaching and modeling,
- to encourage the Cretian believers to good works,
- to motivate outward behavior by focusing on the return of Christ.
- to model several mentoring styles: contemporary model, counselor, teacher, sponsor.

Why Important   Church leadership is needed everywhere at all times. This book points out its fundamental role. A church can not be established without it. For a church to be effective its people must be demonstrating Christian values in their lives. This comes when they are taught them, see them modeled by their leaders, and when they are held accountable to demonstrate them. This book also points out Eerdman's basic idea that the return of the Lord has always been the supreme motivation for consistent Christian living. This book in another cultural setting authenticates the concept of leadership selection dominantly by character--integrity is the key trait which is reflected in all the cultural descriptions. Both Ephesian culture and now this island culture, two varying cultures, show that integrity as reflected in specific cultural traits is the key issue of leadership selection. This book encourages us to believe that high quality leaders are available in any culture no matter what the outward symptoms of the culture are (they are not described very complimentary in Titus).

Where it Fits   In the redemptive drama Titus like Timothy occurs in Part II Salvation proclaimed and chapter 4, the church. Throughout this era God is inviting people everywhere (Acts 15:14) to be reconciled to Himself. His instrument for this is the church. When churches are started, where ever they are, there will always be a need for leadership. Titus shows that leadership is essential to a well ordered church. A church can not function well in society unless

TITUS continued

it is well taught. The teaching must be practically oriented. The teaching involves explanation, demonstration, and application with accountability. Apostolic authority is important. Titus needs Paul's backing so that the Christians on Crete will listen to him.

Leadership Lessons

1. **APOSTOLIC FUNCTION.** Titus gives us insights on what an apostolic function is.
   a. Apostles must appoint sound leaders if a church is to be healthy.
   b. Apostles analyze needs in a situation and bring about training in basic teaching (sound doctrine) that can be applied to problems in the culture.
   c. Apostolic leadership must use modeling which flows from experience.
2. **MENTOR SPONSOR.** Titus shows us how Paul used his spiritual authority to give Titus authority he needed to do the job.
3. **PLURALITY OF LEADERS.** Titus shows us that at least in the churches in Crete (possibly regionally) there was a plurality of leaders.
4. **CONTEXTUALIZATION.** Titus gives insights of how Christian living looks in one culture.
5. **INTEGRITY/CHARACTER.** Titus reaffirms the importance of integrity as a necessary trait for a church leader.
6. **RELEASE.** Paul models the leadership release function with Titus. Titus has heavy responsibility given him. The guidelines are firm but he is left to carry it out on his own. Leaders must increasingly be released if they are to assume initiative for leadership. Paul models the release function and teaches it throughout the book in the guidelines he gives Titus.
7. **HIGH STANDARDS.** High standards for leadership must be held in all cultures. Paul tells Titus to appoint leaders with these qualifications, and he goes on to highlight integrity and its manifestations. He does not lessen the requirements because of the cultures values that pervade. It is not get the best kind you find but get these kind.

For Further Leadership Study

1. Study the mentoring roles that Paul works on in his relationship with Titus as illustrated in this book. What empowering tasks of a sponsor, counselor, teacher, or contemporary mentor are illustrated?
2. Titus is mentioned several times in the Pauline epistles (see especially 2 Corinthians and 2 Timothy). Paul uses an on-the-job training technique

TITUS continued

called a ministry task in Titus' development. A ministry task is an assignment recognized as from God which primarily tests a person's faithfulness and obedience but often also allows use of ministry gifts in the context of the task which has closure, accountability, and evaluation. The ministry task has a two-fold thrust--to develop the leader and to accomplish the task whatever it is. As the leader becomes more proficient the thrust of the task becomes more for the accomplishment of it and less for the development of the leader. Titus has four ministry tasks given (3 at Corinth and one in Crete). He is increasingly released in the tasks. This is whole process is worthy of study.

3. Comparatively study the traits lists of 1 Timothy 3 and Titus 1 to see how culture affects the manifestation of integrity.
4. Study comparatively the kinds of leaders mentioned in 1 Timothy and Titus. Note which one is not present. Why?
5. What are the implications of the closing words for leadership selection and development? (note 3:12-14)

Special Comments
Again as in 1 Timothy this is a book dealing directly with leadership issues--more so on the corporate side of leadership while Timothy deals with the personal side, Timothy himself. The study of this book is a must for personal study and application and for teaching for the church. This book ought to be influential on a leader's foundations for ministry philosophy.

BOOK	**2 TIMOTHY**	**AUTHOR: PAUL**

Characters   Those mentioned include Paul, Timothy, Onesiphorus, Demas, Crescens, Titus, Luke, Tychicus, Carpus, Alexander, Priscilla, Aquila, Erastus, Trophimus, Eubulus, Pudens, Linus, Claudia

Who To/For   To Timothy, a protégé of Paul, who is helping advise church leaders in Ephesus

Literature Type   A personal letter with powerful advice backed by years of experience and pointing to the need to finish well

Story Line   Paul had helped found the church in Ephesus (Acts 19). It became an indigenous church. Later he met with the elders of this church in a stop over on his trip back to Jerusalem (Acts 20). At that time he warned them of problems that would arise in the church. Later he also wrote an epistle to them (along with the ones to Colosse and Philemon). At that time there were no major problems as witnessed by the general nature of the letter. Several years later the problems he warned about have arisen. He sends Timothy to try to minister to the situation and advise the church elders. Timothy runs into a number of problems which he does not know how to handle. Paul writes an epistle to Timothy to help him in that situation. That is 1 Timothy. Now after a period of time, Paul sensing that his end is near writes a second time to Timothy. These last words are powerful because they are just that. They reflect the fruit of a life that counted.

Structure

	I.	(ch 1-2:13)	Exhortations to Persevere And Select Leaders to Carry On in Ministry
	II.	(ch 2:14-26)	Warnings for the Newly Selected Leaders To Aid Them in Persevering
	III.	(ch 3:1-17)	Persevering in Difficult Days Ahead
	IV.	(ch 4:1-8)	End Result of Persevering--A Good Finish
	V.	(ch 4:9-18)	Personal Matters

2 TIMOTHY   continued

Theme   **PERSEVERING IN A MINISTRY**
- should be done to meet God's approval,
- will require the suffering of hardships,
- involves the modeling of righteous living, and
- necessitates the proper use of God's word.

Key Words   faith, faithful (11); good (6); grace (5)

Key Events   An Old Testament, spiritual authority event, is alluded to--see 3:8, Jannes and Jambres who opposed Moses; Paul's first trial which did not go too well.

Purposes
- to summon Timothy to his side,
- to encourage Timothy during these tough days in the Roman empire,
- to give his farewell advice (on numerous issues),
- to highlight the need for transparency in a mentoring relationship (see 3:10,11),
- to give an inspirational model of a leader finishing well.

Why Important   This is the most personal of all of Paul's letters (possible exception, 2 Corinthians). In the midst of his trial at Rome (his first hearing had not gone well) he writes Timothy. Most likely you would expect details as to what happened in the trial and the possible outcomes. But you hear little of that. For Paul is concerned about the church and about Timothy. The letter is filled with that personal concern. Its advice is based upon personal experience. These are the final words of a leader. And they both reveal in his own model and what they say that which is the essence of one who would exercise leadership as a ministry for God. 2 Timothy reveals what true ministry is. It describes a true minister of Jesus Christ. Leaders are *gifted* by the Holy Spirit for ministry and must guard that good deposit by using it and developing oneself to use it. But leaders are not only gifted they must also experience the enabling *grace* of God in life, that is, they must be able to appropriate God's enablement in every kind of situation. Character is crucial both for the minister and for the people to whom ministered. Development in holiness is a priority. The

2 TIMOTHY   continued

Word of God must be known thoroughly and applied to life and ministry. As regards the Word, three marks describe a leader who finishes well. They must: 1. know the Word thoroughly and 2. use it appropriately, and 3. must pass on the stewardship of the Word to others. The stewardship of the Word is crucial. Leaders must pass on to others the responsibility to know and use God's Word. No Christian leader will last long unless he or she abides in the Word. And their work will not abide long after them if they have not passed on the stewardship of the word. Leaders must be diligent--have initiative and discipline to get things done. Finally, leaders must persevere and finish well. All of the above is what Paul did and what he admonished Timothy to do and what comes to us as the abiding message of 2 Timothy.

Where It Fits   This is the last of the Pauline epistles. In the redemptive drama it occurs in Chapter 4, The Church. Messiah has come. The foundational work at the Cross has been done. Peter, the gatekeeper has ushered people into the Church, the manifestation of the Kingdom during this era. Paul the master builder now builds upon that foundation. To Paul is given the task of establishing the church; he will outline its form, its essentials, and its leadership requirements. To John will come the task of restoring that church--renewing it, calling it back to its essentials. But it is Paul who tells us what the church is, what ministry is, and what a leader of that church must be and do. 2 Timothy occurs at the end of Paul's lifetime, about two-thirds way through the first century. It carries the essence of what leadership is all about and it demonstrates what it means for a leader to finish well. No present church or para-church leader can fail to thoroughly grasp this book and still hope to minister well.

Leadership Lessons
1. **FINISH WELL**. This book demonstrates what it means to finish well in a ministry. Paul is the classic New Testament case of a leader finishing well; Daniel is the classic Old Testament one. Christ is still Lord of His life. He is ministering looking for the return of Christ. His

2 TIMOTHY   continued

relationship with God via Christ is still warm and personal. He has finished his task with honor. A destiny has been accomplished; an ultimate contribution left behind. He has a learning posture. You can be sure that his advice to Timothy comes out of one who has done those things himself. He is a pace setter whose advice should be heeded. See 2 Timothy 4:7,8. This is probably the most important contribution of this book. Paul is the architect of the Christian Church as we know it. How did Christianity work out for him? His failure would probably have torpedoed the whole church era. But his finish to his life caps off a triumphant ministry and gives all leaders of this era hope and a challenge to do likewise.

2.   **MINISTRY PRAYER PRINCIPLE.** Paul illustrates the ministry prayer principle first seen in Moses and highlighted in Samuel's ministry. *If God has called you to a ministry then He has called you to pray for that ministry.* This simple responsibility is in seed form the heart of the priestly ministry philosophy model given for leadership in full blown form in Hebrews. See 2 Timothy 1:3.

3.   **GIFTEDNESS DEVELOPMENT.** Giftedness development is highlighted in this book. Christian leaders must constantly keep in balance doing and being. We must produce in our ministry. But we must also develop the production capability. We must develop ourselves. Both our production and our production capability must be tended to. Giftedness can be and must be developed or atrophy sets in (1:6). Gifts can be imparted (1:14) by those having spiritual authority. They should be used with gifted power (1:7). Self-discipline is needed both to develop and use giftedness (1:7 and 4:1-5).

4.   **ULTIMATE ACCOUNTABILITY.** Christian leaders minister always with a conscious view to ultimate accountability to God for their ministry. Paul was conscious of a future day in which God would hold him and others accountable for their actions (see 1:16, 4:8, 4:14). This is more fully developed in 2 Corinthians, and 1, 2 Thessalonians but is affirmed in many epistles.

5.   **LEADERSHIP SELECTION.** Effective leaders see leadership selection and development as a priority function in their life. Paul here (2:2, 2:14ff) advocates top down recruitment of potential leaders. The selection criteria focuses on three major qualities:
a. faithfulness, b. teachableness, and c. ability to pass on to others that which has been life changing for them.

6.   **FOCUS.** To persevere in ministry a leader must have a single minded focus 2:1-4, 10, 21. Life and its many problems can encumber and entangle so as to side track one from a disciplined life that counts for Christ.

2 TIMOTHY   continued

7. **FINANCIAL PRINCIPLE**. A leader's ministry is worthy of remuneration. This is not a big thing with Paul. But a leader who is effective should not be ashamed of reward for having done effective ministry. (2:6,7)
8. **BIBLE CENTERED MINISTRY**. An effective leader who finishes well must have a Bible centered ministry. 2 Timothy 2:15 and 3:16,17 give the keynotes on a Bible centered ministry. It is a God ordained requirement. It brings confident ministry (litotes = not ashamed). It is a matter of integrity (correctly handling). It will change life and ministry (3:16,17).
9. **GENTLENESS**. Gentleness rather than argument is a major influence means for a leader to affect change. There are few gentle leaders. Such a one stands out. Gentle persuasion is a major tool for a change agent. See 2 Timothy 2:22-26.
10. **OPPOSITION**. Effective leaders should expect opposition to their ministry--especially on issues of truth they teach. Forewarned is forearmed. However, major on the majors. See 2:22-26 and 3:8.
11. **MODELING/TRANSPARENCY**. Transparency in modeling God's enabling grace in a life and ministry provides an effective base for influencing followers toward maturity. Paul was conscious of his own life as being a model for others and used it deliberately as such. He shared the ups and downs and always the need for the grace of God to enable one in the midst of them. See 2 Timothy 3:10-14.
12. **ADVENT OF CHRIST**. The return of Christ was a major motivating factor of Paul's leadership. He advocates this for all leader's (all those who love his appearing). See 2 Timothy 4:7,8
13. **LEARNING POSTURE**. Effective leaders maintain a learning posture all during their lives. "*And the books, Timothy, don't forget the books!*" speaks reams about Paul. 2 Timothy 4:13.

For Further Leadership Study
Study each of these suggestive lessons for depth in the book itself and then comparatively throughout Paul's life both for validation, emergence and development.

Special Comments
As is the case with 1 Timothy and Titus, this is a book about leadership. Its basic ideas should permeate a ministry philosophy. Emerging leaders need to immerse themselves in it until they see, feel, believe, and engraft its values.

| BOOK | HEBREWS | AUTHOR: uncertain |

Characters not in focus, though Timothy is mentioned in the closing remarks, and numerous are mentioned in the Hall of Fame Faith chapter including: Abel, Enoch, Noah, Abraham, Isaac, Jacob, Sarah, Esau, Joseph, Moses, Rahab, Gideon, Barak, Samson, Jephthah, David, Samuel

Who To/For Since it is not stated it must be inferred from the book itself. Generally thought to be a group of Jewish Christians who were known personally by the writer. They had made a profession of faith in Christ but were in danger of abandoning it altogether probably due to persecution for the main part but due also to spiritual lethargy.

Literature Type A logical well thought out argument, that is, a sermon-like treatise, which was written to be sent to a group of Jewish believers. Notice his epistle-like closing. And being sermon-like the author's purpose is carried not so much in his argument as in his application of the argument.

Story Line A group of Jewish believers have made a profession of faith in Christ in the past. There are pressures on them now to abandon this claim. Perhaps they are considering reverting to straight Judaism. In any case the writer attempts to persuade them to continue on for God's revelation in Christ is the ultimate and final revelation and supersedes the Old Testament revelation. He argues forcefully and shows an in-depth knowledge of the Old Testament as he marshals his arguments.

Structure The structure follows a cycle of argument and warning (application of the argument). The structure hinges on the warning passages at the end of each argument. See 2:1-4, 3:7-4:13, 5:11-6:20, 10:26-29, 12:14-29. In these warnings the author turns aside from presenting his evidence in order to demand his readers to act in the light of it. These warnings carry the major thrust of the book. Each of the warnings follows a pattern: a chief subject, an Old Testament illustration, and an exhortation.

HEBREWS continued

I.	(ch 1)	Christ, God's Revelation
		1st Warning: Drifting (2:1-4)
II.	(ch 2:5-3:6)	Christ, Greater than Angels, Moses
		2nd Warning: Unbelief (3:7-4:13)
III.	(Ch 4:14-5:10)	Christ, Greater than Aaronic High Priesthood
		3rd Warning: Spiritual Babyhood (5:11-6:20)
IV.	(Ch 7-10:25)	Christ, Greater than Melchizedek and
		Originator of New Covenant and
		Fulfillment of Law
		4th Warning: Willful sin (10:26-29)
V.	(ch 11-12:13)	Christ, the Author and Finisher of Our Faith
		5th Warning: Falling Short (12:14-1-29)
VI.	(ch 13)	Final Words of Encouragement

Theme **GOD'S REDEMPTIVE REVELATION IN CHRIST**,

- is superior to any other,
- is final, and
- therefore, *demands a continued faithful allegiance.*

Key Words perfection roots (11); eternal or forever or for ever and ever or forevermore the same (13); better or similar expressions like more excellent, more glory, so much more. (13); warning words like lest (10); faith (31); partakers (7); sat down or once (phrases emphasizing finality (8+); priest (30+)

Key Events none

Purposes
- to prevent the readers (Hebrew Christians) from abandoning faith in Christ,
- to encourage them to go on in spite of the cost and to fulfill their purpose in God's redemptive program,
- to present the present ministry of the Lord Jesus Christ for his followers, intercessory--high priest,
- to present Christianity as the perfect and therefore the final religion because of its free access to God and hence worthy of its demands,
- to show that the pictures of spiritual reality in the Old Testament were finalized in Christ and His ministry,
- to show the importance of the Old Testament in presenting Christian truth.

HEBREWS continued

Why Important   In all ages God has his redemptive purposes for world
mission. Hebrews in essence is saying that in every age
God has redeemed a people through whom to declare His
message to the world around them. If people fail to fit
into this purpose they will be set aside and God will use
others. With great privilege goes great responsibility.
Because the Christian message is the final and superior
revelation of God to humanity it has exclusive demands.
Those who embrace it and go on to maturity will be used
by God. Those who do not will be set aside. God's great
purposes will continue. Hebrews in applying this great
message presents the greatest teaching in the Scriptures
on the person and work of Christ and shows it to be
superior. Chapter 11 is one of the great inspirational
passages in the Bible on walking with God by faith and
being used by His purposes.

Where It Fits   Hebrews is a New Testament Church Leadership book
probably written sometime before 70 A.D. It is written in
a moment in history when some segment of the church
(unknown as to size) was considering abandoning
Christianity probably to turn back to Judaism or some
form of the law. This book details how Christ and His
work have forever superseded any other religions. This
book has several important leadership lessons in it.

Leadership Lessons

1. **LEADERSHIP AND EXHORTATION.** Exhortation is best done from
a logical/ spiritual/ scriptural basis. The structure of the book centers in
the 5 warnings which break up the flow or presentation. Some lessons on
leadership and exhortation include: a. Each warning contains a *therefore*.
There is a foundation for exhortation. Leaders need more "therefore" in
their leadership influence. b. Precious truths should be accompanied by
solemn warnings--not give always in the same way. The negative
element is needed. c. The Holy Spirit may lead one to digress. Leaders
must be sensitive and flexible. d. The pattern is a three step pattern--state,
illustrate, apply the truth.
2. **RESPONSIBLE WATCHCARE.** A major leadership function is watch
care--making sure that followers are not leaving the faith or missing out
on God purposes for them--whether literally or because of stunted growth

HEBREWS continued

patterns. The book of Hebrews emphasizes the place of leadership in being responsible for followers--both in its illustration and by statement. See 13:17.

3. **DRIFTING.** The first major warning (2:1-4) is a key to the whole book. Leaders need to be aware of the tendency to be bypassed in God's purposes. Both leaders and groups, historically, validate this point. There must be an all out or nothing abandonment to God's purposes or leaders and followers stand to be by-passed and miss the great redemptive stream of God's purposes.

4. **GIFTEDNESS.** Hebrews 2:1-4 mentions giftedness indicating a generic category (signs and wonders) and a specific gift (miracles). This is important for two reasons: a. it gives external confirmation of giftedness beside Peter and Paul, b. it shows that in a transition time, power gifts are used to give God's confirmation of His work.

5. **INTERCESSORY MODEL.** (7:25 and others) The book of Hebrews presents Jesus as a present intercessor. A major on-going leadership act that all leaders can participate in is prayer for the ministry. This is probably the culmination of the ministry prayer principle in the Bible. Much can be learned about intercessory praying by studying the subject in Hebrews. *If God has called you to a ministry then He has called you to pray for the ministry.*

6. **DISCERNMENT.** (5:11-6:12) The book of Hebrews points out that discernment is a developing function. This is an important function in leadership activity. A leader can plateau in this development.

7. **UNION LIFE EMPHASIS.** (ch 8) This truth, which has received treatment from John, Peter, and Paul as an important maturity item for followers again gets emphasis. In Hebrews it is called by the title, New Covenant. Here it is shown to be the source which enables living out truth from within.

8. **HISTORICAL MODELS.** (ch 11) The book of Hebrews emphasizes that one thing historical models do for us is to inspire our faith. One of the high water marks of outstanding leaders in the Old Testament is their faith ventures with God. We need historical models to inspire us. We need to see that faith in an unseen God is legitimate. We need the encouragement that these models bring. We need to see that the essence of faith lies in a faithful God who through the generations will encourage and enable leader after leader to contribute to the on-going purpose and plans of God.

9. **DISCIPLINE/ PROCESSING.** (ch 12) God uses everyday events and people to shape our lives. We can choose to learn from it by responding to God in it or not.

HEBREWS continued

10. **LEADERSHIP MANDATE.** The 13:7,8 passage enforces the importance of studying leaders as models and the importance of being models for others. Both of these ideas have validity because the source of leadership is Jesus Christ who is ever living. This mandate says that we can study leaders, identify those good qualities that enhanced their walk with God, and appropriate those qualities in our own life by trusting Jesus to do it for us. At the same time it holds out the hope that we ourselves will lead just such lives that will impact our own followers. This is the culmination of the modeling principle that has repeatedly occurred in many leader's lives and ministry throughout the Bible.

11. **FINISHING WELL.** The book as a whole shows that the life of faith is not automatic. There are many things that can sidetrack us from finishing well in the Christian faith. We need to take courage from Jesus, our major model, who finished well. We need to take courage from the many Old Testament heroes/heroines who finished well. We need to know that there will be difficulties about what we believe and why we believe it. But we have one who is our advocate interceding on our behalf. One major secret of finishing well is to have a Christ centered life. The book of Hebrews is the most Christ-centered book in the Bible. Leaders who maintain this value will finish well.

For Further Leadership Study

1. The concept of the presence of God as being indispensable in a leader's life is presented in at least two ways in the book of Hebrews. What ways can you think of that enforce this repeated observation concerning leaders?
2. Biographical scans should be made of each of the faith leaders in chapter 11 focusing on lessons of faith seen in their lives as intimated by the Hebrews commentary.
3. Hebrews inspires us to study the Old Testament to identify types of Christ. It also helps us understand the hermeneutical principles for interpreting types. It encourages us to make certain that our Word centered ministries includes the Old Testament as well as the New.

Special Comments

To understand this book will require some serious study of the Old Testament. Bible types, Old Testament pictures of New Testament truth, are used throughout this book. What Hebrews will do for you is to make your Old Testament come alive as you realize it shows us much about the person of Christ and His work.

BOOK	**JUDE**	**AUTHOR:** Jude, Jesus' brother

Characters   none in focus, though many are used in conjunction with Old Testament events to punctuate the author's message

Who To/For   uncertain; possibly to the same kind of audience as the books of James and Peter

Literature Type   This is an exhortive letter.

Story Line   Certain believers were in danger of being led astray by false teachers. Jude writes to warn them of these dangers and to describe the false teachers so that they could be identified and avoided. He alludes to the Old Testament several times in giving his warning. Jude uses faith as a figure of speech standing for basic Christian truth.

Structure   I. (1-16)   The Negative--Warnings From History About Departing From the Faith
II. (17-25) The Positive--Exhortations To Go On In the Faith

Theme   **CONTENDING FOR THE FAITH** (basic Christian truth)
  • involves not only recognition and rejection of ungodly influence to depart from truth, but
  • also positive efforts to live in and learn of this truth.

Key Words   ungodly (6); faith (2); these men (3)

Key Events   The author alludes to several Old Testament events and others occurring in that time but not in Scripture.

Purposes
  • to warn against apostasy (being led astray from the true faith),
  • to give several illustrations of apostasy so as to expose its nature and warn against its results,
  • to show the importance of knowing thoroughly basic Christian truth and acting upon it.

Why Important   This book exposes the danger of apostasy. It gives illustrations of it which suggest its nature and causes:

JUDE continued

unbelief leading to rebellion, not submitting to proper
God-appointed situation; giving over to perversion; self-
righteousness; greed; presumption. We are in danger of
always being led astray. The process is implied: willful
moral declension--some compromise of our convictions,
justification of it in terms of Christian freedom, denial of
Christ.

Where It Fits   Jude was probably written earlier than John's books but
toward the end of the first century of the Church.
Christianity has spread to the Gentiles. As it crosses
cultural barriers there is always the danger that it will be
misinterpreted or become syncretistic (mixed with local
religion in a compromising way). Further there is the
danger of leaders who are not genuine in their faith
leading followers astray. Jude writes to counteract these
leadership issues. He does so not in detail but in terms of
basic issues that have wide application.

Leadership Lessons

1. **CONFRONTATION LEADERSHIP STYLE**: Confrontation (urge
   you) is one of ten Pauline leadership styles identified. Here Jude uses
   that style in confronting a problem of orthodoxic (beliefs) as well as
   orthopraxic (Christian practice) heresy.
2. **INDIRECT LEADERSHIP STYLE.** Another leadership style is
   indirect--one which attempts to do battle in the spiritual realm via
   intercession--rather than a direct confrontation at the human level. The
   word contend (vs 3, epagonizomai) is often used in terms of intercession
   (spiritual warfare)--see Colossians 2:1.
3. **RESPONSIBILITY TO DEFEND CHRISTIAN TRUTH.** There is a
   corporate responsibility (vs 3, entrusted to the Saints) for keeping
   Christianity pure.
4. **BALANCE OF TRUTH AND BEHAVIOR.** Orthopraxy (license for
   immorality) and orthodoxy (deny Jesus Christ) are twin dangers equally
   destructive to the purity of Christianity.
5. **ATTACKS FROM WITHIN/ SUBTLE.** Attacks from within the
   church are more subtle and hence sometimes more dangerous (secretly
   slipped, vs 4).

JUDE continued

6. **ATTACKS FROM WITHIN/ SYMPTOMS.** Symptoms of those who can destroy Christianity from within include:
   a. endorse sexual perversion (vs 4, 7, 8)
   b. reject authority (vs 8, 11)
   c. slander cosmic level warfare (vs 8, 9)
   d. use Christianity as a means of money making (vs 11).
   e. hypocritical practice of Christianity/ leadership (vs 12, 13)
   f. faultfinding (vs 16)
   g. boast about themselves (16)
   h. flatter others for their own advantage (16)
   i. cause splits (vs 19)

For Further Leadership Study

1. See **Conclusions on Leadership styles** for the 10 Pauline styles. Here confrontation and indirect styles are used. Normally the sequence is indirect first then confrontation next.
2. Through the ages the Church has required leadership to sign belief creeds in order to guard against heresy. They have sought to maintain orthodoxy by explicitly defining core tenets which leaders should *believe*. The Church has not been as stringent on Christian practice. Many times its leaders have not demonstrated their Christianity in their relationships with others or in the solving of church problems. One can be orthodox in belief and yet be heretical in practice. The blend, the balance, should be noted. See particularly the Pauline epistles where his practice in solving problems is just as important as what he says about the problems.

Special Comments
This book ends with a special word of encouragement--a doxology often given from the pulpit to close a Sunday morning service. As we attempt to make it our business to live out the Christian faith and grow in it we can rest assured that it is God who will establish us and keep us from apostasy.

BOOK   1 JOHN   **AUTHOR:** John, (one of 3 close disciples)

Characters   None in focus

Who To/For   Not addressed to a local church; general in nature

Literature Type   A treatise or circular letter written generally to Christians, probably in Asia

Story Line   This is probably the last apostolic message to the whole church. In his old age John the Apostle, probably the closest of the twelve to Jesus, writes a general letter explaining what to him is the essential message of Christianity that must not be lost by the church. The tendency to nominalize and to ritualize religion must always be balanced by the life it seeks to impart. So an old leader chats with the family, using intimacy and in-house metaphorical language that is felt by those who have experienced what he is talking about rather than explaining it logically. It deals with the essential of Christianity--a personal and real relationship with Christ--and addresses the feelings, the will, and the experience of the listener rather than the intellect.

Structure   The structure is difficult as John does not write from a logical, analytical framework but chooses rather to weave his message into metaphorical language which has overlap from section to section. His purpose is stated clearly in 1 John 5:13. He weaves his subjects together to carry out that purpose. In general, John follows a cyclical methodology. He gives a metaphorical description of God always implying relationship with this God, tests whereby we can assess our personal understanding and experience of it, and then warns against what may block our fully entering into that relationship. According to John, eternal life is a now experience, a relationship with God in which we experience an increasingly new perspective on life now, and a future experience in which we will fully know God and be like God.

1 **JOHN** continued

    I.   (ch 1, 2) Eternal Life--As Personal Relationship With the God of Truth

    II. (ch 3,4) Eternal Life--As Personal Relationship With the God of Love

    III. (ch 5) Eternal Life--As Personal Relationship With the God of Life

Theme   **KNOWING FULLY THAT YOU HAVE ETERNAL LIFE**

- involves your knowing Jesus as the God of truth which can be tested by your love for God as seen in obedience to Him and your discernment of issues that can sidetrack your relationship--worldliness and a spirit against Christ,
- is based on a love relationship rooted in your adoption into God's family as tested by your demonstration of love and inner peace in a world opposed to it,
- inherently depends on your having God's life as confirmed by truth and love and tested by your confidence in God--typically demonstrated in your intercession with God.

Key Words   know and cognates (35); world (23); love (21); light (and truth) (16); write (8) to: little children, Fathers, young men, everyone;

Key Events   none

Purposes

- to help Christians know for certain of their relationship with God,
- to help Christians to confidently manifest their relationship with God,
- to warn Christians of those things that can sidetrack that relationship and rob a Christian of assurance,
- to show the essence of Christianity, a vital relationship with God.

Why Important   The outward traditions of any religion are much easier to pass on to new followers than the essence of the religious experience. Movements usually lose force after they have been institutionalized into a society. John toward

1 JOHN continued

the end of the first century wants to guard against this
loss of life in the Christian movement. He wants to assert
the essence of Christianity, individual believers having a
personal relationship with God. A transforming union
with Christ experienced in life is stressed. Throughout
the history of the Old Testament this degenerative
process is seen. The Christian movement, as
institutionalized in the church is going to spread around
the world. John's book helps to assure that where ever it
goes and no matter what culture it enters there will be
basic manifestations of its life and vitality that can serve
to assess its reality.

Where It Fits   First, Second and Third John are written toward the end
of the first century. Christianity has spread into Asia
minor and Europe. John, the oldest living disciple of
Christ authored these books after a long life. His
reflective thinking most likely centers on what he
considers to be essentials of the faith. Truth and life and
love are hallmarks he espouses. In 1 John he wants to
make certain that followers know they have a vital
relationship with Christ.

Leadership Lessons
1. **GENRE.** This is a book containing no biographical nor direct leadership
   sources. It is an old leader chatting with the family, using intimate and
   in-house metaphorical language that is felt by those who have
   experienced what he is talking about. It is a book which deals with the
   affect, conative, and experiential side of learning rather than the
   cognitive. As such it is difficult to draw out specific leadership lessons.
2. **PHILOSOPHICAL MODELS.** Two philosophical New Testament
   leadership models include the Harvest Model and the Shepherd Model.[23]
   Normally a leader identifies with one of these models more strongly
   depending on giftedness and experience in ministry. Paul identifies
   primarily with the Harvest Model and secondarily with the Shepherd.
   John identifies primarily with the Shepherd Model and secondarily with

---

[23]These models are presented in Handbook I of the leadership series. The models derive from Christ's
teaching in the Gospels. The models are presented in terms of statements of values. Leaders usually
identify with these values when they see them. The Harvest model is an outreach model seeking to bring
people into the Kingdom. The Shepherd model is seeking to help those within the Kingdom grow up to
be mature participants.

1 JOHN continued

the Harvest. It is Shepherd Model values which come out so strongly in this book. Some of these include: a. Believers in fellowship with God can't continue to be dominated by sin in their lives. b. Believers obey truth. c. Believers manifest love in their relationships with others. d. Believers have an indwelling Holy Spirit who convicts about and clarifies truth. e. Believers in fellowship will have clear consciences. f. Believers can know that they are related to God.

3. **FINISHING WELL**. John is a leader who is finishing well. This book highlights the first four of the descriptors of those finishing well. (1) It is clear that John has a <u>personal vibrant relationship</u> with God through Jesus and wants his hearers to experience the same. (2) He evinces a <u>learning posture</u> as seen from his drawing lessons from life. (3) He certainly shows forth <u>Christ likeness in character</u>. Love as an evidence of Christianity is one of John's strong emphasis. (4) Truth is lived out in his life so that <u>convictions</u> and promises of God are seen to be real. This model of a leader who is passionate about maturity in lives and who is finishing well is probably the single most important overall leadership lesson in the book.

For Further Leadership Study
1. What indications of shepherd values do you see in the book?
2. What levels of maturity do you see?
3. Most leaders recognize that there will be differing levels of intimacy with their followers. What evidence of intimacy levels do you see in this book?

Special Comments
John's in-house language though difficult to see analytically strikes a resonant chord to those who have experienced what he is talking about. What he says can be felt and valued and acted upon even though it may not be dissected analytically.

BOOK **2 JOHN** **AUTHOR:** John, (one of 3 close disciples)
Characters   none named directly

Who To/For   unclear; possibly a local church and its members (if salutation is taken metaphorically or a Christian woman if taken literally) or the Church generally.

Literature Type   a letter

Story Line   As in 1 John, John deals with core issues of Christianity. One such is what do people believe about Jesus and the incarnation. Jesus is God in human form. John asserts that as a core doctrine for assessing validity of followers of Christ.

Structure I. (1-3)   Greeting Emphasizing Inner Reality of Truth and Love In a Believer
             II. (4-6)   Cardinal Truth--Believers Love One Another
             III. (7-11)   Cardinal Truth--Incarnation of Christ

Theme   **WALKING IN TRUTH**
    • involves both loving one another, and
    • rejecting those who deny essential truth.

Key Words   truth or teaching (8); love (4)

Key Events   none

Purposes
• to affirm the hearers of their vital walk with Christ,
• to encourage relationships between believers,
• to warn against false teachers in general by using a cardinal doctrine of Christianity as a test (this is probably typical of other such cardinal doctrines),
• to show what must be done to those who do not hold such cardinal doctrines--reject them.

Why Important   Movements usually lose force as they are institutionalized in society. The church can lose its vitality in two basic ways--from without by being secularized, that is allowing the values of the society

2 JOHN continued

around it to permeate its value system and from within by having its own leaders lose the essence of its teaching. John always simplifies things to the basics. Two such basics are that believers must love other believers and reject those who can erode their beliefs. These are always tests that can be applied to the vitality of the Christian movement in what ever culture it goes.

Where It Fits   This book occurs toward the end of the first century of the Christian era. The church has gone through some persecutions. John recognizes that the church has great tendencies toward nominality. 1, 2, 3 John and the Revelation are written, all from that perspective--How to stir up the church and move it back to its original commitment. John stresses the basics--fundamentals, truth and love with consistency in 2 John.

Leadership Lessons

1. **DIRECT DEALINGS.** Some leadership issues require face-to-face resolution. Some are too complex; some are too delicate; some require relational more than analytical skills (vs 12 See also 3 John).
2. **BASIC TRUTH.** Followers need to be repeatedly reminded of simple basic truth.
3. **BALANCE.** Consistency between what is known and what is lived out is an ideal that must be held before followers.
4. **CORE/ PERIPHERY.** There are standards, core issues, on which separation from others is necessary. Leaders can be tolerant on periphery issues while holding firm on core issues. First, one has to recognize that not all truth is core (i.e. requiring total agreement).
5. **FULL TIME CHRISTIAN WORKERS.** Itinerant Christian workers visit churches. Whether to receive them or not is an issue. The "teaching" is the basic criterion. I would suppose this "teaching" has to do with basic truth and is given in 1 John. That there is a category of full time Christian workers is not questioned but assumed.
6. **MODEL OF HUMILITY.** The author of the book, we assume it to be John the closest disciple to Christ, identifes himself as *The Elder*. He could have identified himself as the most important living Christian, the one closest to Jesus, the one with the greatest grasp on Christology. Instead he identifies himself as The Elder, a term of respect, but

2 JOHN continued

    identified with any others who are helping guide the church. He does not use his status to impress.

7. **CHURCHES/ REGIONAL LEADERSHIP.** The fact that John addresses this letter and 3 John to churches identifies the concept of regional leadership (perhaps tied only by spiritual authority). But here John's concerned with churches and their orthodoxy and orthopraxy. Higher levels of leadership are possible.

For Further Leadership Study

1. What is the "teaching?" If essentials, then that give in 1 John is probably it. What are these essentials? Here we are dealing with the concept of core and periphery doctrine.
2. The concept of Rewards, is it for corporate church or for leaders? (vs8)
3. The use of *the elder* (vs1) has implications for leadership style, role, relationship to these followers (see also 3 John).

Special Comments
John implicitly recognizes that there are core truths and peripheral truths, that is, essentials that all must hold to, and things on which there may be differences. John's tone in 1 John, 2 John, and 3 John is to major on the majors. The incarnation is certainly a major (but not the only major) and is probably typical of others.

BOOK   **3 JOHN**   **AUTHOR:** John, (one of 3 close disciples)

Characters	Gaius, Diotrephes, Demetrius
Who To/For	Gaius, a Christian friend of John
Literature Type	A personal letter giving affirmation and emphasizing the importance of Christian conduct, showing love.
Story Line	In the early Christian era, frequently Christian teachers, evangelists, apostles, pastors, and prophets visited other churches. Travel and accommodations being what they were, Christians were expected to show hospitality to these travelling ministers. Diotrephes, evidently a leader in a local church situation did not welcome some travelling ministers, in this case probably sent by John. He was either personally threatened by them or did not want to hear their views which might have contradicted his own. In any case he did not allow them to have influence in the church. In fact, he excommunicated members who did have fellowship with the visitors. On the other hand, Gaius and Demetrius, two close friends of John do act with hospitality and are open to truth from visiting church ministers. John writes to affirm their conduct and to

Structure   I. (1-4)   Greeting To Gaius--Affirming HisTestimony
　　　　　　II. (5-8)   The Point of Tension--Visiting Christian Workers
　　　　　　III. (9-10)   Diotrephes Negative Model
　　　　　　IV. (11-12)   Demetrius' Positive Model
　　　　　　　　　　　　Closing (13,14)

Theme   **YOUR RESPONSE OF RECEIVING CHRISTIAN WORKERS**
- demonstrates obedience to Christian truth, and
- should be imitated by other Christians.

Key Words   truth or true (7);

Key Events   none

3 JOHN   continued

Purposes
- to stress the importance of models--good and bad--for influencing the church,
- to show the need for external accountability in a given isolated local church situation,
- to emphasize a basic Christian truth of loving one another,
- to warn Diotrephes that his conduct is unacceptable,
- to give notice of his coming visit (and the impending conflict with Diotrophes).

Why Important   The body of Christ is wider than just its manifestation in a local community. A core truth to John is relationship between believers. Love between believers is a manifestation of the reality of the presence of Jesus. In the years to come, when the church is spread around the world and in many differing cultures--this core truth will remain. No group can exclusively reject other Christians. apart from their failing to hold essential doctrines. John asserts this truth in one given situation so that it will typically hold true in the years to come.

Where It Fits   Like 1 and 2 John, this letter is written toward the end of the 1st century. The church, in its 2nd, 3rd, and following generations, has moved toward a nominality of Christian expression. There is a need for renewal and commitment toward the earlier basics that gave Christianity its vital appeal. Itinerant Christian workers perform just such renewal efforts. John is endorsing the reception of these workers in a local church.

Leadership Lessons

1. **MODELS.** Models are important in a local church. Here three models are contrasted. Demetrius and Gaius both positive are contrasted to Diotrephes, a negative model. The issue is financial support (hospitality) of these itinerant, full-time Christian workers (vs 11).
2. **FULL TIME SODALITY WORKERS**. Full time Christian leaders exist at the end of the 1st century. These appear to be oriented toward a

3 JOHN   continued

sodality function (parachurch/ mobile function) that a modality (church/ local function).

3. **POWER.** Power can be used for good or abused (vs 9,10). Here John is using it for good. Diotrephes is abusing it.

4. **NON PLURALITY OF LEADERSHIP.** An ideal plurality of leadership is not evident in this church--one leader dominates.

5. **PRIDE.** The before mentioned barrier, pride, seems to be a problem with Diotrephes. Pride is one of 6 major hindrances identified as keeping leaders from finishing well.

6. **CHALLENGE/ THREAT.** Often leaders are threatened by other leaders such as the visit of these external Christian workers. There is always an implied evaluation.

7. **CROSS-POLLINIZATION.** Cross-pollinization is a healthy counter balance toward exclusive tendencies of local independent congregations or organizations.

8. **MODEL OF HUMILITY/RELATIONAL.** The author of the book, we assume it to be John the closest disciple to Christ, identifes himself as *The Elder*. He could have identified himself as the most important living Christian, the one closest to Jesus, the one with the greatest grasp on Christology. Instead he identifies himself as The Elder, a term of respect, but identified with any others who are helping guide the church. He does not use his status to impress. And it is this person, this important Christian, who demonstrates the imporance of relational empowerment. The book is written to a close friend and demonstrates the importance both of networking power and relational empowerment.

For Further Leadership Study

1. Are there other *full-time* leaders mentioned in the New Testament (maybe Acts)? What were their gifts? What were their roles? What were their functions? Who were they accountable to?

2. Study the Greek, philopotrotuo (vs 9), in order to understand a potential barrier to ones growth in leadership.

3. There is no mention of the Holy Spirit in 2, 3 John. Implications?

Special Comments
John is seen giving hard truth in love.

BOOK **REVELATION** **Author:** John, (one of 3 close disciples)

Characters	not in focus

Who To/For   Seven churches in Asia are given as recipients: Ephesus, Smyrna, Pergamum, Thyatira, Sardis, Philadelphia, Laodicea

Literature Type   A long treatise involving visions, exhortations, and future happenings. Much is given in symbolic language. It is a highly pictorial form of writing. The events are not given in strict chronological order. Allusions to Old Testament Scriptures.

Story Line   John, in his old age, was exiled to the island of Patmos, apparently as part of some punishment for being a Christian leader. He had much time for meditation and reflection. He was concerned with the future of the church. During this period of time he was given a revelation of what was to happen to the churches in the future. He saw it as an encouraging word which brought God's working in the Old and New Testament to a fitting conclusion

Structure   The Visions of the Churches follows a cyclical pattern: address, description of writer, affirmation, confrontation, exhortation, warning, promise. The Visions of part III are not chronologically ordered.

I.	(ch 1)	The Vision of Christ Himself
II.	(ch 2,3)	The Vision of Christ to the 7 Churches
III.	(ch 4-22)	Christ and His Kingdom Established
	(ch 4,5)	A. Unveiling of Heavenly Activity
		1. Worship of God (ch 4)
		2. Worship of Christ (Lamb) (ch 5)
	(ch 6,7)	B. Opening the 7 Seals
	(ch 8-11)	C. Seeing the 7 Trumpets
	(ch 12-14)	D. Influentials in Last Days
	(ch 15,16)	E. Spilling the 7 Vials
	(ch 17,18)	F. Fall of Babylon
	(ch 19-22)	G. Moving to the Eternal State

REVELATION continued

Theme   **GOD'S ULTIMATE PURPOSES FOR HIS REDEMPTIVE PROGRAM**
- center in the Person of His Son,
- involve His churches,
- will take place in a context of persecution and struggle-- as described cryptically by many visions,
- will focus on the triumph of Jesus and his judgment of all things in harmony with his divine attributes, and
- will be realized in final victory for His people and ultimate justice accomplished in the world.

Key Words   I saw, beheld, viewed, looked etc. (49); seven(th) (59), Angel (70); Lamb (29)

Key Events   Many future events indicated symbolically in visions

Purposes
- to reveal future purposes of Jesus Christ and the power He will unleash in accomplishing His purposes,
- to show those purposes and power to be in harmony with His divine attributes,
- to encourage the Asian churches (and all churches throughout history) to persevere and purify themselves knowing that ultimately they are on the winning side,
- to warn the Asian churches (and all churches throughout history) that judgment will fall on them if they do not correct themselves to fall in with Christ's purposes,
- to bring a fitting climax to the redemptive story developed throughout Scripture.

Why Important   God's intent from the first of Genesis on has been to bless His people with His eternal presence. Ezekiel closes his book with that thought in mind. Numerous of the prophets point to a future day in which things would be made right and God would dwell with His people. The plan has had many twists and turns but through it all God has sovereignly moved on to His purpose. Some have followed hard after God and were included in His

REVELATION continued

purposes. Others refused to follow God. They were cast aside. God moved on. In the New Testament God prepares a way where He can reveal Himself in justice and love and reconcile all people unto Himself. The Cross climaxes all of God's preparation to bless the world. The message of the Cross is seen to be for all. The church goes out into all the world. It has its problems. But always it seeks to be part of God's future purposes looking forward to Christ's return. Were there no Revelation, the Redemptive Story would be incomplete. The Revelation brings to a fitting climax all of God's working to bless the world. There is seen to be an ultimate purpose in history. Justice is meted out. And there is the final blessing--the eternal presence of God with His people.

Where It Fits   The Revelation is the culmination of the written word from God and as such tops off the N.T. Church Leadership Era. Lessons for church leaders occur more directly in the first three chapters and obliquely in the remainder of the chapters. And it describes the next portion of the Redemptive Drama, The Kingdom Age. It brings to a fitting climax the end of God's Redemptive Drama. Although written in a difficult Genre for our day and time we know for certain the big picture--how it will all end, even if the details are not that clear. We are on the winning side!

Leadership Lessons
1. **GENRE.** The book of Revelation contains no biographical information. The visions which proliferate the book yield very little direct leadership ideas. However, chapters 1-3 do talk about churches, standards of assessing validity and effectiveness, and relate the responsibility to leadership. Hence they are useful in drawing out some overall lessons.
2. **PERSPECTIVE**. Perspective is one of the most important characteristics of leadership. That has been a repeated observation on leadership throughout all the leadership eras. This book gives a major future perfect paradigm which is needed by leaders of all time. All leaders need hope. They need to know that God will make things right. That He indeed will complete His work. There will be an eternal future that is bright. Leaders need to inspire followers and give hope. That is a

REVELATION continued

needed function in all leadership eras. This book models that notion as well as giving information about it. While it may contain many, many unclear things. One thing is clear. God will triumph in Christ. Victory is certain.

3. **CHRIST CENTERED.** This book, along with Hebrews, is the most Christ-centered book in the Scriptures. It shows that Christ will triumph. All our future hopes must be tied up with Christ. It is a different kind of Christ-centered aspect. The New Testament Church Leadership era develops the notion of an individual relationship with Christ that puts Christ at the center of ones life. Here, we see a different kind of Christ-centeredness. Here we see that all of God's culminating work centers in Christ. And because of that we have confidence and know that justice will be lovingly administered.

4. **APOSTLESHIP.** (ch 2, Ephesus church). Apostleship must be tested. It seems clear here that John expects this gift to continue. Authoritarian leadership is not always right.

5. **PLATEAUED.** (ch 2, Ephesus church). Churches can plateau. The major cause is lack of commitment (left first love).

6. **SUFFERING.** (ch 2, Smyrna church). Christ's model (first and last who died and came to life again and identifies with their suffering) is the major motivation to endure suffering.

7. **SPIRITUAL WARFARE.** (ch 2, Smyrna, Pergamum, Thyatira and Philadelphia churches). Spiritual warfare is real. Churches as corporate bodies must recognize and resist. Expect slander. Expect physical persecution. Do not compromise with false teachers.

8. **STANDARDS.** (ch 2, Thyatira church) The surrounding society will pressure towards sexual immorality and will justify it with false teaching.

9. **RESPONSIBILITY OF LEADERSHIP, PROPER EVALUATION.** (ch 3, Sardis church) Leaders must have a proper evaluation of their works. External reputation in the eyes of others is not enough.

10. **RESOURCES.** (ch 3, Philadelphia church) Churches that are pleasing Christ will have resources and opportunities and must by faith exploit them. Perseverance is a major factor in churches succeeding.

11. **COMMITMENT.** (ch 3, Laodicea) Nominal commitment as the dominant feature of followership is an unworthy standard for leadership.

12. **AVAILABILITY.** Christ stands ready to meet any leadership and churches that are willing to turn to Him and follow him. There is hope if leaders and churches are willing to commit themselves to His purposes.

REVELATION continued

For Further Leadership Study
1. From a leadership perspective, what are the implications of the seven golden lampstands with the son of man in the midst of them (1:12-16)?
2. From a leadership perspective, what are the implications of the seven stars in his right hand (1:16)?
3. Study each of the church descriptions in chapters 2 and 3 in detail and with a leadership focus. While some things will be unclear, what is clear?

Special Comments
As noted before, John does not write from an analytical viewpoint. He writes to move the reader, to create feeling, and to motivate to action. He deals more with the affective (feelings) and the conative (volitional) than he does the cognitive (intellectual or analytical). So while his writings are difficult to understand, especially in detail, they are clear in the central teachings. There are many interpretations of the diverse visions and symbols contained within them. But there is general agreement on the bigger issues as stated in the thematic analysis of this outline. So major on the majors-- many of the details will probably clear up as these times approach. Some may wait eternity for clarification. In the meantime be encouraged with the larger picture and confidently expect it.

The Big Picture—Comparative Study Across All The Books

Comparative study across all the suggested leadership ideas for each book resulted in identification of high level leadership values or guidelines which probably apply to leadership everywhere. I call these macro-lessons. They are, of course, open to validation. But even if only suggestive they can be quite helpful to leaders today who are struggling with answers to complex leadership problems and need Biblical centered authority for making decisions and carrying on ministry.

BIBLICAL MACRO-LESSONS

Lesson Name	Era First Seen	Statement Of Lesson
1. Blessing	Patriarchal	God mediates His blessing to His followers through leaders.
2. Shaping	Patriarchal	God shapes leader's lives and ministry through critical incidents.
3. Timing	Patriarchal	God's timing is crucial to accomplishment of God's purposes.
4. Destiny	Patriarchal	Leaders must have a sense of destiny.
5. Character	Patriarchal	Integrity is the essential character trait of a spiritual leader.
6. Faith	Patriarchal	Biblical leaders must learn to trust in the unseen God, sense His presence, sense His revelation, and follow Him by faith.
7. Purity	Patriarchal	Leaders must personally learn of and respond to the holiness of God in order to have lasting effective ministry.
8. Intercession	Pre-Kingdom	Leaders called to a ministry are called to intercede for that ministry.
9. Presence	Pre-Kingdom	The essential ingredient of leadership is the powerful presence of God in the leader's life and ministry.
10. Intimacy	Pre-Kingdom	Leaders develop intimacy with God which in turn overflows into all their ministry since ministry flows out of being.
11. Burden	Pre-Kingdom	Leaders feel a responsibility to God for their ministry.
12. Hope	Pre-Kingdom	A primary function of all leadership is to inspire followers with hope in God and in what God is doing.
13. Challenge	Pre-Kingdom	Leaders receive vision from God which sets before them challenges that inspire their leadership.
14. Spiritual Authority	Pre-Kingdom	Spiritual authority is the dominant power base of a spiritual leader and comes through experiences with God, knowledge of God, godly character and gifted power.
15. Transition	Pre-Kingdom	Leaders must transition other leaders into their work in order to maintain continuity and effectiveness.

BIBLICAL MACRO-LESSONS continued

Lesson Name	Era First Seen	Statement Of Lesson
16. Weakness	Pre-Kingdom	God can work through weak spiritual leaders if they are available to Him.
17. Continuity	Pre-Kingdom	Leaders must provide for continuity to new leadership in order to preserve their leadership legacy.
18. Unity	Kingdom	Unity of the people of God is a value that leader's must preserve.
19. Stability	Kingdom	Preserving a ministry of God with life and vigor over time is as much if not more of a challenge to leadership skills than creating one.
20. Spiritual Leadership	Kingdom	Spiritual leadership can make a difference even in the midst of difficult times.
21. Recrudescence	Kingdom	God will attempt to bring renewal to His people until they no longer respond to Him.
22. By-pass	Kingdom	God will by-pass leadership and structures that do not respond to Him and will institute new leadership and structures.
23. Future Perfect	Post-Kingdom	A primary function of all leadership is to walk by faith with a future perfect paradigm so as to inspire followers with certainty of God's accomplishment of ultimate purposes.
24. Perspective	Post-Kingdom	Leaders must know the value of perspective and interpret present happenings in terms of God's broader purposes.
25. Modeling	Post-Kingdom	Leaders can most powerfully influence by modeling godly lives, the sufficiency and sovereignty of God at all times, and gifted power.
26. Ultimate	Post-Kingdom	Leaders must remember that the ultimate goal of their lives and ministry is to manifest the glory of God.
27. Perseverance	Post-Kingdom	Once known leaders must persevere with the vision God has given.
28. Selection	Pre-Church	The key to good leadership is the selection of good potential leaders which should be a priority of all leaders.
29. Training	Pre-Church	Leaders should deliberately train potential leaders in their ministry by available and appropriate means.
30. Focus	Pre-Church	Leaders should increasingly move toward a focus in their ministry which moves toward fulfillment of their calling and their ultimate contribution to God's purposes for them.
31. Spirituality	Pre-Church	Leaders must develop interiority, spirit sensitivity, and fruitfulness in accord with their uniqueness since ministry flows out of being.
32. Servant	Pre-Church	Leaders must maintain a dynamic tension as they lead by serving and serve by leading.
33. Steward	Pre-Church	Leaders are endowed by God with natural abilities, acquired skills, spiritual gifts, opportunities, experiences, and privileges which must be developed and used for God.

BIBLICAL MACRO-LESSONS continued

Lesson Name	Era First Seen	Statement Of Lesson
34. Harvest	Pre-Church	Leaders must seek to bring people into relationship with God.
35. Shepherd	Pre-Church	Leaders must preserve, protect, and develop those who belong to God's people.
36. Movement	Pre-Church	Leaders recognize that movements are the way to penetrate society though they must be preserved via appropriate on-going institutional structures.
37. Structure	Church	Leaders must vary structures to fit the needs of the times if they are to conserve gains and continue with renewed effort.
38. Universal	Church	The church structure is inherently universal and can be made to fit various cultural situations if functions and not forms are in view.
39. Giftedness	Church	Leaders are responsible to help God's people identify, develop, and use their resources for God.
40. Word Centered	Church	God's Word is the primary source for equipping leaders and must be a vital part of any leaders ministry.
41. Complexity	All eras	Leadership is complex, problematic, difficult and fraught with risk which is why leadership is needed.

Conclusion

The identification of structure, themes, and purposes is never a finished job. So too, with the identification of principles, guidelines, and values pertaining to leadership. The books of the Bible are complex. Perspectives that the student brings to them both open and block one from seeing all that is there. And so it is with leadership lessons also. New experiences in life allow us to gain new perspective. That in turn allows us to see fresh truth from the Scriptures, even in old familiar territory. So we continue to walk obediently. We act upon the truth as we have seen it and can expect God to both honor our understanding and obedience and to reveal further clarification and/or modification as we sensitively move in response to the Holy Spirit.

The Word of God can never be authoritative in a leader's life, no matter what doctrine they may hold about the Scriptures, if they do not know and use it. And to that end these notes are given. It is not that they are the final word on anything. But they may stimulate leaders to search the Scriptures for themselves, to see whether these things be so. I close with the two reminders that have come to mind many times as I typed these notes with the hope that they may become your intent also.

Make every effort to present yourself to God as one approved, a workman who does not need to be ashamed and who correctly handles the word of truth. 2 Timothy 2:15

All Scripture is God inspired and is useful for teaching, rebuking, correcting and training in righteousness, so that the leader of God may be thoroughly equipped for every good work. 2 Timothy 3:16, 17.

BIBLIOGRAPHY

Clinton, Dr. J. Robert
1985   **Spiritual Gifts**. Available through Christian
Publications in Philadelphia.

1989   **Leadership Emergence Theory**. Altadena: Barnabas
Publishers.

1986   **Coming to Conclusions on Leadership** Styles.
Altadena: Barnabas Publishers.

1992   **Bridging Strategies--Leadership Perspectives for
Introducing Change**. Altadena: Barnabas Publishers.

1993   *The Paradigm Shift* --God's Breakthrough Processing
That Opens New Leadership Vistas. Altadena: Barnabus
Publishers.

1993   *Social Base Processing*—The Home Base Environment
Out of Which a Leader Works. Altadena: Barnabus
Publishers.

Clinton, Dr. J. Robert and Clinton, Richard
1992   **The Mentor Handbook**. Altadena: Barnabas Publishers.

Doohan, Helen
1984   **Leadership in Paul**. Wilmington, Del: Michael Glazier,
Inc.

Gerlach, L.P. and and Hine, V.H.,
1970   **People, Power, Change: Movements of Social
Transformation**. New York: Bobbs-Mderrill Co.
Luck, G. Coleman
1955   **The Bible Book By Book--An Introduction to Bible Synthesis**.
Chicago: Moody Press.

Morgan, G. Campbell
  1964   **The Analyzed Bible**. Westwood, N.J.: Fleming H. Revell Co.

  1990   **Handbook for Bible Teachers and Preachers**. 5th Printing.
          Original 4 Volume Series, 1912. Grand Rapids, Michigan: Baker
          Book House.

Scroggie, W. Graham
  1976   **The Unfolding Drama of Redemption**. Third Zondervan Printing
          of September 1976. Grand Rapids, Michigan: Zondervan.

Sells, Frank
  1968   **New Testament Syllabus**. Unpublished notes. Columbia, S.C.:
          Columbia Bible College.

Wimber, John
  1986   **Power Evangelism**. San Francisco: Harper and Row.

Wrong, Dennis
  1980   **Power: Its Forms, Bases, and Uses**. New York: Harper and Row.

BIBLIOGRAPHY

Clinton, Dr. J. Robert
1985   **Spiritual Gifts**. Available through Christian
                Publications in Philadelphia.

1989   **Leadership Emergence Theory**. Altadena: Barnabas
                Publishers.

1986   **Coming to Conclusions on Leadership S**tyles.
                Altadena: Barnabas Publishers.

1992   **Bridging Strategies--Leadership Perspectives for
                Introducing Change**. Altadena: Barnabas Publishers.

1993   *The Paradigm Shift* --God's Breakthrough Processing
                That Opens New Leadership Vistas. Altadena: Barnabus
                Publishers.

Clinton, Dr. J. Robert and Clinton, Richard
1992   **The Mentor Handbook**. Altadena: Barnabas Publishers.

Doohan, Helen
1984   **Leadership in Paul**. Wilmington, Del: Michael Glazier,
                Inc.

Gerlach, L.P. and and Hine, V.H.,
1970   **People, Power, Change: Movements of Social
                Transformation**. New York: Bobbs-Mderrill Co.

Luck, G. Coleman
1955   **The Bible Book By Book--An Introduction to Bible Synthesis**.
        Chicago: Moody Press.

Morgan, G. Campbell
1964   **The Analyzed Bible**. Westwood, N.J.: Fleming H. Revell Co.

1990   **Handbook for Bible Teachers and Preachers**. 5th Printing.
        Original 4 Volume Series, 1912. Grand Rapids, Michigan: Baker
        Book House.

Scroggie, W. Graham
1976   **The Unfolding Drama of Redemption.** Third Zondervan Printing
       of September 1976. Grand Rapids, Michigan: Zondervan.

Sells, Frank
1968   **New Testament Syllabus.** Unpublished notes. Columbia, S.C.:
       Columbia Bible College.

Wimber, John
1986   **Power Evangelism.** San Francisco: Harper and Row.

Wrong, Dennis
1980   **Power: Its Forms, Bases, and Uses.** New York: Harper and Row.